SELL YOUR HOUSE THROUGH CREATIVE FINANCING WITHOUT A BROKER!

by Richard Haskell

SIMON AND SCHUSTER
NEW YORK

This publication is designed to provide accurate, authoritative
information with regard to the subject matter covered. It is
sold with the understanding that the publisher is not engaged in
rendering legal, accounting, or other professional advice. Laws
vary from state to state, and if legal advice or other expert
assistance is required, the services of a competent professional
person should be sought.

Published by Simon and Schuster
A Division of Gulf & Western Corporation
Simon & Schuster Building
Rockefeller Center
1230 Avenue of the Americas
New York, New York 10020

SIMON AND SCHUSTER and colophon are trademarks of
Simon & Schuster
Manufactured in the United States of America
10 9 8 7 6 5 4 3 2 1
Pbk. 10 9 8 7 6 5 4 3 2 1

Library of Congress Cataloging in Publication Data

Haskell, Richard (Richard A.)
   Sell your house through creative financing without a
broker!

   1. House selling.   2. Housing—Finance.   3. Mortgages.
I. Title.   II. Title: Creative financing without a
broker!
HD1379.S345   333.33′8   82-5537
ISBN 0-671-44524-3   AACR2
      0-671-45077-8 pbk

CONTENTS

INTRODUCTION

I am a real-estate broker specializing in selling residential property. In the past several years, I've sold millions of dollars' worth of homes, from modest single-family dwellings to expensive houses with elaborate grounds. And I'm going to tell you one simple truth: *the bulk of what most real-estate brokers and agents do could be done by someone who has never seen the inside of a real-estate school.*

What do real-estate agents do? They follow simple directions and fill in the blanks on some forms. It's as easy as that.

That's why I think you can bypass the real-estate agent, do the job yourself, and save thousands of dollars in brokerage fees in the process!

In addition, there is an important key to closing the sale that many real-estate agents overlook: *helping the buyer get the financing* he or she needs to buy your home. I know from experience that almost *anyone* can sell his own home and help a buyer arrange the necessary financing in just a few weeks—despite what the real-estate agents might lead you to believe. That's why I am writing this book. And, too, I'm writing this book because I realize that in today's tight economy, almost all of us could put that extra money we'd save on brokerage commissions to much better use.

WHAT THIS BOOK WILL DO FOR YOU

Simply stated, this book will *save you money*. Lots of it. The typical commission charged by a real-estate broker or agent who sells your home for you is 6%. Sometimes the fee can be as high as 7%. In dollars, what this means is that if you sell your home for, say, $100,000, you're forfeiting $6,000 or even $7,000 right off the top. And in the tight-fisted economy we're living in, that's a hefty chunk.

The good news for homeowners is that you can save that $6,000 or $7,000 by following the advice and easy step-by-step instructions in this book. You can pocket the money you would have spent on a real-estate broker and invest it to increase your nest egg instead. Just think, you could put that money in one of the high-yielding new savings vehicles available to consumers—a money fund, for example. Now who wouldn't want to get a high-interest return on $6,000 or $7,000 of found money? When you look at it this way, the few *tax-deductible* dollars you're spending for this book may be one of the best investments you'll ever make.

WHY YOU NEED THIS BOOK

Your local library or bookstore probably has half a dozen volumes that claim to tell you how you can sell your home without using a broker. I've looked at these books and I can tell you something about them: they are overrated and outdated. For the most part, these books tell you how to clean up your house to impress potential buyers, and give advice on when it's best to sell. Well, that's fine, but it won't help you when it comes right down to the specifics of actually putting your home on the market, negotiating with a potential buyer, making sure you get the best possible price for your home, and, most important of all, *making sure your buyer can get the financing to purchase your property.*

Today, when the trend in the United States is to smaller households, and new households are forming at a rate three times that of the overall population growth, you, as a seller, are at a distinct advantage. According to the Census Bureau, the population increased more than 11% in the past decade. And although the actual number of housing units increased by about a third, the number of people living in those homes dropped significantly (from 3.11 in 1970 to 2.75 in 1980). For a number of reasons—the rising divorce rate, increased longevity, the decision of many people to postpone marriage and delay starting a family, and, above all, the millions of more affluent Americans born during the post–World War II baby boom who choose to live alone—more and more of us are looking for housing.

At the same time, galloping inflation and sky-high interest rates have made the cost of borrowing money to purchase a home a difficult issue for hundreds of thousands of potential homebuyers. As a seller, it's vital for you to be aware of this important fact. No matter how interested he or she may be in buying your home, if your buyer cannot get the financing needed, there won't be a sale. So obviously it's to your advantage as well as your buyer's for you to know how to help obtain that money, as quickly and easily as possible. Remember, the money you're going to get for your current house will most likely be used to buy another home for you and your family. Being able to get the highest possible price for your home is in your best interest now and in the future.

FORMS THAT HELP YOU SELL YOUR HOME LIKE A PROFESSIONAL

This book is unique in two ways. First, it gives you the *step-by-step instructions* you'll need to market your home, with the forms necessary to carry out those steps with the confident assurance of a professional. Samples of the appropriate forms for all kinds of financial situations are filled out in detail and are included throughout the book for your easy reference.

These forms, in addition to the information contained in the chapters, give you the accurate guidelines you'll need to carry out your sale, from the moment you decide to put your home on the market, to negotiating with a buyer, right through to the happy day when you sit down with your lawyer or escrow agent and your buyer to conclude the deal. You'll find forms to help you set a realistic selling price, forms to help you accurately evaluate whether the buyer can afford to purchase your home, forms to help the buyer choose the right kind of financing, forms to document the sale, and forms to help you tax-shelter your profit.

All these forms are simple to read and understand. Best of all, they'll save you money.

USING CREATIVE FINANCING TO SELL YOUR HOME IN A TIGHT MONEY MARKET

The second thing that makes this book unique is that it tells you all the ways to sell your home through *creative financing*. Creative financing is a brand-new idea in real estate, and at a time when the high cost of borrowing money for home loans (anywhere from 17% to a staggering 19.5%) and high down-payment requirements (25% to 40% of the total purchase price) are discouraging thousands of would-be homeowners, it's arrived just in time. Creative financing plans have done more to open up housing and make it affordable for average Americans than any other method of financing in recent years.

What *is* creative financing? Well, it's simply a term used to refer to the new breed of financing plans developed by bank officials and lending regulators that enable buyers to get mortgage money at more advantageous rates. Creative financing, or creative mortgaging as it's sometimes known, offers buyers four irresistible features:

1. lower interest rates,
2. lower monthly payments for the first few years of the loan,
3. longer loan periods, and often
4. lower down payments.

These plans, including mortgage assumptions, shared-appreciation mortgages (SAM), graduated-payment adjustable mortgages (GPAM), rollover mortgages (ROM), variable-rate mortgages (VRM), renegotiable-rate mortgages (RRM), and others, are characterized by their flexibility and liberalized payment schedules. They offer a greatly increased number of financing options to homebuyers—often allowing the buyer and seller to arrange for financing without going to a bank or other commercial lender for a loan. Let's see what this can mean to you, the seller.

Suppose you've just landed a terrific new job. It's a promotion, with more responsibility, and most attractive of all, you'll be earning $12,000 more per year. Your new company is located 150 miles away from where you now live, in a nicer, less congested residential area where the kids will be happier. So you have to sell your home. You advertise and an interested buyer comes around. You're asking $125,000 and he seems serious about buying. There's just one problem. Your buyer qualifies for a

$60,000, 30-year, adjustable rate mortgage with the first three years' interest fixed at a rate of 17%. He's going to have an almost unmanageable monthly payment and he has to come up with a $65,000 down payment. He can't do it. Or can he?

Here's where creative financing can make the difference between selling your house at the price you want and no sale at all. You check with your bank and find out that your mortgage which you hold at a low 9% interest rate is "assumable," that is, you can transfer it to the buyer. That helps him out a lot. Then your buyer goes to your bank and asks about obtaining a new loan. Because it's in the bank's interest to get rid of an old low-interest-producing loan (your mortgage), they agree to give the buyer a new loan for the total amount at 14%, thus wiping out your old 9% mortgage. Banks and other commercial lenders are anxious to eliminate all their long-standing, unprofitable mortgages and will reduce the interest rate as much as 3% on a new loan to accomplish just that. Your buyer now has the needed financing at 14% and his monthly payments have been reduced by a substantial chunk. He can buy your house at the price you're asking.

Or for a different approach, let's say you decide to use another creative financing technique called owner financing. In this case you would be taking a first mortgage on your own home, using your house as security for the mortgage. You go to your bank and take out a loan for the amount your buyer needs, say a three-year loan at 16%. Again, the advantage to your buyer is that he now has to come up with less financing and so can cut the amount of the down payment. Your buyer will then make monthly payments to you, say at 14%. You invest the down payment in a high-yielding money market mutual fund, and even though you've given the buyer a discounted interest rate, you make a profit. The buyer pays you monthly installments on your mortgage and has three years to come up with the additional financing he needs. If he fails to do this, you can either work out a second mortgage or repossess the property. In the meantime, you've made a nice profit by selling your home at the price you want.

According to the National Association of Realtors, *over half of all the single-family homes bought today are purchased with some type of creative financing.* And when you consider that by the time a traditional mortgage of, say, $100,000 for a 30-year life at 18% interest is paid off, the home will have cost $542,552.40, it's not hard to see why.

By learning the many new options offered by the creative financing techniques described in this book, you'll have a big head start in selling your home for the maximum amount possible.

HOW TO USE THIS BOOK

On the next page you'll find the key: the *twelve simple steps* to selling your own home without a broker. Read these steps carefully. Then read on. The following chapters explain these twelve important steps in depth. As you read this book, it's a good idea to keep paper handy to note any questions you might have (especially those you might want to ask an attorney).

Be sure as well to pay particular attention to the tax information located in the appendixes. It can help you *legally* shelter the profit you make on your sale from the ravenous clutches of the IRS.

In Appendix G you will also find a complete set of money-saving *blank house-sale contract forms* which are reprinted for your personal use in selling your home.

Finally, a glossary giving precise definitions of all the terms used in the book is also included for your convenience. (*Note:* real-estate jargon, like all professional jargon, can sound strange at first. Don't let these unfamiliar terms bamboozle you! There's nothing in this book a grade-schooler can't understand.)

Today's real-estate market is a fortunate one for any seller who is willing to take a little time and effort to properly arrange the sale of his or her home. With thousands of corporate relocations every month, hundreds of thousands of senior citizens opting for different climes in which to enjoy their retirement, and a housing shortage that puts a premium on family dwellings, you, as a homeowner, are in the driver's seat. Armed with the information in this book, you will discover that you can sell your home as well as a professional and in addition have the satisfaction and pride of knowing that you did it without the costly brokerage fees most homeowners reluctantly pay.

Good luck!

THE TWELVE SIMPLE STEPS TO SELLING YOUR OWN HOME

Did you know that every year hundreds of thousands of Americans sell their own homes without the help of a real-estate agent or broker? According to the most recent survey conducted by the National Association of Realtors, in 1980 nearly 15% of the 2½ million existing single-family homes sold that year were sold by ordinary homeowners.

That's about 375,000 people—all of whom had no special real-estate expertise and all of whom saved the commission a broker or agent would have charged!

You can join these people. To do it, all you need to know is that selling your own home is as simple as the following twelve steps:

1. **Clean your house thoroughly and make any necessary repairs to prepare it for showing.**

2. **Set a realistic selling price.**

3. **Find out if you can transfer your existing mortgage to the buyer.**

4. **Prepare a Listing Worksheet detailing all the features of your home to give to prospective buyers.**

5. **Use advertising to help sell your house for the maximum profit.**

6. **Help your buyer get financing in the three basic ways.**

7. **Help your buyer get financing using creative financing techniques.**

8. **Qualify your buyer for a new mortgage loan.**

9. **Document your buyer's serious intent to buy with the earnest-money contract.**

10. **Hire a lawyer to review your sale agreement.**

11. **Set up an escrow account at your local title company.**

12. **Transfer the deed to the property to your buyer at the closing.**

Sound easy? Well, it is. With these twelve steps and the step-by-step instructions in this book you're well on your way to selling your own home.

Now it's time to begin . . .

PREPARE YOUR HOUSE FOR SHOWING

The way your house and property look and the condition that they are in are the very first things an appraiser and a prospective buyer will notice. To have your home appraised for the maximum value, it must be in tip-top condition *before* the appraiser arrives and before you begin to show it to prospective buyers.

When you show your house, it should be as clean and neat as possible, both inside and out. Thoroughly clean all closets, throwing out any accumulated junk that's just hanging around collecting dust. Replace old or torn wallpaper and shelf paper. Wash the floors. Windows and mirrors should glisten. Shampoo and vacuum the rugs and carpets. Tidy the garage and yard (a few new shrubs or flowers can be inexpensive and will make a pleasant first impression on a buyer). Repaint any rooms where embedded fingerprints or wear and tear from children is especially noticeable. Spray, if necessary, to eliminate any odors from pets or excess dampness (it's a good idea to leave the windows open for a few minutes prior to the buyers' arrival). And since major appliances such as dishwashers and refrigerators are often included in the price of a home, make sure they're in good working order. If you don't, the buyer will, and will bill you later for the repairs—and you will then be at the mercy of the buyer's repairman.

REPAIRS

Repairs are important and can affect your ability to get the sales price you're asking, but when making repairs on your home don't go overboard. As a seller, you are primarily responsible for making sure that the major systems of the home—plumbing, electrical, air conditioning, and heat—are in working order and that there are no serious defects in the foundation or structure of the house, such as major cracks or holes in ceilings or walls. If you sell your home knowing that any of these items is faulty without informing your prospective buyer, you open yourself up to a whopping lawsuit down the road.

Keep in mind that any repairs you make in order to improve the marketability of your home are *tax-deductible* expenses from your profit on the sale. What exactly is a "repair" under the law? A good rule of thumb is that a repair is a small job, like fixing a leaky faucet. Jobs that are significantly bigger than this, such as adding a new room, installing central air conditioning, or building a swimming pool, are known as "improvements." Any repair you make in order to sell your home is a full, immediate tax deduction. An improvement, on the other hand, can be depreciated over its useful life. To the extent that an improvement is not depreciated before you sell the property it is added to the property's tax basis, which helps reduce your taxable profit on the sale. The expenditures involved in making improvements or in remodeling your home are great and are not advisable unless they are absolutely necessary to the sale.

The real tax-savings rule about repairs is this: any expense that keeps your property in efficient operating condition is a tax-deductible repair. Make sure that any repairs, especially cosmetic ones like repairing and repainting cracks in sheetrock, that you deem necessary to improve the salability of the property are done *before* the appraiser arrives.

In deciding what repairs you're going to make, the two guiding principles should be:

1. How much will it cost?
2. Does making the repair significantly improve the chances of selling the house at a good price?

HOME REPAIR RECORD

Here is a handy schedule for recording repairs and their costs. Be sure to save all receipts for materials and labor and any canceled checks. You can deduct only what you pay others; your own labor does not qualify. Some people take pictures of the property before and after any major repairs are made. Fixing leaky faucets and roofs, repairing freon leaks in air-conditioning units, replacing broken windowpanes, and repairing and repainting cracks in sheetrock are all examples of repairs.

KIND OF REPAIR	DATE DONE	COST

Most of the time the cost of making repairs is well worth it. Ask yourself if *you* would buy a home in the condition your home is now in. If the answer is no, chances are a buyer will feel the same way and repairs are in order.

Because repairs are legitimate tax deductions, be sure to keep all canceled checks for payments to outside repairers and for all materials, and, if possible, photographs of any major work done, in the event of an IRS audit. (*Note:* labor you perform yourself is *not* tax-deductible.)

PAINT

Whether or not to repaint your house is a major decision every homeowner faces before putting his home on the market. To repaint the outside of an average house can cost anywhere from $2,000 to $5,000. This sounds like a lot of money, and it is. But the truth of the matter is that paint probably increases the value and appeal of your house more than anything else. A bright new coat of paint can cover a multitude of sins, making an old house look newer, or, by painting your house a single color, making it look larger than it actually is. If the exterior of your house is in poor condition and badly in need of fresh paint, it is definitely worth the investment. If your house needs to be painted and you decide not to, you run the risk of discovering that prospective buyers are few and far between or, worse, that you are forced to sell your house for less than it's worth.

If you do decide to paint, use a moderately priced brand. What counts is that the house look clean and fresh, not how expensive the paint is (besides, the new owners may want to repaint it in another color once they move in).

HOW LONG DOES IT TAKE?

If you have maintained your house and property reasonably well, one month should be enough time for you to get everything in good order before showing it to prospective buyers. If, on the other hand, you need to have major repairs done or you have a particularly busy schedule and can't afford the time, you might allow anywhere from six to eight weeks to be certain everything gets done. At the very least, give yourself two full weeks to devote to the job of cleaning and sprucing up.

Surprisingly, children can be your best allies in this fix-up process. Once it's explained to them that the sale of your house is for their benefit too, they can usually be marshaled into duty quite willingly. In a household where both spouses work, alternate shifts may be the best method of equalizing the work load. You might also consider hiring neighborhood teenagers to help out. For a reasonable cost—$2 to $3 per hour—they can make the work go much faster.

The trick in getting your house ready for showing is to be as organized as possible. *Plan ahead* and delegate responsibility for specific tasks to each family member. It's a good idea to organize your schedule on a weekly basis, allotting one or two chores per day. Start with the more time-consuming projects, such as major repairs and outside or touch-up painting the first week, working your way toward the less arduous chores like washing windows.

Before the appraiser comes and you show your home, make sure you've covered all the items on the handy checklist which follows.

One more word about preparing to show your home: get set for some surprises. Homebuyers (and especially home*lookers*) can be a singularly difficult species. The businessman in the expensive suit with the suede attaché case may not mind dropping ashes on your newly shampooed rug, but he may turn on his heel if he sees a large dust ball under the piano. That lady whose kids usually look like refugees from the Salvation Army may hum a different tune when she sees that the draperies in your living room are soiled. Women, in particular, can be tough customers when it comes to buying a new home.

You can go a long way toward conquering even the most critical potential buyer if you merely observe some commonsense rules, like making sure everything is spic and span, placing bright (100-watt) bulbs in the lamps, arranging for children and pets to be elsewhere when buyers start to arrive (the sound of shrill voices or yapping, no matter how friendly, diminishes the tranquil atmosphere you're trying to create), strategically placing flowers and plants throughout the house, even baking bread or cookies shortly before buyers arrive so the inviting aroma will spell "home."

In the final analysis, you are the best judge of what is necessary to get your house in the proper shape to show. Once you're satisfied that all is ready to face the outside world, you're ready for the next step: *setting a realistic selling price.*

FIX-UP CHECKLIST

E X T E R I O R

LANDSCAPING

☐ lawn in good condition with no bald spots or weeds ───────────

☐ lawn newly fertilized ───────────────────────

☐ grass mowed and trimmed around the edges ───────────────

☐ leaves raked ─────────────────────────

☐ garden raked and tidied ──────────────────────

☐ new shrubs, or flowers planted ─────────────────────

☐ shrubs pruned or trimmed ──────────────────────

☐ dead or dying tree branches removed ──────────────────

☐ yard sprayed to remove insects ─────────────────────

☐ fences or rails painted and unbroken ──────────────────

GARAGE

☐ floor swept and mopped with disinfectant ──────────────

☐ oil spots removed from floor ───────────────────────

☐ bikes, toys, etc. neatly against the wall ──────────────────

☐ all junk removed ───────────────────────────

☐ garbage cans disinfected and lids secured ──────────────────

☐ tools and equipment stored or neatly arranged on shelves ──────────

☐ electric lights working ─────────────────────────

☐ doors open and close easily ──────────────────────

DRIVEWAY

☐ cars washed and waxed ──────────────────────────

☐ asphalt smooth with no pits or holes ────────────────────

☐ gravel smooth and full ─────────────────────────

☐ weeds removed ────────────────────────────

☐ bikes, toys, etc. removed ─────────────────────────

PATIO, PORCH, TERRACE

☐ surfaces clean and clear of debris ─────────────────────

☐ wood stained or painted ──────────────────────────

☐ screens untorn and secure ——————————————————

☐ no water or dampness ——————————————————

☐ area sprayed to remove insects, termites, etc. ——————————

☐ potted plants or hanging flower baskets ——————————

☐ lights working ——————————————————————

SIDEWALK

☐ swept clear of leaves and hosed ——————————————

☐ weeds trimmed from edges ——————————————————

☐ curb and gutter clear ——————————————————————

OUTSIDE OF HOUSE

☐ freshly painted ——————————————————————————

☐ no peeling or cracking paint ————————————————

☐ shutters straight and secure ————————————————

☐ missing shutters replaced ——————————————————

☐ gutters secure with no clogging, debris, or rust ————————

☐ roof clear of miscellaneous objects ——————————————

☐ antenna upright ——————————————————————————

☐ chimney secure and clear ——————————————————

☐ shingles fastened ————————————————————————

☐ missing shingles replaced ——————————————————

☐ windows washed ——————————————————————————

☐ windows open and close easily ————————————————

☐ window panes uncracked ——————————————————

☐ door painted ——————————————————————————————

☐ doorknob and hinges polished ————————————————

☐ doorbell working ————————————————————————

☐ steps swept ——————————————————————————————

☐ steps smooth and secure ——————————————————

☐ mailbox upright ——————————————————————————

☐ mailbox polished or painted ————————————————

☐ lights working ——————————————————————————

I N T E R I O R

ATTIC

- ☐ floor swept _____
- ☐ sprayed to remove mold _____
- ☐ trash or junk removed _____
- ☐ storage items packed neatly in boxes _____
- ☐ windows washed _____
- ☐ beams secure and dusted _____
- ☐ floor planks secure _____
- ☐ doors open and close freely _____
- ☐ lights working _____

BASEMENT

- ☐ walls and ceilings uncracked _____
- ☐ beams secure _____
- ☐ no water or dampness _____
- ☐ floors swept and mopped _____
- ☐ storage items packed neatly in boxes _____
- ☐ trash or junk removed _____
- ☐ no termites _____
- ☐ area sprayed to remove mold or must _____
- ☐ furnace and boiler inspected and cleaned _____
- ☐ handrail and stairways secure _____
- ☐ windows washed _____
- ☐ lights working _____

ENTRANCE HALL

- ☐ ceiling and walls uncracked _____
- ☐ paint on walls unchipped, uncracked _____
- ☐ wallpaper adheres tightly to walls _____
- ☐ walls clean _____
- ☐ floors swept and waxed _____
- ☐ carpet shampooed and vacuumed _____
- ☐ carpet tacked down securely _____
- ☐ draperies or curtains clean _____
- ☐ windows washed _____
- ☐ mirrors shined _____
- ☐ area dusted thoroughly _____

☐ closet clean

☐ closet light working

☐ lights working

STAIRWAYS

☐ ceilings and walls uncracked

☐ paint on walls unchipped, uncracked

☐ wallpaper adheres tightly to walls

☐ walls clean

☐ all steps secure

☐ missing or chipped wood replaced

☐ handrails or bannisters secure

☐ railings dusted

☐ stairs swept and covering vacuumed

☐ lights working

FIREPLACE

☐ free of debris and soot

☐ hearth swept and mopped

☐ pokers and irons upright

☐ screen clean and upright

☐ logs neatly placed

LAUNDRY ROOM

☐ ceilings and walls uncracked

☐ paint on walls unchipped, uncracked

☐ wallpaper adheres tightly to walls

☐ walls clean

☐ appliances clean and in working order

☐ boxes, storage items neatly arranged

☐ shelves neat

☐ windows washed

☐ lights working

KITCHEN

☐ ceilings and walls uncracked

☐ paint on walls unchipped, uncracked

☐ wallpaper adheres tightly to walls

- [ ] walls clean
- [ ] floors washed and waxed
- [ ] missing tiles replaced
- [ ] sink immaculate
- [ ] sink drain unclogged and in working order
- [ ] appliances clean and in working order
- [ ] stove or range lights working
- [ ] stove or range hood, filter, and exhaust working
- [ ] counters clean and clear
- [ ] cupboards neat
- [ ] torn shelf paper replaced
- [ ] all dishes washed and stored
- [ ] windows washed
- [ ] lights working

DINING ROOM

- [ ] ceilings and walls uncracked
- [ ] paint on walls unchipped, uncracked
- [ ] wallpaper adheres tightly to walls
- [ ] walls clean
- [ ] floors swept and waxed
- [ ] carpet shampooed and vacuumed
- [ ] carpet tacked down securely
- [ ] draperies or curtains clean
- [ ] windows washed
- [ ] area thoroughly dusted
- [ ] woodwork repainted
- [ ] furniture dusted and polished
- [ ] tablecloth clean
- [ ] flowers on table
- [ ] furniture arranged to show room to best advantage
- [ ] lights operating

FAMILY ROOM, DEN, STUDY

- [ ] ceilings and walls uncracked
- [ ] paint on walls unchipped, uncracked
- [ ] wallpaper adheres tightly to walls

- ☐ walls clean
- ☐ floors swept and waxed
- ☐ carpet shampooed and vacuumed
- ☐ carpet tacked down securely
- ☐ draperies or curtains clean
- ☐ windows washed
- ☐ area thoroughly dusted
- ☐ woodwork repainted
- ☐ furniture dusted and polished
- ☐ furniture arranged to show room to best advantage
- ☐ lights operating

LIVING ROOM

- ☐ ceilings and walls uncracked
- ☐ paint on walls unchipped, uncracked
- ☐ wallpaper adheres tightly to walls
- ☐ walls clean
- ☐ floors swept and waxed
- ☐ carpet shampooed and vacuumed
- ☐ carpet tacked down securely
- ☐ draperies or curtains clean
- ☐ windows washed
- ☐ area thoroughly dusted
- ☐ woodwork repainted
- ☐ furniture dusted and polished
- ☐ furniture arranged to show room to best advantage
- ☐ lights operating

BATHROOM # 1

- ☐ ceilings and walls uncracked
- ☐ paint on walls unchipped, uncracked
- ☐ wallpaper adheres tightly to walls
- ☐ walls clean
- ☐ floors washed
- ☐ missing tiles replaced
- ☐ joints caulked
- ☐ grouting cleaned

- ☐ sink immaculate
- ☐ sink drain unclogged and in working order
- ☐ bathtub drain unclogged and in working order
- ☐ faucet repaired if leaky
- ☐ counters clean and clear
- ☐ closets clean and neat
- ☐ drawers and cabinets clean and neat
- ☐ mirrors shined
- ☐ new shower curtain
- ☐ fresh towels
- ☐ all supplies stored
- ☐ windows washed
- ☐ new soap in dishes
- ☐ all fixtures cleaned
- ☐ area disinfected
- ☐ lights working

BATHROOM # 2

- ☐ ceilings and walls uncracked
- ☐ paint on walls unchipped, uncracked
- ☐ wallpaper adheres tightly to walls
- ☐ walls clean
- ☐ floors washed
- ☐ missing tiles replaced
- ☐ joints caulked
- ☐ grouting cleaned
- ☐ sink immaculate
- ☐ sink drain unclogged and in working order
- ☐ bathtub drain unclogged and in working order
- ☐ faucet repaired if leaky
- ☐ counters clean and clear
- ☐ closets clean and neat
- ☐ drawers and cabinets clean and neat
- ☐ mirrors shined
- ☐ new shower curtain
- ☐ fresh towels

- ☐ all supplies stored
- ☐ windows washed
- ☐ new soap in dishes
- ☐ all fixtures cleaned
- ☐ area disinfected
- ☐ lights working

BEDROOM # 1

- ☐ ceilings and walls uncracked
- ☐ paint on walls unchipped, uncracked
- ☐ wallpaper adheres tightly to walls
- ☐ walls clean
- ☐ floors swept and waxed
- ☐ carpet shampooed and vacuumed
- ☐ carpet tacked down securely
- ☐ draperies or curtains clean
- ☐ windows washed
- ☐ mirrors shined
- ☐ woodwork repainted
- ☐ furniture dusted and polished
- ☐ bed made neatly
- ☐ bedspread clean
- ☐ area thoroughly dusted
- ☐ closet clean
- ☐ closet light working
- ☐ doors open and close easily
- ☐ furniture arranged to show room to best advantage
- ☐ lights working

BEDROOM # 2

- ☐ ceilings and walls uncracked
- ☐ paint on walls unchipped, uncracked
- ☐ wallpaper adheres tightly to walls
- ☐ walls clean
- ☐ floors swept and waxed
- ☐ carpet shampooed and vacuumed
- ☐ carpet tacked down securely

☐ draperies or curtains clean ⎯⎯⎯⎯⎯⎯⎯⎯⎯⎯⎯⎯⎯⎯⎯⎯

☐ windows washed ⎯⎯⎯⎯⎯⎯⎯⎯⎯⎯⎯⎯⎯⎯⎯⎯⎯⎯⎯⎯

☐ mirrors shined ⎯⎯⎯⎯⎯⎯⎯⎯⎯⎯⎯⎯⎯⎯⎯⎯⎯⎯⎯⎯

☐ woodwork repainted ⎯⎯⎯⎯⎯⎯⎯⎯⎯⎯⎯⎯⎯⎯⎯⎯⎯

☐ furniture dusted and polished ⎯⎯⎯⎯⎯⎯⎯⎯⎯⎯⎯

☐ bed made neatly ⎯⎯⎯⎯⎯⎯⎯⎯⎯⎯⎯⎯⎯⎯⎯⎯⎯⎯

☐ bedspread clean ⎯⎯⎯⎯⎯⎯⎯⎯⎯⎯⎯⎯⎯⎯⎯⎯⎯⎯

☐ area thoroughly dusted ⎯⎯⎯⎯⎯⎯⎯⎯⎯⎯⎯⎯⎯⎯

☐ closet clean ⎯⎯⎯⎯⎯⎯⎯⎯⎯⎯⎯⎯⎯⎯⎯⎯⎯⎯⎯

☐ closet light working ⎯⎯⎯⎯⎯⎯⎯⎯⎯⎯⎯⎯⎯⎯⎯

☐ doors open and close easily ⎯⎯⎯⎯⎯⎯⎯⎯⎯⎯⎯⎯

☐ furniture arranged to show room to best advantage ⎯⎯⎯⎯

☐ lights working ⎯⎯⎯⎯⎯⎯⎯⎯⎯⎯⎯⎯⎯⎯⎯⎯⎯⎯

BEDROOM # 3

☐ ceilings and walls uncracked ⎯⎯⎯⎯⎯⎯⎯⎯⎯⎯⎯

☐ paint on walls unchipped, uncracked ⎯⎯⎯⎯⎯⎯⎯⎯

☐ wallpaper tightly adheres to walls ⎯⎯⎯⎯⎯⎯⎯⎯⎯

☐ walls clean ⎯⎯⎯⎯⎯⎯⎯⎯⎯⎯⎯⎯⎯⎯⎯⎯⎯⎯⎯⎯

☐ floors swept and waxed ⎯⎯⎯⎯⎯⎯⎯⎯⎯⎯⎯⎯⎯⎯

☐ carpet shampooed and vacuumed ⎯⎯⎯⎯⎯⎯⎯⎯⎯

☐ carpet tacked down securely ⎯⎯⎯⎯⎯⎯⎯⎯⎯⎯⎯

☐ draperies or curtains clean ⎯⎯⎯⎯⎯⎯⎯⎯⎯⎯⎯⎯

☐ windows washed ⎯⎯⎯⎯⎯⎯⎯⎯⎯⎯⎯⎯⎯⎯⎯⎯⎯

☐ mirrors shined ⎯⎯⎯⎯⎯⎯⎯⎯⎯⎯⎯⎯⎯⎯⎯⎯⎯⎯

☐ woodwork repainted ⎯⎯⎯⎯⎯⎯⎯⎯⎯⎯⎯⎯⎯⎯⎯

☐ furniture dusted and polished ⎯⎯⎯⎯⎯⎯⎯⎯⎯⎯

☐ bed made neatly ⎯⎯⎯⎯⎯⎯⎯⎯⎯⎯⎯⎯⎯⎯⎯⎯

☐ bedspread clean ⎯⎯⎯⎯⎯⎯⎯⎯⎯⎯⎯⎯⎯⎯⎯⎯

☐ area thoroughly dusted ⎯⎯⎯⎯⎯⎯⎯⎯⎯⎯⎯⎯⎯

☐ closet clean ⎯⎯⎯⎯⎯⎯⎯⎯⎯⎯⎯⎯⎯⎯⎯⎯⎯⎯

☐ closet light working ⎯⎯⎯⎯⎯⎯⎯⎯⎯⎯⎯⎯⎯⎯

☐ doors open and close easily ⎯⎯⎯⎯⎯⎯⎯⎯⎯⎯⎯

☐ furniture arranged to show room to best advantage ⎯⎯⎯

☐ lights working ⎯⎯⎯⎯⎯⎯⎯⎯⎯⎯⎯⎯⎯⎯⎯⎯⎯⎯

SET A REALISTIC SELLING PRICE

You may have heard a lot of talk about setting an "asking price," a "minimum price," and any of a number of other negotiating prices, but if you want to get the best possible price for your home, the fact of the matter is that it can be done quickly and simply, without endless negotiating. The way to do it is to have your home appraised by a member of the American Institute of Real Estate Appraisers (AIREA), a national accreditation organization for real-estate appraisers, affiliated with the National Association of Realtors.

The Institute has stringent standards and offers the MAI (member of the Appraisal Institute) and RM (residential member) designations to those who qualify. The MAI designation is the primary category of accreditation. Candidates for the MAI must be at least 21 years old; have graduated from an accredited four-year college or have the equivalent of a four-year advanced education; and have received a passing grade on the Institute's rigid required examinations. Appraisers holding the designation RM have certified skills in appraising only single-family residences, in contrast to the MAI designation, which covers all types of property.

The average fee for having your home appraised by an AIREA member ranges from $150 to $220. This fee, which is tax-deductible from the profit you make on the sale of your house, is worth every penny. There are two reasons for this. First, a written appraisal from an AIREA-accredited member is proof positive to any prospective buyer that you are offering your home at its fair market value. Showing the written appraisal to prospective buyers will convince them that, perhaps unlike some real-estate brokers or sellers in your community, you really are asking an objective price for your house and are not attempting to artificially inflate your property's value. Gaining this kind of

trust from prospective buyers can help you out later as well, when an offer has been made and fine points are being negotiated.

The second reason why a professional appraisal is advisable is that it will be realistic. Trying to appraise the value of your home and property yourself can result in costly errors. If you price the property too high, by the time you realize it, you'll have lost valuable time, energy, and momentum. If, on the other hand, you price it too low, you're going to lose money. Knowing the true value of your home from the beginning is well worth the modest cost.

The amount at which you price your property should never be higher than the appraisal. Sometimes, however, there may be a valid reason for pricing your property somewhat below the appraised value—for example, if it is necessary that you sell within a very short time period. If this is the case, you might consider requesting a concession from your buyer in exchange—for example, a larger cash down payment. This kind of concession on your part need not mean a loss. Your willingness to drop your asking price from the fair market value of your home can sometimes be the basis of advantageous negotiations.

To find an appraiser who is accredited by the AIREA, call your local Board of Realtors or county courthouse, or simply look up the listing in the telephone directory. Be sure, however, that the person you pick is officially accredited by this national organization.

One last point: don't forget to talk to your neighbors or any friendly realtors you might know and to check your local paper to see what comparable houses in your area are selling for. If you are considering asking $125,000 for a 1,650-square-foot house when just last week a 1,650-square-foot house two blocks away sold for $97,000, you may have to rethink your asking price. Ask your neighbors what they know about prices currently being advertised for houses in your neighborhood. You may discover that the time you have chosen to sell your home coincides with a current lull in real estate in your area or, perhaps, that just at the time you've chosen to sell, prices are beginning to climb. Realtors, too, may be willing to give you some advice. After all, it's their business and they will probably agree to give you some free professional advice if they think you will turn to them later if you need help in selling.

FIND OUT IF YOUR MORTGAGE CAN BE ASSUMED

Your mortgage company is the party to whom you are making the monthly loan payments for your home. Most homeowners have mortgages with savings and loan associations or commercial banks; others may have a mortgage with a separate mortgage company or even with an individual.

By law, whoever holds your existing loan *must* inform you under what conditions, if any, the new buyer of your home can take over (assume) your existing loan, whether the interest rate for the loan will escalate, and how often and at what rate it will escalate. Financing is probably the single most critical step in buying and selling a home and it's essential that you find out what financing options are available to you and your prospective buyer as soon as you decide to sell. If you have a mortgage that is transferable, you have a head start in helping the buyer get the financing he or she needs to buy your home.

The Mortgage Information form which follows is the best way to obtain this information, and it's important to have this completed form in hand before talking to buyers. As you can see, on the form the mortgage company or lender must state the requirements for the new buyer to assume your existing loan. There should be no guesswork in regard to whether the new buyer will have to pay a higher interest rate and submit to a loan committee for its approval. The information on this form is also vital for the officer at the title company and for the lawyer who will be handling the closing of your transaction.

To complete this simple form, call the mortgage or assumption department of your bank or mortgage company and ask them for your mortgage loan number (or if you have good records, simply look up this number on your copy of the loan agreement). Then, as owner, fill out the top portion of the form only and sign your name at the bottom. Mail the form to the holder of your loan. If you don't hear from them promptly, call them up. This information is necessary for you to proceed quickly with the sale of your home.

MORTGAGE INFORMATION

_____   _____
(Name of Mortgage Company)   (Date)

_____
(Address)

_____

Gentlemen:

We are placing our property at _____ on the market for sale. Please mail to us,

_____, _____, [city, state]

_____, the following information regarding our loan, #_____, which we have with you:
(zip)

KIND OF LOAN Conv. ( ) FHA ( ) VA ( )   MONTHLY PRINCIPAL PAYMENT $_____

ORIGINAL DATE OF LOAN _____   MONTHLY INTEREST PAYMENT $_____

ORIGINAL AMOUNT $_____   MONTHLY DEPOSIT FOR TAXES $_____

TERM (YEARS)   _____   MONTHLY DEPOSIT HAZ. INS. $_____

INTEREST RATE   _____   MONTHLY DEPOSIT FHA INS. $_____

BALANCE DUE   _____   TOTAL MONTHLY PAYMENT $_____

AS OF (DATE)   _____   TRUST FUND BAL._____ $_____
                                                                     (Date)

CAN LOAN BE ASSUMED? YES ( )   NO ( )   TYPES OF HAZARD INS. _____

REQUIREMENTS FOR LOAN ASSUMPTION: EXPIRATION DATE OF HAZ. INS. _____

_____   PREPAYMENT PRIVILEGES _____

_____

_____   _____

CITY & SCHOOL TAXES   19____ $_____   _____

STATE & COUNTY TAXES 19____ $_____   TRANSFER FEE $_____

MAINTENANCE FEE   19____ $_____

                                              Thank you for your courtesy,

_____   _____
(Name of person furnishing information)   (Owner)

DATE: _____

GIVING THE BUYER THE FACTS— THE LISTING WORKSHEET

Once you have received the completed Mortgage Information form back from your bank or mortgage company, you are ready to fill in the sample Listing Worksheet reprinted in this chapter.

This concise, encapsulated form gives the prospective buyer all the information he or she needs to know about your home at a glance. The Listing Worksheet is not just a courtesy to the potential buyer—it shows that you are handling the sale of your home in a professional manner. Forms similar to this one are used by realtors all over the country and are indispensable aids in selling a home. The information on the form pinpoints all the key selling features of your home, and filling it out will help you organize your thoughts for the time when you actually show your home.

The Listing Worksheet includes critical information about every facet of your home and property, including room size, special features of your home, the availability of nearby schools and services, and so on. In addition, there is a space to include a photograph of your home. Color photographs are preferable (especially if the grounds or landscaping are a strong selling point) but a clear black-and-white photograph will also serve the purpose. Polaroid snapshots are fine; the main objective is that the photo present a clear, attractive picture of your home.

After you have completed this form, make enough copies so that you can hand it out to prospective buyers. Buyers will probably be looking at other houses besides yours, and this form enables them to refresh their memories about any specific details they might have forgotten. It is especially valuable for out-of-town prospects who cannot easily make a second visit to your home.

LISTING WORKSHEET

FOR SALE BY OWNER	**(PHOTOGRAPH)**	Owner _____ Telephone Bus: _____ Res: _____ . . . . (headline describing key selling features)

Street _____ County _____ City _____ State _____ Zip _____

Age ____ Style _____ Construction _____ Lot Size _____ Sq. Feet _____

Total Rooms ____ No. Bedrooms ____ No. Baths ____ Garage _____ Basement _____

Special Features _____ Major Improvements _____

Zoning/Building Restrictions _____ Legal _____

Price _____ Terms _____ Occupancy Date _____

Kitchen _____	Roof _____
Breakfast Room _____	Foundation _____
Dining Room _____	Sidewalk _____
Living Room _____	Curb/Gutter _____
Family Room _____	Sewer _____
Bedroom #1 _____	Street Surface _____
Bedroom #2 _____	Patio _____
Bedroom #3 _____	Pool _____
Bedroom #4 _____	Fence _____

Floors —————————————————

Attic —————————————————

Closets —————————————————

Draperies —————————————————

Carpet —————————————————

Antenna —————————————————

—————————————————

Total Annual Taxes

City ——— State ——— County ———

Annual Maintenance Fee —————————

Utilities (Average per month):

Elec. ———————— Water ————————

Fuel ———————— Trash ————————

Gas ———————— Other ————————

Schools:

Elementary —————————————

Junior High —————————————

Senior High —————————————

College —————————————

Air Conditioning

Central ———————— Units ————————

Heat —————————————————

A/C Units —————————————————

Fireplace —————————————————

Exhaust Fan —————————————————

Dishwasher —————————————————

Disposal —————————————————

Clothes Washer —————————————————

Clothes Dryer —————————————————

Utility Room —————————————————

Oven —————————————————

Range —————————————————

Water District —————————————————

Churches:

Catholic —————————————

Protestant —————————————

Jewish —————————————

Other —————————————

Remarks:

SELLING YOUR HOME THROUGH ADVERTISING

Now you're ready to let people know about the good offer that's become available to them. In a word: *advertise.*

Advertising the sale of your home involves two things:

1. buying a "For Sale by Owner" sign, and
2. placing an advertisement announcing the sale of your home in a newspaper.

"FOR SALE BY OWNER"

A "For Sale by Owner" sign is a tax-deductible selling cost and a very good idea. This sign will attract neighbors who will tell their friends and acquaintances about the home that has recently gone on the market, and it will catch the eye of passersby who might be driving around the neighborhood in search of a new dwelling.

You can purchase such a sign at your local hardware store. You can even paint your own on a piece of wood (just be sure the lettering is dark and neat). A "For Sale by Owner" sign lets people know that you, the homeowner and the person most knowledgeable about all the features of your home, are the one who's selling it. Post the sign prominently in your front yard. (*Note:* if aggressive real-estate agents start to come by the carful, politely but firmly tell them you intend to sell your house yourself.)

ADVERTISEMENTS

Advertisements in newspapers announcing that your home is for sale are also a tax-deductible expense from the profit you make when you sell. You can place any of a number of different types of ads, depending upon what your sales objectives are. If your number-one priority is to sell your home quickly, ads can and should be written with this in mind. Often, people who must sell their homes in a prescribed period of time are willing to slightly lower their prices or make other concessions to a buyer. If this is true in your case, be sure to say so in the ad. It's a terrific way to get your phone to start ringing.

In your ads, it pays to emphasize the most important or attractive features of your home in the ad headline. In today's economy, for example, a low-interest assumable mortgage might just be the best calling card you've got. Use it to maximum advantage in your ad.

Where Do You Advertise?

The best place to advertise is in your local paper. If you live in an urban or suburban area you should also place an ad in the nearest large metropolitan daily newspaper. Community and college newspapers and published announcements and bulletins (church newsletters, for example) can also bring results. You, as the seller of your home, are familiar with your neighborhood and the kind of publications potential buyers are most likely to read. But be sure to advertise in the major local and nearby metropolitan papers.

When Do You Advertise?

Many people choose to advertise exclusively in the weekend real-estate sections of their paper. Weekends are the time when potential homebuyers or those already looking are best able to sit down with the paper and peruse the "For Sale" announcements carefully. On the other hand, people who are seriously looking to purchase a new home may well be reading the announcements in the daily papers also. Depending upon how much you want to spend—$300 is about average—it's a wise idea to place ads in the Friday, Saturday, Sunday, and Monday editions. Again, the cost is tax-deductible and good ad space may be less expensive than you expect (ad rates vary greatly throughout the country). Call the advertising department of the paper or papers you want to advertise in and ask them to tell you their rates for daily and weekend editions. A well-written ad with a strong headline that announces the sale of an attractive, affordable home—especially one with a low assumable mortgage—will usually start to pull in responses immediately. Your ad may run for only one week before you are inundated with calls for appointments to come and see.

Finally, don't forget about the free advertising that you can get from friends and neighbors who'll spread the word. You might even decide to have an "open house" to get the ball rolling.

The following guidelines will help you to write and place advertisements that *sell* your home. Read the examples carefully. Remember, a well-written ad can have an immediate effect.

TIPS ON ADVERTISING

A well-written advertisement will do the following:

1. list the selling points of the home,
2. mention the benefits it offers the buyer,
3. single out the one feature that stands out above all the others, and
4. take that outstanding feature and make it the central theme of the advertisement.

Every advertisement should include: (1) the location, (2) the price, (3) the style (whether colonial, ranch, etc.), (4) the number of bedrooms and baths, (5) the size of the lot, (6) the condition of the property, (7) transportation facilities, and (8) nearness of schools, churches, and stores.

To get attention for your ad, the headline of the ad should be done in big, bold, black type. Some good examples are:

PRICED FOR QUICK SALE
MOST UNUSUAL VALUE
OWNER'S LOSS YOUR GAIN
MUST LIQUIDATE IMMEDIATELY
I'VE GOT TO MOVE
OWNER OUT OF TOWN—MUST SELL NOW
NOT A ROW-UPON-ROW DEVELOPMENT
BUILT WHEN BUILDING WAS AN ART
NOT A CRACKER BOX
FUSSY BUILDER
ONE ACRE OF LAND AND A HOME
REMODELING NOW COMPLETE
SPECULATORS, ATTENTION
EXTRAORDINARY SACRIFICE
BE YOUR OWN MASTER
FREE YOURSELF FROM THE LANDLORD
A CHILD'S PARADISE
SECURITY IS THE WATCHWORD
TREES GALORE
EXECUTIVE NEIGHBORHOOD WITH PRESTIGE HOMES
EXCLUSIVE AREA OF ESTABLISHED FAMILIES
PROFESSIONALLY LANDSCAPED

Descriptive phrases within the ad itself also increase its appeal. Examples are:

- built-in barbecue pit, waiting for a cookout
- fenced yard, providing a safe play area for children
- breathtaking great room, with ample windows that bring the outdoors inside
- plush carpet and expensive drapes included in price
- cozy fireplace nestled in brick wall
- step-saving kitchen with name-brand, built-in appliances that make even a man want to cook
- the charming formality of a closed-off dining room
- a king-size sultan's hideaway with elegant private bath, his and hers walk-in closets, located far away from the children's area
- walk-in closets with space for much more than clothes
- a dignified dining area that makes every meal a banquet
- a family room located for maximum access to the outdoors and kitchen
- police and fire protection nearby
- planned traffic patterns and entryways designed to prevent guests from staring into the kitchen

Whatever you do, don't pinch pennies with your ad. By selling your home yourself, you'll be saving thousands of dollars in real-estate commissions, so you can afford to give the ad your best show. Don't use abbreviations. Tell the newspaper to give the ad a black border around it. Leave plenty of white space. Here are some good examples:

THREE YEARS OF A MAN'S LOVE AND LABOR FOR
ONLY $10,000

Young 9-room split-level for a growing family. Set in 1/4 acre corner of West Islip, with stand-out landscaping. Original cost was $65,000. Brand new just three short years ago. $10,000 more buys love, labor, and the cash the owner poured in to make his the neighborhood showcase:

    Year 1: laid the flagstone patio
    Year 2: custom-finished the recreation room
    Year 3: built shelves and storage bins in the garage

Many, many other custom touches, like oak flooring. Owner widowed, must abandon lovely home for L.A.

SACRIFICE PRICE: $75,000

Call the owner now for showing: LE 1-2902

JUST MARRIED? JUST RETIRED? Here's a home that's as spacious as you need, and as gracious as you could want. There's just enough of a yard to take your ease in without causing you trouble. It's shady, too, for barbecues, but sunny enough for rose gardening. You'll also be snug and content within under a new roof and blanketed by new insulation. And there's an extra bedroom for company as well as room for another car in the garage. You can stroll to stores within minutes. It's not old (5 years), but the mortgage is—one of the good old low-interest ones. Price is right too, $70,000. Call the owner now, 463-7050.

TOP SECRET

Don't let anyone else hear about the spacious, all-brick Colonial we're selling in River Oaks. We want you to be the first to see this once-in-a-lifetime buy.

It's got that convenient but still secluded location you've dreamed about, near Westheimer and River Oaks Boulevard.

It's got 7 bedrooms, 5 baths, and we don't know how many trees sealing out the rest of the world.
Call Owner at 666-6767.

ROOM TO ROAM

Here's the home for the growing family   3 bedrooms, 2½ baths

There's a den, too

Everyone can get off by himself whenever he wants to . . .
                                  Call the owner 889-9898

Shorter ads without borders can also be effective. Here are some examples of how type can be used persuasively to help sell your home:

WORRIED ABOUT SOARING GASOLINE PRICES? Here's a 3 bedroom beauty within blocks of all bus lines and so close to Northwest Mall you can walk there and back in no time. Only blocks away from schools too . . . Call owner 333-4545.

YOU WON'T BE BURNING MONEY HEATING THIS HOME, with its high-efficiency air conditioner and its extra-thick (R.23) insulation. Call owner 223-2323.

SLEEP AS LATE AS YOU WANT on this quiet block. No traffic to speak of. And with 2 bedrooms, you can take your pick. If you wish to discourage guests, turn the other into a den. Haven't you always wanted one? Now's your chance in a home of your own . . . Call owner 444-4545.

FORGET ABOUT HIGH FUEL BILLS . . . extra insulation and solid brick construction make this 3-bedroom ranch a dream-come-true for today's energy-conscious homebuyer . . . Call owner 212-1122.

At a time when interest rates are high, probably the most effective ad of all is the one that emphasizes the easy assumption of your existing mortgage, as in the following advertisement:

RIVER OAKS 10½%
$30,000 assumes the non-qualifying, non-escalating loan on this exquisite 4BR, 2-story Colonial in stately River Oaks. Call the owner at 666-6666 after 6PM before you lose the finance opportunity of a lifetime. No agents please!

If you have an assumable loan, this ad alone could very well bring you dozens of qualified buyers.

TWO FINAL TIPS

1. Always specify in the ad that you are the owner of the home advertised, not a realtor. Many buyers prefer dealing directly, in the belief that they will save money by avoiding a sales commission.
2. Be prepared for a deluge of calls from realtors requesting your listing. Politely but firmly decline.

HOW TO HELP YOUR BUYER GET A LOAN— THE THREE BASIC WAYS

In the old days before inflation hit us hard, it seemed that almost any salaried couple or individual could qualify for a home mortgage. Interest rates were 6% or 7% and the average cost of a new house was $30,000 to $40,000. Nowadays, with sky-rocketing interest rates of 17% and 18% and houses selling for double the price they fetched just a few years ago, the problem of obtaining financing is *the single greatest stumbling block* to actually selling your home.

It is the question uppermost in every potential buyer's mind, and unless you can help him or her solve that question, you may not make the sale. I can't emphasize this enough. A buyer's ability to get the needed financing is more often than not the deciding factor in whether or not the seller can sell his home.

One of your primary concerns as a seller should be to find out all you can about the different possibilities for home financing. After all, the money your buyer obtains will go directly to you, most likely toward the purchase of your own new home. Your buyer's ability to get that loan is directly related to your profit on the sale and to how well you and your family will be able to live in the future.

In this chapter we will discuss the three *basic* types of loans available:*

---

* Real-estate laws vary from state to state. Certain states have special eligibility requirements or conditions under which loans can be approved. Before making a final decision about the method of financing to be used, consult your lawyer.

1. *conventional,*
2. *FHA (Federal Housing Administration),* and
3. *VA (Veterans Administration).*

CONVENTIONAL LOANS

A conventional loan is a loan obtained from a commercial lender (generally a bank or a savings and loan association) in which the mortgagee (the institution lending the money) establishes a fixed interest rate for the life of the loan, usually 25 or 30 years. The interest rate charged varies according to the money market. In 1981, the interest on conventional mortgages ranged from 16% to as high as 20%. This steep interest rate made it difficult for many prospective buyers to afford a new home, although the good news on the horizon is that many experts now predict that a downward trend in rates will soon begin.

If your buyer expects to go this route for financing, you'll need to know where these loans are currently available and the kind of rates your local lenders are offering. Banks and S&Ls often announce their rates and loan policies in newspapers and on the radio, but the most direct way to get this information is to comparison-shop by phone. You'll want to make a thorough survey of all the major lenders in your area to ascertain the availability of mortgage money in the near future, current interest rates being charged for new home loans, and so on. Keep in mind that different lenders have different policies on such important items to a buyer as the rate of interest and the term of the loan. It pays to shop around.

When investigating conventional loans, keep your ears open for the mention of *points*. Some commercial lenders apply points (also called "discount points" and "origination" or "loan fees") when they agree to lend money. A point is a percentage of the mortgage's value; one point is one percent of the mortgage's value. On a $50,000 loan, for example, one point would be $500. This cost adds up surprisingly rapidly and even though it is charged only once (at the time the loan is made), the question of who pays the point—you or your buyer—can crop up later. If your buyer gets a loan from a lender that charges points, make sure it is stated in your sale agreement that the buyer does not charge you for this amount. At the least, it should be negotiated between you so that you, as seller, are not responsible for the entire amount.

FHA LOANS

FHA loans are loans for which the federal government establishes the interest rate; the government insures the loan as well. Despite the name, the financing for these loans comes not from the Federal Housing Administration but from a commercial lender—a bank, savings and loan association, or other mortgagee. If you have an FHA loan, it can be assumed by your new buyer without any approval from the mortgage company.

The FHA appraises your property by comparing it with homes of similar size (square footage), style (one- or two-story), and features (numbers of bedrooms, baths, etc.) located in the same subdivision (preferably on the same street) that have recently been sold. The FHA appraiser receives this information, as well as the selling price of the comparable property and the date it was sold, from the local Board of Realtors. The FHA appraiser will inspect your house and inform you in writing of any repairs that are required; usually such repairs involve the major systems of your house—plumbing, heating, etc. Any repairs cited by the FHA appraiser must be completed *before* the FHA will issue a loan.

Facts About FHA Financing

• FHA loans may be assumed at the same rate of interest as the original loan. Escalation of interest rates is not allowed.

• FHA loans may be paid in part or in full before maturity without any prepayment penalties.

• FHA loans may be assumed without the buyer having to qualify. Also, the assumer need not occupy the property.

• FHA buyers do not have to be United States citizens to use FHA financing; they must only reside in the United States or its possessions.

• Buyers can use FHA financing outside the United States if the property is located in a possession of the United States (Puerto Rico, Guam, etc.).

• Virtually anyone 18 years of age or older may use FHA financing. Even wealthy individuals may use FHA financing; you cannot be financially overqualified for an FHA mortgage.

• Unmarried co-mortgagors are allowed to combine their incomes and purchase homes with FHA-insured financing.

• National Guardsmen and Reservists are allowed a reduced down payment on FHA loans for serving their country: no down payment on the first $25,000 of the sales price and only 5% down payment required on the balance over $25,000.

• The FHA has a non-owner-occupied program (investor) for one- to four-family unit structures. This program requires an additional 15% down payment over what an owner-occupant would be required to make as a down payment.

• The FHA allows co-mortgagors to purchase property together and only requires that one of the co-mortgagors must occupy the property in order to obtain the maximum mortgage amount.

• Mortgage companies require 30 days notice from the seller that he intends to pay off his FHA loan. Failure to give this notice may result in 30 days additional interest being charged.

• The FHA may refund a portion of the 0.5% mortgage insurance premium (MIP) if the loan has been held at least 12 years.

• The FHA has a program for home-improvement loans, but these are usually underwritten by commercial banks rather than by savings and loans or mortgage companies.

• FHA loans may be refinanced, subject to state laws. Any home with any type of mortgage or no mortgage may be refinanced using FHA financing, subject to state laws.

FHA Buyer Qualifications

Credit: The applicant must have established a satisfactory credit history for at least two years, unless he or she has just graduated from college or has just become of legal age to buy property. Several slow ratings on a credit report would normally be a basis for rejection, unless there are extremely good reasons for the slow ratings.

Employment: The lender must be able to verify two years of satisfactory employment; if the applicant was in the armed services or in school this usually will count.

Bankruptcy or foreclosures: If the bankruptcy or foreclosure occurred seven or more years go and the applicant has since re-established good credit, he or she may be acceptable. Bankruptcy or foreclosures within the past three years will usually be unacceptable.

Monthly payments: Any monthly payments on other loans or charge accounts of less than 12 months in duration will not count against the applicant. The FHA will look at the minimum monthly payment required rather than the actual amount being paid on revolving accounts.

Cash required: The buyer must verify that he has enough cash to pay the down payment and closing costs prior to approval by the FHA.

Gift letters: Gift letters from relatives or business associates are acceptable, but they must state what the gift is intended for, the amount, the relationship to the buyer, and that the money does not need to be repaid. Parents may give children money for down payments, but the money must be a *gift,* not a loan.

Child support: Child support received will usually count toward income. It is necessary to show proof of child support, such as canceled checks or payment through the courts.

Rental income: Rental income (income from another property owned by applicant, such as a house, a duplex or apartment building) may count if there is a lease or rental agreement from the tenant verifying payment.

Caution: actually only approximately 50% of the rental income that exceeds the applicant's mortgage payment ends up being counted after taxes, maintenance, and a factor for vagrancy are figured in. If the applicant's income is borderline, it may be to his advantage to sell the original property in order to qualify for a loan to buy the new property.

Co-borrowers: Co-borrowers are allowed even if they are not related. There is no limit to the number of co-borrowers and only one of the co-borrowers must occupy the property in order to obtain the maximum mortgage amount allowed by the FHA.

Non-owner-occupied: The FHA will allow investors to purchase property that they will not occupy, but requires an additional 15% down payment on top of the normal FHA down payment.

FHA Property Qualifications

Age: In general, the house should not be more than 20 years old; particularly well-constructed homes may exceed 20 years in age.

Price range: The value should be above $35,000 and below $120,000 in most cases. Homes below $35,000 in price generally require excessive repair or will not be appraised at the requested value. Homes priced above $40,000 and less than 20 years old have a much better chance of being appraised for full price or without repairs.

Units: One- to four-family units as long as they are attached.

Acreage: Limited to a maximum of five acres.

Specifications: The property should have modern plumbing, heating, and electrical systems. Modern floor plans are mandatory, and the number of bedrooms should be adequate for the buyer's family size. Ceilings must be a minimum of 7'2" throughout. The property should not adjoin commercial areas or railroads or underdeveloped areas. If near incinerators, factories, or airports, or if in a neighborhood shifting to rooming houses or commercial use, the property may be unacceptable.

Appraisals: FHA appraisals are valid for 6 months on existing homes and for 12 months on proposed construction. No extension of the appraisal is allowed.

How to Figure Maximum Mortgage Amounts on FHA Level-Payment Mortgages

If an FHA buyer is going to pay his own closing costs, he may receive a higher mortgage amount than you have figured. This higher mortgage amount is allowed in order to offset the buyer's closing costs. (In effect, this permits the costs to be financed.) This allows the buyer to purchase the property with a smaller cash outlay than if the standard mortgage amount is used.

Here is the way the total acquisition cost is figured, to arrive at the maximum mortgage amount:

The buyer must pay his own closing costs and prepaid items. The sale price must be equal to or less than the FHA appraised value.

Sale price:	$60,000
FHA appraised value:	60,000

The closing costs are added to the sale price to arrive at the total acquisition cost:

Sale price:	60,000
Estimated closing costs:	950
Total acquisition cost:	$60,950

FHA MORTGAGE TABLE FOR LEVEL PAYMENT MORTGAGES

FHA Appraised Value	FHA Standard Mortgage Amount	FHA* Maximum Mortgage Amount	FHA-VET Standard Mortgage Amount	FHA-VET* Maximum Mortgage Amount	Estimated Buyers Closing Costs	Estimated Buyers Prepaid Costs
$ 35,000	33,750	34,400	34,500	35,000	700	425
36,000	34,700	35,350	35,450	36,000	700	450
37,000	35,650	36,300	36,400	37,000	700	450
38,000	36,600	37,300	37,350	38,000	750	475
39,000	37,550	38,250	38,300	39,000	750	475
40,000	38,500	39,200	39,250	39,950	750	500
41,000	39,450	40,150	40,200	40,900	750	500
42,000	40,400	41,100	41,150	41,850	750	525
43,000	41,350	42,050	42,100	42,800	750	525
44,000	42,300	43,050	43,050	43,750	800	550
45,000	43,250	44,000	44,000	44,750	800	550
46,000	44,200	44,950	44,950	45,700	800	575
47,000	45,150	45,900	45,900	46,550	800	575
48,000	46,100	46,850	46,850	47,600	800	600
49,000	47,050	47,800	47,800	48,550	800	600
50,000	48,000	48,800	48,750	49,550	850	625
51,000	48,950	49,750	49,700	50,500	850	625
52,000	49,900	50,700	50,650	51,450	850	650
53,000	50,850	51,650	51,600	52,400	850	650
54,000	51,800	52,600	52,550	53,350	850	675
55,000	52,750	53,600	53,500	54,350	900	675
56,000	53,700	54,550	54,450	55,300	900	700
57,000	54,650	55,500	55,400	56,250	900	700
58,000	55,600	56,450	56,350	57,200	900	725
59,000	56,550	57,400	57,300	58,150	900	725
60,000	57,500	58,400	58,250	59,150	950	750
61,000	58,450	59,350	59,200	60,100	950	750
62,000	59,400	60,300	60,150	61,050	950	775
63,000	60,350	61,250	61,100	62,000	950	775
64,000	61,300	62,200	62,050	62,950	950	800
65,000	62,250	63,200	63,000	63,950	1,000	800
66,000	63,200	64,150	63,950	64,900	1,000	825
67,000	64,150	65,100	64,900	65,850	1,000	825
68,000	65,100	66,050	65,850	66,800	1,000	850
69,000	66,050	67,000	66,800	67,750†	1,000	850
70,000	67,000	67,950†	67,750†	69,150	1,000	875
71,000	67,950†	68,900	68,700	69,660	1,000	875
72,000	68,900	69,850	69,650	70,500	1,050	900
73,000	69,850	70,800	70,600	71,550	1,050	900
74,000	70,800	71,750	71,550	72,500	1,050	925
75,000	71,750	72,700	72,500	73,450	1,050	925
76,000	72,700	73,700	73,450	74,450	1,100	950
77,000	73,650	74,650	74,400	75,400	1,100	950
78,000	74,600	75,600	75,350	76,350	1,100	975
79,000	75,550	76,550	76,300	77,300	1,100	975
80,000	76,500	77,500	77,250	78,250	1,100	1,000
81,000	77,450	78,450	78,200	79,200	1,100	1,000
82,000	78,400	79,450	79,150	80,200	1,150	1,025
83,000	79,350	80,400	80,100	81,150	1,150	1,025
84,000	80,300	81,350	81,050	82,100	1,150	1,050
85,000	81,250	82,300	82,000	83,050	1,150	1,050
86,000	82,200	83,250	82,950	84,000	1,150	1,075
87,000	83,150	84,250	83,900	85,000	1,200	1,075
88,000	84,100	85,200	84,850	85,950	1,200	1,100
89,000	85,050	86,150	85,800	85,900	1,200	1,100
90,000	86,000	87,100	86,750	87,850	1,200	1,125
91,000	86,950	88,050	87,700	88,800	1,200	1,125
92,000	87,900	89,050	88,650	89,800	1,250	1,150
93,000	88,850	90,000	89,600	90,750	1,250	1,150
94,000	89,800	90,950	90,550	91,700	1,250	1,175
95,000	90,750	91,900	91,500	92,650	1,250	1,175
96,000	91,700	92,850	92,450	93,600	1,250	1,200
97,000	92,550	93,800	93,400	94,550	1,250	1,200
98,000	93,600	94,750	94,350	95,500	1,250	1,225
99,000	94,550	95,700	95,300	96,450	1,250	1,225
100,000	95,500	96,650	96,250	97,400	1,250	1,250

* Based on buyer paying own closing costs. Buyer can obtain a higher mortgage amount to offset his closing costs. If the seller pays any of the buyers closing costs the maximum mortgage amount must be reduced by the amount paid by the seller.
† Loan amounts are available in excess of $67,500 in some areas. Check with area lenders.

The FHA will allow the buyer to finance 97% of the first $25,000 and 95% of the balance of the total acquisition cost:

97% of $25,000:	24,250
95% of the balance (35,950):	34,152
Maximum mortgage amount:	$58,402

Always round down your answer to the nearest $50 increment. Thus the maximum mortgage in this example would be $58,400. And the down payment would be $1,600.

Using the FHA-Vet program, the veteran (Reservist with 90 days of active duty or a regular VA-qualified veteran) is allowed to finance 100% of the first $25,000 and 95% of the balance of the total acquisition cost.

Sale price:	$60,000
Estimated closing costs:	950
Total acquisition cost:	$60,950
100% of the first $25,000:	25,000
95% of the balance (35,950):	34,152
Maximum mortgage amount for vet:	59,152
Rounded down to:	$59,150

Thus the maximum loan for an FHA-Vet in this example would be $59,150 and the down payment would be $850.

VA LOANS

With a VA loan a commercial lender makes the actual payment, but the Veterans Administration regulates the interest rate and guarantees the loan up to a maximum of $110,000 (when there is no down payment) or $135,000 (when there is a down payment of at least 25% of the sales price of the home) in case of default.

Eligibility

To be eligible for a VA loan, a veteran must meet the following criteria: be a World War II veteran, Korean War veteran or Vietnam War veteran who served in the armed forces of the United States a) between September 16, 1940, and July 25, 1947, or b) after June 26, 1950, and before February 1, 1955, or c) during the Vietnam War and was discharged under conditions other than dishonorable, after at least 90 days' active service (less than 90 days with a service-connected disability).

Pre-Korean veterans. Those who served a) after July 25, 1947, and before June 27, 1950, for a period of more than 180 days and were discharged under conditions other than dishonorable (less than 180 days with a service-connected disability).

Surviving spouses. An unremarried surviving spouse of a veteran who died as a result of service is also eligible for a VA loan.

Other persons. American citizens who served in the armed forces of a government allied with the United States in World War II and who a) have not received any loan-guarantee benefits from a foreign government in whose armed forces they served and b) are residents of the United States at the time they file for a GI loan.

Veterans may have more than one GI loan provided the first home they purchase with their VA eligibility has been sold and the former loan paid off or another eligible ex-GI buys the home and assumes the first VA loan using his or her own eligibility.

Caution: A veteran who allows a nonveteran to assume his or her VA loan may lose part or all of his or her eligibility for a future VA home purchase. Check with your local VA office before allowing a nonveteran to assume your VA loan.

As a veteran, your maximum eligibility for a loan with no down payment is $27,500 × 4 = $110,000; with a down payment of 25% of the toal purchase price, the maximum eligibility is $135,000. Unlike a conventional loan, where the payment of points is negotiable between buyer and seller, with a new VA loan, the seller is required by law to pay the points charged by the lender.

Like FHA loans, a VA loan can be assumed by a new buyer without the mortgage company's approval.

If your buyers meet the above criteria for VA eligibility, have them contact their local VA office and ask for a certificate of eligibility. Have the buyers take this to the mortgage lender at the time they make the loan application to purchase your home.

Facts About VA Financing

- Approximately 40% of the adult population of the United States either are veterans or are married to veterans.
- With 30 million eligible veterans and 20 million spouses, there are enough veterans to purchase all of the estimated 30 million single-family homes in the United States.
- Widows of veterans may be eligible for VA home loans if the veteran died while in service or of a

service-connected injury or illness. Widows of veterans who are listed as missing in action (MIA) may be eligible for VA loans. In the majority of these cases they are eligible.

- Veterans of certain allied countries who fought with us in World War II are eligible for VA loans even though they may not be U.S. citizens. The countries are: Australia, Canada, England, Formosa (Taiwan), France, India, Northern Ireland, and South Africa.
- Veterans usually get home loans from private lenders, but in areas where there are no private lenders making VA loans the veteran can get a direct loan from the Veterans Administration.
- A veteran and a nonveteran may purchase a home together as co-borrowers. However, the VA will *not* guarantee the nonveteran's portion of the loan. Consequently most lenders will not make this type of loan.
- The VA allows co-signers on VA loans but the co-signer must be exceptionally well qualified and be able to qualify for the loan by himself. Co-signers will not hold any title to the property but will have liability for repayment of the loan.
- The VA allows secondary financing in some situations if the secondary loan is secured by real property or by some other asset owned by the veteran.
- The VA makes business loans to veterans.
- The VA has a mobile-home loan program. Some private lenders participate but most do not.
- VA loans can be refinanced. On a VA refinance, buyer and seller can negotiate who pays the discount points. There is no prepayment penalty on VA loans.
- The interest rates on VA loans do not escalate on loan assumptions.
- Some veterans who served during the Korean War era (1950–55) and purchased a home with a VA loan prior to March 3, 1966, need not have that VA loan paid in full to regain full eligibility, but they must have disposed of the property.
- The VA allows common-law marriages without reduction of the loan guaranty for the nonveteran.
- VA grants of up to $30,000 are available for veterans who are restricted to a wheelchair or otherwise handicapped, to use for specially adapted housing.
- Veterans may purchase townhomes (or townhouses, in which the owner has title to the land, the home, and all improvements on it) or condominium units (in which a percentage of the whole building and the land, and the air space is owned), however, the homeowners association would have to be VA-approved and few of them are approved.
- A veteran may purchase a home with improvements or additions to be made, usch as: adding a garage, adding a bedroom, finishing the basement, insulating, or adding solar heat. These additions may be financed in the VA home loan.

ADVANTAGES AND DISADVANTAGES OF FHA AND VA FINANCING

Advantages

Low cash outlay: On most transactions, no down payment is required for a VA mortgage, and only a low down payment is required for an FHA, allowing buyers who are short on cash to obtain financing—or allowing a buyer who has plenty of cash to use his money for other endeavors.

Favorable interest rate: The maximum interest rate is lower for veterans than for FHA or conventional loans in most cases.

Liberal qualifying formula for VA: The veteran usually can qualify for considerably higher loan amounts due to the progressive and liberal qualifying formula employed by the VA. In some cases veterans can qualify for up to $40,000 more on a VA loan than on a conventional loan.

Loans are assumable: VA or FHA loans can be assumed without the interest rate escalating or the buyer's having to qualify. This feature makes the home more salable in the future, and if the buyer later resells it on an assumption, saves him from paying discount points (as no mortgage company is involved). Veterans who assume other veterans' loans and substitute eligibiity will have to qualify.

No prepayment penalty: With VA and FHA loans there is no prepayment penalty if the buyer pays off all or part of the loan before maturity.

Disadvantages

The seller may demand full price: Because the interest rate to the buyer is lower with a VA or FHA loan than with a conventional loan, the seller is required to pay the discount points on these loans. As a result of this expense to the seller, he or she may not be willing to accept less than the full price being asked for the home.

Some sellers fear VA or FHA appraisals: Some sellers prefer not to sell their homes to VA or FHA buyers because of a fear that their house will not be appraised at the full value or that the VA or FHA will require that they make numerous repairs.

Processing time: The time necessary to process and close a VA or FHA loan is from four to six weeks, compared to two to four weeks on most conventional loans.

SUMMARY OF VA, FHA, AND CONVENTIONAL MORTGAGE FINANCING

Program	Maximum Loan Amount	Maximum Term	Interest Rate	Down-payment Requirement	Type of Housing	Notes
VA	$110,000 with no down payment $135,000 with a 25% down payment on the amount above $110,000	30 years	set at time of loan	No down payment required	1–4 family homes over 1 year old, or built under VA supervision, or homes built under Home Owners Warranty Program (HOW)	There are approximately 30 million veterans; only 10 million VA loans have been made to date. Seller is required to pay all of the veteran's closing costs and prepaid items.
FHA	1-family home: $69,500* 2-family home: $78,000 3-family home: $95,000 4-family home: $109,500	30 years	set at time of loan	Down payment will vary from 2% to 5%	1–4 family homes over 1 year old, or built to FHA specifications, or built under HOW program	For properties not over 1 year old or built under FHA specifications, a 10% down payment is required unless built under HOW program.
FHA Vet	69,500*	30 years	set at time of loan	Down payment will vary from 0% to 3%	1-family homes over 1 year old, or built to FHA specifications, or built under HOW program	Vet need only serve 90 days of active duty. Basic training time counts. National Guard and Reserves are eligible. Regular vets are also eligible for this program.
FHA Graduated Payment†	69,500*	30 years	set at time of loan	Down payment will vary	1-family homes only, same as above	For properties not over 1 year old or built under FHA specifications, a 10% down payment is required unless built under HOW program.
80% Conv.	$93,750	30 years	set at time of loan	20%	1–4 family	Non-owner-occupied duplexes
90% Conv.	$93,750	30 years	set at time of loan	10%	1–4 family	Owner-occupied duplexes
95% Conv.	$75,000	30 years	set at time of loan	5%	1–4 family	Owner-occupied duplexes

* FHA maximum loan amounts may be higher for designated high-cost areas. Check with local FHA office.
† FHA Graduated Payment loans allow the buyer a reduced payment during the first five years of the loan. Thereafter, the payment is increased each year until it reaches the note rate level. For example, FHA loans are currently at 16½%, but under this plan, the buyer might start paying an effective rate of, say, 12%, and over five years build to slightly over the 16½% note rate.

HOW TO HELP YOUR BUYER GET A LOAN— WITH CREATIVE FINANCING

For homebuyers, the obvious advantage of creative financing plans is that they make it possible to obtain the money needed to purchase a home that otherwise would simply be too expensive. These creative financing techniques are a real boon for American homeowners, and as a seller, it's important to realize, if a prospective buyer tells you he or she wants to purchase your home but is afraid it won't be possible to get the necessary financing, that a number of creative alternatives *are* available.*

There are six standard types of creative financing programs:

1. *Assumption of existing mortgage* (by far the easiest and most highly recommended program for the average homeowner)
2. *contract for sale or deed*
3. *second mortgage*
4. *owner financing*
5. *wraparound mortgage*
6. *secondary financing with a new VA mortgage*

In the following pages, each of these six creative means of helping your buyer qualify for a loan is discussed in detail—and then we'll explore some other possibilities.

---

* Real-estate laws vary from state to state. Certain states have special eligibility requirements or conditions under which loans can be approved. Before making a final decision about the method of financing to be used, consult your lawyer.

MORTGAGE ASSUMPTION

With an assumption the buyer takes over the responsibility for making payments on the mortgage currently held by the seller. The buyer will pay the difference between the sales price and the present loan balance in cash to the seller. (*Example:* Sales price = $70,000, loan balance = $40,000. Buyer would have to give seller $30,000 to assume his mortgage.)

Advantages

The buyer may avoid having to qualify for the loan. He may be able to assume a lower interest rate, and he avoids the closing costs associated with a new loan.

The seller avoids paying discount points, reduces his closing costs, and does not usually have to worry about the buyer qualifying. Also there is no appraisal to worry about.

Disadvantages

Many mortgages are either not assumable or are assumable only if the interest rate is increased to the current rate. Some lenders require the buyer to qualify for the loan. (VA and FHA loans are always assumable without the interest rate escalating.) The seller still remains liable for repayment of the loan if the new buyer fails to pay. (However, if the buyer defaults, the seller keeps the entire down payment and can sell the house again.)

Example

VA and FHA loan assumptions are generally the most desirable because there is no prepayment penalty, no interest escalation, and generally the buyers do not have to qualify. Investors may assume FHA and VA loans with no intention of occupying the property. Here is an example of a VA loan assumption:

Sales price:	$70,000
Existing VA loan balance:	40,000
Cash needed to assume:	$30,000
Interest rate at 8%	
Total mortgage payment:	$400/mo.

An assumption contract is written with the buyer to pay the seller $30,000 in cash and the buyer takes over the existing mortgage payment of $400 per month. There is absolutely no qualifying required for the buyer, or any appraisal required on the property. The seller will not have to pay discount points and the buyer will not have to pay closing costs (origination fee, credit report, etc.).

In the event that another veteran is going to assume the VA mortgage and has agreed to substitute his eligibility for the original veteran's, the buyer would be required to qualify.

NOTE: the buyer may rely on other methods of creative financing to obtain the $30,000 required on this assumption example.

CONTRACT FOR SALE OR DEED

In a contract for sale or deed the seller continues to hold title to the property and continues to make payments on the original mortgage. A sales price is agreed upon by the buyer and seller; the buyer usually makes a down payment and agrees to pay the balance owed in monthly payments. The buyer "owns" the property but the title does not pass to the buyer until all the terms of the contract are satisfied and the balance owed is paid in full. There may be some type of agreement that the buyer will refinance the loan within a specified period of time or that a balloon payment will be due on a specified date. The contract for deed may or may not be recorded in the county courthouse.

Advantages

The buyer usually can purchase under contract for deed with less cash than on a new loan. The buyer is not subject to qualifying with a lending institution, although the seller will want to be satisfied that he will be repaid in full by the buyer. The buyer's interest rate may be below what he could get with new financing.

The seller avoids paying any discount points, and avoids worry about an appraisal or fear that the buyers will not qualify. The seller can create his own financing in a period of tight money.

Disadvantages

The buyer is not the owner of record until all terms of the contract are satisfied. Because the buyer does not have title until the payments are completed, he runs the risk of losing his entire interest in the home (including the down payment and any equity buildup) if he defaults on even a single payment. And when the conditions have been met, some problems could arise if the seller is unable to deliver a valid title to the buyer—due to judgments against him, divorce settlements, or any liens filed on the property.

The seller takes a chance because the buyer may not make his payments, although if this occurs the seller may repossess the property and sell it again.

Example

Sales price:	$70,000
Down payment:	10,000
Contract for deed loan amount:	$60,000
Interest agreed at 10%	
Principal and interest:	$526.80
Plus taxes and insurance:	73.20
Total payment per month:	$600.00
Existing loan on home:	$30,000
Present payment:	$300/mo.

Buyer and seller agree on a $70,000 sales price. The buyer has $10,000 for his down payment but cannot qualify for a new loan of $60,000. Since the seller needs to sell his property and is getting full sales price and feels he is getting good security with a $10,000 down payment, he agrees to receive mortgage payments of $600 per month from the buyer for a period of time (say five years). This pays his present mortgage payment of $300 and the seller pockets the additional $300 per month. At the end of the term agreed upon (five years in this example), the contract states that the note becomes payable in full. The buyer then has to obtain financing for the balance of the money due (approximately $30,000 cash) or sell to someone, thus paying off the $60,000 loan he has to the seller. If the buyer is able to repay the seller in full at this time, the deed would be transferred to the buyer and he would now become the owner of record.

SECOND MORTGAGE

Second mortgages are used when the buyer is short on cash, whether the buyer is getting new financing or is assuming the seller's existing mortgage.

One of the best sources of second mortagages is the seller of the property. When interest rates are high or new second liens are difficult to obtain, a seller may be able to make the sale of his home more attractive by offering to take a second mortgage. The rate and terms vary greatly, but usually the duration of the second mortgage is less than ten years. Occasionally a balloon payment is required at the end of the term.

Advantages

The buyer can purchase a higher-priced home with a second mortgage than he could with new financing or on an assumption, due to his available cash. The buyer may also be able to get a more favorable interest rate on the second mortgage, particularly from a motivated seller.

The seller is able to sell his home more easily in a tight money market.

Disadvantages

The buyer's payments might be larger than on new financing due to the shorter term of the second lien. The buyer may have to come up with a lump sum when the term expires.

The seller does not receive as much cash as he would if he sold his home with new financing or on an assumption.

Caution: not all lenders permit second mortgages. Normally, second mortgages are not allowed on new financing of FHA, 90% conventional, or 95% conventional loans. The VA may allow a second mortgage on a case-by-case basis.

Example

Sales price:	$70,000
Existing loan balance:	40,000
Cash needed to assume:	$30,000
Interest rate on first lien 8%	
Current payment	$400/mo.

The prospective buyer has only $20,000 cash, which is not enough to assume the existing mortgage, so he applies to a second mortgage company for a loan of $10,000. They make a second lien of $10,000 for ten years at a monthly payment of $150. He now has the $30,000 to assume the loan but will have two payments totaling $550/per month. The first payment of $400 pays the first mortgage and the $150 pays the second mortgage.

OWNER FINANCING

When the seller has a very low loan balance or owns the home free and clear, he may wish to provide a first mortgage to the buyer, particularly in a tight money market. The buyer and seller can agree on any sales price, interest rate, and mortgage term. The monthly payments are made to the seller or to an escrow agent (such as a title company) instead of to a mortgage lending institution. Funds may be escrowed for taxes and insurance or the buyer may pay these himself, depending upon the agreement with the seller.

Advantages

The buyer can purchase a home without the traditional qualifying. The buyer may be able to negotiate a better interest rate than the prevailing rate on new loans. The buyer's down payment may be less than with new financing and he can avoid the closing costs associated with new financing.

The seller can name his own terms and sales price without worrying about an appraisal or about the buyer qualifying. The seller avoids paying discount points on the sale.

Disadvantages

The buyer has no apparent disadvantages.

The seller does not get all the proceeds in cash immediately, only the down payment. However, he will receive steady monthly income. The seller may have to abide by state usury laws.

Example 1

Sales price:	$70,000
Loan balance:	0
Cash needed to purchase:	$70,000
Buyer's available cash:	$20,000

The buyer makes a down payment to the seller of $20,000 and the seller agrees to hold a first mortgage of $50,000, payable monthly at 12% interest amortized over, say, 30 years. The buyer's payment to the seller, who in effect becomes the mortgage lender, is $514.50 plus taxes and insurance. Other provisions may be written into the contract that the mortgage will become due and payable in a specific time frame.

Example 2

Sales price:	$70,000
Existing loan balance:	40,000
Cash needed to assume:	$30,000
Buyer's available cash:	$10,000
Seller carries second lien of:	$20,000

In this case the buyer assumes the first mortgage and the seller is carrying a second mortgage. The buyer is not required to qualify for the second mortgage.

WRAPAROUND MORTGAGE

This is a special kind of contract for deed. A wraparound mortgage covers the amount of the original mortgage balance and an additional amount agreed on by the buyer and seller. The new loan amount is said to envelop, or "wrap," the original mortgage. The buyer makes a down payment and will pay a monthly payment which is large enough to pay the seller's existing payment plus some additional amount which goes to the seller each month. The seller continues to make his original mortgage payment each month and pockets the difference. In addition, the interest rate on the wraparound note is generally higher than the interest rate on the seller's first mortgage, which gives the seller a greater profit.

Advantages

The buyer's overall payment may be lower than if he obtained new financing. The buyer's cash outlay is generally lower than on new financing. Further, the buyer may not be required to qualify for this type of financing.

The seller can sell his property in a tight money market and benefits from a monthly income from the payments.

Disadvantages

If the buyer does not take title to the property at the time of the closing, he may find defects in the title later on. (The buyer may or may not take title at closing, depending on the contractual agreement.)

The seller does not receive as much cash as he would with new financing or an assumption. Also, the seller's first mortgage could be called due if that lender does not permit their loans to be wrapped. *Caution:* check with the lender to see if they allow wraparounds in order to avoid legal problems.

Example

Sales price:	$70,000
Existing loan balance:	30,000
Cash needed to assume:	$40,000

Interest rate at 9% but will escalate to 13% if assumed.
Buyer has only $10,000 to put down.

The buyer puts down $10,000 and takes a $60,000 wraparound mortgage at 10% interest. The buyer's total payment to the seller would be about $500 per month. The seller's existing mortgage payment would be about $300 per month, so he would pay his mortgage and pocket the additional $200. This would also avoid or postpone the seller's having to pay a prepayment penalty on his own mortgage, and he has no discount points to pay.

Sometimes a mortgage company will make a new mortgage loan to the buyer for the $60,000 wraparound, and the mortgage company assumes the existing mortgage. In this case the buyer makes his payment to the mortgage company and the mortgage company would pay the payment on the $30,000 mortgage. This enables the seller to receive all of his proceeds at the time of sale, and avoids a prepayment penalty and discount points. *Caution:* lenders will usually limit this sort of transaction to VA or FHA first liens only.

SECONDARY FINANCING WITH A NEW VA MORTGAGE

In many instances the Veterans Administration will allow a veteran buyer to obtain a new VA first mortgage loan and a second mortgage simultaneously. The second mortgage loan could be from a lending institution or from the seller as long as the interest rate does not exceed the maximum VA rate and the buyer qualifies for both payments. This second mortgage must be secured by real property, either property already owned by the buyer or the property being purchased with the new VA financing. This type of financing can be of great value in reaching the $150,000-and-over price ranges, since the maximum VA loan that most lenders will make is $135,000.

Advantages

The buyer is able to get VA financing at a favorable interest rate in excess of current VA loan limitations, using less cash than he would normally be able to arrange.

The seller is able to sell his home in a tight money market.

Disadvantages

If the second mortgage is carried by the seller, the seller would not receive all of his proceeds at closing.

Example

A veteran buyer wishes to purchase a home for $180,000 and has $40,000 to use as a down payment. He would like a mortgage of $140,000 but most VA lenders will loan only up to a maximum of $135,000. If the seller is willing to take a second mortgage at the current VA interest rate, and the buyer qualifies for both payments (using the VA's more liberal qualifying formula), you could put this transaction together like this:

Selling price:	$180,000
VA first mortgage:	$135,000
Buyer's down payment:	40,000
Seller's second mortgage:	5,000
	$180,000

The buyer would thus have first and second mortgages totaling $140,000.

Caution: most VA lenders will require that the buyer's down payment be equal to at least one half of the purchase price that exceeds what the veteran would qualify for with no down payment. For example, if the veteran has VA entitlement of $27,500 enabling him to obtain $110,000 with no down payment, and wishes to purchase the $180,000 home in the above example, the lender would require that the veteran put down at least $35,000 from his own funds.

ALTERNATIVE METHODS OF CREATIVE FINANCING

In addition to the six methods of creative financing already discussed, there are a variety of other brand-new creative financing mortgage techniques now available. Though the names may sound slightly confusing, don't be put off. Graduated-payment mortgages (GPMs), graduated-payment adjustable mortgages (GPAMs), shared-appreciation mortgages (SAMs), rollover mortgages (ROMs), variable-rate mortgages (VRMs), pledged-account mortgages (PAMs, FLIPS, and ACTIONS), reverse-annuity mortgages (RAMs), and renegotiable-rate mortgages (RRMs) are all valuable techniques for helping your buyer obtain the needed financing under advantageous terms.

If you decide to use one of these creative financing techniques, contact your local mortgage company for a written statement detailing its specific terms. Plans vary widely depending upon the lender. And, as you will see from the summary chart on pages 48–49, there are distinct advantages to each one. Often such advantages depend on the buyer's age. For example, some plans are preferable for young homeowners whose income is likely to increase, others for seniors living on a fixed income. Consulting this summary chart will give you a head start on helping your buyer pinpoint the best type of financing.

NOTE: if your buyer uses one of these plans, add the following to your conventional earnest-money contract form under the heading "Special Provisions":

This sale is expressly contingent upon the buyer securing a [variable rate mortgage, rollover mortgage, etc.] as defined in the attached description from [name of mortgage company].

Both the buyer and the seller should initial copies of the description furnished by the mortgage company you decide to use. (For more about earnest-money contracts, see Step Nine.)

SHARED-APPRECIATION MORTGAGE (SAM)

This type of mortgage is now being offered in many states. The SAM can reduce the buyer's monthly payment, allowing the buyer to purchase a home that he or she might not otherwise be able to obtain. The lender reduces the buyer's interest rate by a fixed percentage, such as 30%. If the going interest rate is 13%, the buyer would receive a rate of approximately 9%. In return for this lower interest rate and correspondingly lower monthly payment, the buyer must give up a percentage of the profit when he in turn sells the house. The percentage is usually the same as the reduction in interest rate. So in this case, the buyer, when he sells the house in the future, shares the profits (the appreciation) with the lender. In other words the lender would be entitled to 30% of any profit received upon the sale of the home.

If the buyer remains in the home for ten years, he will owe the lender a lump sum—called "contingent interest"—equal to the agreed share of the appreciation, as determined by an appraiser, less any improvements the homeowner may have put into the home and less the cost of the appraisal. The lender would be required to refinance the home for the remaining 20 years if the borrower wishes, with the new loan covering at least the unpaid balance of the mortgage plus the amount of contingent interest.

Advantages

The buyer is able to obtain a lower monthly mortgage payment than current market rates would allow, and thus may be able to purchase a home which he might not otherwise have been able to qualify for.

The lender has the opportunity to receive large profits if the home appreciates substantially.

Disadvantages

The buyer is not entitled to all of the home's appreciation. The lender may not gain if the home does not appreciate much.

Example

The current interest rate is about 12%, and the buyer wants to obtain a $60,000 mortgage loan. At 12% interest the payment for principal and interest

would be $617.40 per month. However, the lender agrees to reduce his interest rate by one third to 8% interest, in return for 33% of any appreciation on the sale of his home. This reduces his payment for principal and interest to $440.40 per month. Therefore the buyer saves $177 per month each year. (In this example the buyer would have saved about $10,600 in payments to help offset the appreciation that the lender is entitled to.) However, when the home is sold he must share the gain by appreciation with the lender. Suppose he sells the home in five years, at a selling price of $100,000. The lender would receive $11,550 in addition to the payoff of the mortgage loan.

Selling price:	$100,000
Less costs:	65,000
Appreciation:	35,000
Lender's share 33%:	$11,550
Homeowner's share 67%:	$23,450

GRADUATED-PAYMENT MORTGAGE (GPM)

In this type of mortgage the Department of Housing and Urban Development (HUD) insures mortgages to facilitate early home ownership for households that expect their incomes to rise substantially. These graduated-payment mortgages allow homeowners to make smaller monthly payments initially and to increase their size gradually over a period of a few years, after which they level off. Five different plans are available, varying in duration and rate of increase, the most popular of which are FHA 245–Plan 3 and FHA 245–Plan 3B.

Contact your local HUD office, give them the selling price (appraised value) of your home, and ask for their help in computing the down payment, the *initial* monthly payment, and the *maximum* monthly payment your buyers will be making. In qualifying the buyer, use only the *initial* monthly payment for the principal and interest.

GRADUATED-PAYMENT ADJUSTABLE MORTGAGE (GPAM)

This type of mortgage is a cross between a graduated-payment mortgage and a variable-rate mortgage. The payments will gradually increase as with a GPM, but the interest rate also is adjusted every three, four or five years. The mortgage balance will increase approximately 10% over five years like FHA 245–Plan 3. The interest rate may be adjusted up or down for each year in the adjustment period. If the adjustment period is three years, then the rate could be adjusted up or down a maximum of 1.5% at renewal, since the rate may be adjusted no more than 0.5% per year.

Advantages

The buyer is able to attain a slightly lower interest rate because the lender is not locked into a fixed-rate mortgage for 30 years.

Disadvantages

The buyer's payments may increase more than projected if the interest rate climbs.

RENEGOTIABLE RATE MORTGAGE (RRM)

This mortgage is a cross between a rollover and a variable-rate mortgage. A 30-year term mortgage is renewed in three-, four- or five-year terms for the balance of the years remaining. The interest rates are adjusted upon renewal based on an index rate. The adjustment cannot exceed an average of 0.5% per year.

Advantages

The buyer may be able to obtain a lower interest rate initially, and if rates go down he will benefit further.

Disadvantages

The interest rates may continue to climb, increasing the buyer's payments upon renewals.

Example

On a three-year renewable mortgage plan the interest rate could be adjusted up or down 1.5% on renewal. The maximum increase or decrease cannot exceed 5% over the life of the loan.

PLEDGED ACCOUNT MORTGAGE (PAM), ALSO CALLED FLEXIBLE LOAN INSURANCE PLAN (FLIP)

Both are very similar to the conventional graduated-payment mortgage. Separate funds are deposited in a savings account and this fund plus interest is used to subsidize the mortgage payments.

Advantages

The buyer can obtain a decreased payment for several years.

Disadvantages

The buyer must make a greater down payment or cash deposit than would normally be required, or than he would have with other types of financing.

ROLLOVER MORTGAGE (ROM)

This is a renewable mortgage that is a fixed-rate mortgage which is due in full every five years. However, the lender must renew the loan or "roll over" for another five years at the prevailing interest rate. The new monthly payments are then computed for 20 years on the unpaid balance. This loan is rolled over every five years until the loan is paid off. The buyer has the option at the five-year intervals to renew the mortgage with the original lender or refinance the loan with another lender. This type of loan originated in Canada and is commonly referred to as the Canadian Rollover Mortgage. Three- and four-year rollovers are also available.

Advantages

The buyer may be able to obtain a lower interest rate since the lender does not have to guarantee an interest rate for 30 years. The lender is not saddled with a "bad investment" for 30 years.

Disadvantages

The buyer may be faced with higher payments after the first five years.

Example

A buyer wishes to take out a rollover mortgage of $60,000 at 11% interest during a time when 30-year fixed-rate mortgages are running at 12% interest. The rollover mortgage payment will be $571.80 per month for principal and interest compared to a fixed-rate mortgage payment of $617.40. If the buyer sells before the end of the fifth year he

SUMMARY OF NEW CREATIVE MORTGAGE FINANCING

Type of Mortgage	Explanation	Term	Prime Users	Advantages	Disadvantages
Graduated-payment mortgage (GPM)	Payments start out lower than on level-payment mortgages and gradually increase over a 5- or 10-year period. Then payments level out for balance of term.	30 years	Buyers who want more for their money. Young homebuyers whose income is likely to increase rapidly.	Buyer can qualify for higher loan amounts due to lower first-year payment. Buyer can purchase up to $20,000 more house for same first year's monthly payment.	Loan balance increases initially instead of decreasing. Buyer's payments increase each year.
Variable-rate mortgage (VHM)	Buyer's payments are adjusted at least every 12 months in relation to current interest rates under some index beyond control of lender.	30 years	Buyers who do not plan to stay in the home for a long period. Buyers who believe interest rates will decline.	Buyer may obtain slightly lower interest rates because lender is not locked into fixed-rate mortgage for 30 years.	Buyer's payments will go up each year if interest rates go up each year.
Rollover mortgage (ROM)	Comes due every 5 years. On renewal, loan is rolled over for another 5 years at prevailing interest rates.	30 years (3-, 4-, or 5-year renewals)	Buyers who do not plan to stay in home for more than 5 years. Buyers who want lower payments now.	Buyer may obtain slightly lower interest rates and lower payments as lender is not locked into a fixed rate for 30 years.	Buyer's payments will probably go up on the renewal periods as interest rates historically have gone up.
Shared-appreciation mortgage (SAM)	Lender reduces prevailing interest rate by a fixed percentage. This reduces the buyer's payment and in return buyer shares any appreciation with lender in the same ratio.	30 years (contingent interest is due in 10 years)	Buyers who want lower payments or buyers who cannot qualify at prevailing interest rates.	Buyer is able to qualify for higher loan amount and have lower monthly payments.	Buyer must give up part of his proceeds to lender upon sale of home or after 10 years, whichever comes first.

Type of mortgage	Description	Term	Suitable for	Advantages	Disadvantages
Pledged-account mortgage (PAM, FLIP, ACTION)	Payments start out lower than on level-payment mortgages and gradually increase over 5- or 10-year period. Then payments level out for balance of term.	30 years	Buyers who want more house for their money. Young home-buyers whose income is likely to increase rapidly.	Buyer can qualify for higher loan amounts due to lower first-year payment. Buyer can purchase up to $20,000 more house for same first year's monthly payment. No increase in principal balance.	Buyer is required to make a larger down payment which is deposited into a pledged savings account. Down payment required is 10–15%.
Graduated-payment adjustable mortgage (GPAM)	Payments start out lower than on level-payment mortgages and gradually increase over 5- or 10-year period. However, interest rate and payments are also adjusted on 3-, 4-, or 5-year intervals.	30 years (3-, 4-, or 5-year renewals)	Buyers who want more house for their money. Young home-buyers whose income is likely to increase rapidly.	Buyer can qualify for higher loan amounts due to lower first-year payment. Buyer can purchase up to $20,000 more house for same first year's monthly payment.	Buyer is required to make a larger down payment and his interest rate and payment may increase on renewal.
Reverse-annuity mortgage (RAM)	Opposite of most mortgages: buyer receives a monthly income from the equity he has accumulated. This equity may be used to liquidate any remaining mortgage balance.	Life of owner or specified term of sale	Retired couples or individuals nearing retirement who need additional income.	Owner can obtain additional income without selling his home.	Owner is pledging his property to a lending institution in return for monthly income.
Renegotiable-rate mortgage (RRM)	Renewed on 3-, 4-, or 5-year intervals. Interest rates are adjusted in accordance with an index rate. Maximum adjustment is 0.5% per year over adjustment period.	30 years (3-, 4-, or 5-year renewals)	Buyers who do not plan to hold the property more than five years. Buyers who believe interest rates will decline.	Buyer may be able to obtain slightly lower interest rate since lender is not locked in for 30 years.	Buyer's payments will probably go up on the renewal periods as interest rates historically have gone up.

Note: interest rates will vary greatly from plan to plan.

will come out ahead. If, however, he is in the house on the renewal of the mortgage (after five years) his payment may increase or decrease, but will probably increase since a 20-year amortization schedule is used on renewals. If the prevailing rate is 12% at renewal, the buyer's new payment for principal and interest would be approximately $660.60, an increase of $43.20 per month for the next five-year period.

VARIABLE-RATE MORTGAGE (VRM)

As the name implies, the rate will fluctuate according to some reference index beyond the lender's control. An example of a reference index being used for federally regulated savings and loans is the National Cost of Funds Index published by the Federal Home Loan Bank.

If the index increases, the lender may at its discretion increase the borrower's interest rate up to 0.5% per year. The buyer then has a choice of paying the higher monthly payment or extending the loan maturity to keep the payment the same, or a combination of these choices.

If the index decreases, the lender must lower the interest rate, but not to exceed 0.5% per year.

Advantages

The lender's yield on the mortgage will closely correspond to its cost of borrowing the money. The buyer will have lower payments if the interest rate goes down.

Disadvantages

The buyer's payments will increase if the interest rate goes up.

Example

A buyer takes out a $60,000 mortgage at 12% interest. His monthly payment during the first year would begin at $617.40, principal and interest. The second year the going interest rate falls to 11.5%, so the lender reduces the buyer's payment to $594.60 per month, principal and interest. The third year the interest rate goes back up to 13%, but the lender is allowed to raise the payment only by 0.5% per year, so the buyer's payment would be calculated at 12% interest, the original rate in this example.

REVERSE-ANNUITY MORTGAGE (RAM)

This is a form of mortgage that permits a homeowner to draw on the accumulated equity in his home. For example, a retired homeowner might borrow against his equity under an arrangement by which the lender (e.g., a federal S&L) makes periodic payments to the homeowner. Thus, cash inflows and outflows under a RAM are in reverse of those associated with a conventional mortgage loan. The mortgagee makes periodic payments (the number and amount of which are fixed) to the mortgagor, who contracts to repay the amount loaned, plus interest, on the maturity date of the mortgage or the mortgagor's death, whichever comes first. If the mortgagor should die before the maturity date, repayment generally comes through settlement of the mortgagor's estate. A RAM introduces a risk of loss not inherent in a conventional mortgage loan because the principal balance increases over its term. It is very rare to find a bank that will make this kind of loan, but if you are retiring and have had a long-standing relationship with your bank, it's certainly worth your time to ask them to work with you on this basis. It is a great method to use for supplementing retirement income without selling your home.

STILL MORE WAYS TO CREATIVELY FINANCE!

The Federal National Mortgage Association (FNMA, popularly known as Fannie Mae), the Federal Home Loan Mortgage Corporation (FHLMC), and some smaller lenders are making a strong bid to woo homebuyers with advantageous interest rates, consolidation loans, and other innovative financing programs. That old standby, the life-insurance policy, can even offer buyers unexpected financial assistance. Read on . . .

NEW BELOW-MARKET LOANS THROUGH FANNIE MAE

Home loans at two to four points under the market are available for many homebuyers right now. The only basic requirement is that the home to be sold must carry a first mortgage that is currently owned by the Federal National Mortgage Association (FNMA), the largest single purchaser of residential mortgages. (Banks seldom hold loans for 25 or 30 years; they almost always sell their loans to FNMA, thus freeing up more capital to lend to new buyers.) If this condition is met, then Fannie Mae under its Resale Finance Program can make it possible for your buyer to get one home loan of up to $98,500 for as little as 5% down—and at a below-market rate. To find out if Fannie Mae owns your mortgage, call your lender.

Q. Why is Fannie Mae making this offer?
A. Because it wants to clear its portfolio of old, low-interest loans made years ago at rates six to eight points lower than today's. Without the resale finance program, the homebuyer would assume the seller's old mortgage and continue paying Fannie Mae the old, low rate. Of course, the buyer would have to make a big down payment or get a second mortgage—or both.

Under the new program, the buyer gets one mortgage—no assumption, no second mortgage—at a rate lower than the market. But low as it is, the new rate gives Fannie Mae a higher return (if it doesn't, no deal).

Q. Will the interest rate on these new loans always be low?
A. It will almost always be under the current rate because of the way it is determined. Fannie Mae will use the lower of two money-market indexes, and one or the other of these is generally below the market. The rate will be reviewed monthly.

Q. But why would the bank cooperate and make a below-market loan?
A. The bank won't actually put up any cash—Fannie Mae does that—but the bank will earn loan-origination and servicing fees. Incidentally, the buyer needn't deal with the seller's original bank. If another Fannie Mae–approved lender charges less, the buyer can use it.

Q. Can you give me an example of how this works out?
A. All right. Let's say the seller, whose 9% mortgage is owned by FNMA, wants to sell for $70,000; he still owes $45,000 and monthly payments are $362. If the buyer assumed this loan, paid $3,500 down, and financed the balance with a ten-year second mortgage at 16%, his total monthly payment would be $722. If he tried to finance the whole package at the going rate, say 14.5%, monthly payments would have to be $814 on a $66,500 loan. But under the Resale Finance Program, the monthly payments would be only $699—for one 30-year 12.3% loan. This program covers FHA, VA, and conventional loans, providing at least $10,000 is still due.

CONSOLIDATION LOANS THAT OFFER LOW INTEREST RATES

You can obtain a lower interest rate for the buyer by ingeniously combining an old fact with a new change just announced by Federal National Mortgage Association (FNMA).

Fannie Mae will now buy from banks those home loans made to enable a homebuyer to consolidate first and second mortgages into one new first mortgage. Up until now, FNMA would not purchase such mortgages. This switch in policy means that S&Ls now will make more consolidation loans because there's a big market for them—FNMA. And that change in policy will mean less worry for homeowners who need such loans when the balloon on the second mortgage comes due.

Q. This new policy is going to make a big difference to past sellers and buyers, all right. But what's that old fact you mentioned?
A. It's this: the banks are stuck with plenty of low-rate, long-term loans issued some years ago. That fact and FNMA's new policy can be combined with some ingenuity to make a big difference to future sellers and buyers.

Here's an example. You want to sell your home for $90,000. You owe $30,000 on an 8.5% 30-year mortgage. You need $75,000 cash to finance your new home purchase and move. A buyer likes your home, but has only $15,000 cash and can't possibly swing a $75,000 mortgage at current rates.

Here's what you do. You remind your lender that it's stuck with a $30,000 mortgage at 8.5% if you can't sell your home. Then you make this suggestion. The lender should give the buyer a 30-year mortgage at 12%. You will get your $60,000 cash along with the buyer's $15,000 down payment, but you will also have to give the buyer a $15,000 second mortgage, with a balloon due in five years.

Q. But why should the lender give the buyer a $60,000 mortgage at a low rate like 12%?
A. Because $30,000 of the loan is actually bringing the lender the equivalent of around 15% on his money. Remember that the old $30,000 mortgage was earning only 8.5%. But at 12% that old $30,000 is actually pulling in 3.5% more a year. In short, the lender is actually getting approximately 15% return on his money, where

he was getting only 8.5% before. Tell the buyer he now stands a better chance than ever of being able to refinance before the second mortgage balloon comes due, thanks to FNMA's new policy. He may even be able to refinance at a lower rate.

BREAK THE ROADBLOCK OF HIGH DOWN PAYMENTS

Here's another way to break the roadblock of high down payments. Have homebuyers and lenders work with Home Capital Funds (HCF) of Austin, Texas.

When lenders won't go beyond a 75% or 80% mortgage, HCF can step in with what it calls a "joint loan" to help your buyer get a 90% or even 95% loan on the home you have for sale. Here's how it works:

1. The buyer wants to purchase an $86,500 home. All he can afford, though, is a 5% down payment. Although the buyer is an executive with a rising income, the lender won't go beyond an 80% loan.
2. HCF steps in and saves the day. How? The lender will make an 80% senior loan ($69,200) and HCF will make a separate, junior loan of 15% ($12,975).
3. The joint loan is bound by private mortgage insurance which will cover, say, the top 20% of the loan. The lender hasn't gone beyond his 80% limit, and thanks to HCF's junior loan, the buyer got what he wanted: a 95%, $82,175 loan on the home of his dreams.

Isn't HCF's loan a second mortgage? Definitely not! HCF does not supply a loan that has a higher interest rate and a shorter term than the lender's. The buyer gets everything in one package. He pays only the lender. It's just like a regular loan except that out of each payment, the lender is limited to 80% (HCF receives that extra 15%).

This big combination means more expensive homes will also be within reach of more prospects. They may have to pay a slightly higher fee (1% more, typically), but it's a small price to pay for having that dream home today, not years from now!

How high will HCF go? It will go up to a $142,-000 mortgage on a 95% loan deal (with lender granting a 75% or 80% loan and HCF making up the 20% or 15% difference). Your prospects can get,

in effect, a 95% loan on a home costing up to $150,-000. If the mortgage runs higher, HCF will help the buyer get up to a 90% loan with no specified outside limit.

HCF President, Hugh K. Higgins, Jr., tells me that the Home Loan Bank Board allows Federal S&Ls as well as most state-chartered institutions, to cooperate with his firm in getting a homebuyer a loan that's above their legal limit. And HCF can work with your local commercial bank or mortgage lender, too. (They've done work with insurance companies, as well.)

There's no special red tape involved in going along with HCF on a 95% mortgage, either. "The lender controls the loan qualifications and borrower interest rates on both joint loans when he works with us," Higgins says. "We do not interfere. Nor do we technically participate since our notes are separate, are never owned by the lender, and are completely subordinated to its loans." Home Capital Funds presently functions in some 40 states and it operates quickly, too. "We generally have same-day processing with our cooperating lenders," Higgins says. Tell your lender, or write to Home Capital Funds, P.O. Box 9963, Austin, Texas 78766. Or phone: (512) 345-5500.

SPEEDY, INEXPENSIVE MORTGAGE INSURANCE

A new private mortgage insurance company that can insure conventional loans up to 95% in as little as two days is now in operation. The delays of FHA processing can be a thing of the past if your lender will turn to Continental Mortgage Insurance, Inc.

What does CMI do? It steps in to insure the top 20% of a loan, so that 95% loans would leave the lender holding only 75% "exposure" as they say. And its insurance premium, as well as its processing time, is much less than FHA's. What's more, your lender can terminate CMI's insurance whenever they feel your buyer's equity is now sufficient. To speed up processing time even more, CMI tells me it frequently accepts your lender's appraisal instead of insisting upon one of its own.

Your lenders can phone CMI collect at its home office, (608) 257-2527, or write to 2 East Gilman Street, P.O. Box 2017, Madison, Wisconsin 53701.

Or they can try the regional office, (404) 523-2825, at 40 Marietta Street, N.W., P.O. Box 1105, Atlanta, Georgia 30301. These offices can give them the name of their nearest CMI representative, along with further details.

GOOD NEWS FROM WASHINGTON

Three recent events from Washington can make a big difference to you and your potential buyer:

1. The Federal Home Loan Mortgage Corporation, a large purchaser of home loans, told banks they can increase such mortgages and FHLMC will still buy them. FHLMC is now in the market for single-family-home loans of up to $98,500, two-family loans of $126,000, three-family loans of $152,000, four-family loans of $189,000 . . .
2. On single-family houses and duplexes, FHLMC's new policy will allow buyers to put down only 4% for conventional loans. FHLMC also increased the amount of home-improvement loans it will buy. They can be up to $15,-000 for condos, $30,000 for single-family homes, and $60,000 for two- to four-family homes.
3. Energy-savers can rescue home sales. Federal Home Loan Mortgage Corporation reports that 68% of lenders surveyed now have appraisers consider the home's energy efficiency when evaluating it. Also 59% of the lenders say energy costs can influence their approval of a mortgage, with 12% blaming soaring fuel bills as a major drain on the homeowner's budget and a major cause of the recent increase in mortgage delinquencies. Remember this and stress every energy-saving feature in your home when you're trying to get financing for your buyer. Hang on to those facts and figures about the new furnace or the insulation, and cite them all over again for both the lender and the future buyer.

HOW TO PERSUADE YOUR BUYER TO TAP A FOOLPROOF SOURCE OF LOW-COST FINANCING

There is one method of raising home-buying cash that many prospects may be reluctant to use. They can borrow on their life-insurance policies and save thousands of dollars in interest. If you took out your policy before 1975, you can pay only 5% or 6% interest (8% if you took it out later). That's a substantial saving—a cut in interest of over 50%.

Some policyholders should not borrow because the full face value of the policy is needed for family protection. Others, however, can afford to borrow the cash value of their policies—they may have more than one policy. But they may still hesitate to do so. They know their family protection will be reduced until the loan is paid off.

Here is how you can offset this fear without making buyers feel you are interested in nothing but selling them your home. Let's say Mr. Brown has his eye on your house, which is selling for $100,000. He has a problem. He doesn't have the $25,000 he needs to close the deal.

"Mr. Brown, there is one source of cash we haven't considered."

"What's that?"

"Your $100,000 cash-value insurance policy. You may be able to borrow $25,000 against it."

"Oh, no. I don't want to borrow on that. What if something happened to me before I paid it back? I'd leave my family with a third less coverage. Forget it."

"I certainly understand your feeling that way. But I assure you I would never suggest your reducing your insurance coverage if I didn't believe it a very smart move. Look at it this way: if you put that $25,000 into this house and something happened to you next year, you would leave your family a bigger estate."

"How do you figure that?"

"Because of $100,000 insurance, you'd get $75,-000 insurance plus the $25,000 invested in your home. And the $25,000 will have grown as your home appreciates in value—probably faster than if it had stayed as part of the cash value of the policy. It's less liquid when invested in your home. Nevertheless, you are not reducing your family's security. And if you have mortgage payoff insurance, you've lost nothing."

HOW TO QUALIFY YOUR BUYER FOR A LOAN

You know what kinds of financing are available to your buyer, and now you're ready to determine whether the buyer can meet the loan requirements the lender poses before issuing the loan. The checklists and worksheets in this chapter will enable you to do this easily, thereby avoiding the unhappy situation of being forced to remove your home from the market for someone who will never be able to get an adequate loan. As we've said, the inability of an interested prospect to qualify for the needed financing is perhaps *the* greatest pitfall for real-estate agents and homeowners alike. By following the guidelines in this chapter you can eliminate any questions about your buyer's ability to get financing right at the start. The time and aggravation this preliminary step saves you can make the difference in assuring a smooth sale with no last-minute hitches.

To establish that your buyer will qualify for a home loan, read the credit application checklist and give a copy to your buyer to serve as a handy reminder of the information and/or documents he or she will need to have when going to the lender. Then ask the buyer to fill out a copy of the form entitled "Prequalification Questions." When these questions have been answered you will have a good idea of whether or not you've actually got a valid buyer on your hands.

Next, sit down with the buyer and complete a qualification worksheet for the appropriate type of loan. Forms and requirements for the three basic types of loans—conventional, FHA, and VA—are included here. Monthly payroll tax tables are also included to help you compute federal withholding. If the buyer has a copy of a recent pay stub, that can be used instead.

If you think you have a bona fide buyer but he or she fails to qualify for a basic loan, immediately refer him or her to a lender that offers one of the creative financing techniques discussed in Step Seven. And make sure that he or she applies for a mortgage within *five* working days.

CREDIT APPLICATION CHECKLIST

Some or all of the following items are needed when the bank accepts a credit application from your buyer. You as seller can help expedite the processing of the loan if you make the buyer aware of these items prior to his or her application for credit.

EMPLOYMENT:

Employment addresses for two full years.
Gross monthly income.
If more than 3 employers, W-2's should be furnished. (Especially in the case of an individual who subcontracts.)
If an applicant is self-employed, 1040 tax returns for the past two years.
Plus a current year profit-and-loss statement with balance sheet.
Proof of pensions, social security, disability, retirement, etc.
Proof of income from rentals, investments, etc.
Proof of child support or alimony paid or received.

CREDITORS:

Creditors' names and types of accounts.
Account numbers.
Monthly payments and approximate balances.

BANKING:

Names and addresses of saving institutions.
Account numbers for all accounts.
Types of accounts and present balances.

MISCELLANEOUS:

List of assets in stocks, bonds, land, life-insurance cash value.
If applicant is also selling a home, a copy of the sales contract.
Social Security numbers for husband and wife.
Veterans should furnish Certificate of Eligibility or copy of Separation Paper (DD-214).
Cash or check to pay for credit report and appraisal.

PREQUALIFICATION QUESTIONS

NAME_____ HOME PHONE_____ WORK_____

OCCUPATION_____ LENGTH of EMPLOYMENT_____

GROSS MONTHLY INCOME_____ PAID SALARY, HOURLY, COMMISSION

SECONDARY JOB?_____ LENGTH of EMPLOYMENT_____ EARNINGS_____

WILL THERE BE a CO-BUYER?_____ IS CO-BUYER EMPLOYED?_____

CO-BUYER'S OCCUPATION_____ LENGTH of EMPLOYMENT_____

GROSS MONTHLY INCOME_____ BONUSES_____ OTHER COMP._____

ANY OTHER SOURCE of INCOME?_____ DESCRIBE_____

NUMBER of FAMILY MEMBERS_____ IN HOUSEHOLD_____

MONTHLY INDEBTEDNESS PAYMENTS (MINIMUM PAYMENT DUE)_____

ANY CHILD SUPPORT OWED?_____ ANY CHILD SUPPORT RECEIVED?_____

HAVE YOU EVER HAD CREDIT PROBLEMS?_____ BANKRUPTCY?_____

ARE YOU a VETERAN?_____ WERE YOU in RESERVES?_____

HAVE YOU EVER USED a VA HOME LOAN BENEFIT?_____ IN WHAT YEAR?_____

WHAT DID YOU PAY FOR the VA HOME?_____ HOW MUCH DID YOU

    BORROW?_____ WAS the VA LOAN PAID IN FULL?_____

DO YOU STILL OWN the HOME?_____

HOW MUCH CASH DO YOU WANT to INVEST in a HOME?_____

HOW MUCH PAYMENT WILL YOU BE COMFORTABLE with?_____

WHAT PRICE RANGE ARE YOU LOOKING in?_____

WHAT ARE YOUR SPECIAL NEEDS OR PREFERENCES in a HOME?_____

WHAT DID YOU LIKE MOST ABOUT OUR HOME?_____

_____

_____ Least?_____

SAMPLE CONVENTIONAL BUYER QUALIFICATION WORKSHEET

NAME: _Joseph L. Prospect_   MORTGAGE AMOUNT _93,550_

GROSS MONTHLY INCOME _____ 4,000 _____ A.

MORTGAGE PAYMENT

    PRINCIPAL AND INTEREST _____ 1108 _____

    TAXES _____ 230 _____

    INSURANCE _____ 40 _____

    PRIVATE MORTGAGE INSUR.* _____ 20 _____

    TOTAL MORTGAGE PAYMENT _____ 1398 _____ B.

INCOME QUALIFICATION. TAKE 25% of the
total mortgage payment (A.) to compute (C.).
Line (B.) must not exceed (C.). _____ 1,000 _____ C.

    NOT QUALIFIED!

DEBT QUALIFICATION

    TOTAL MORTGAGE PAYMENT (B.) _____ 1398 _____

    AUTO PAYMENTS** _____ 300 _____

    INSTALLMENT CHARGES** _____ 50 _____

    LOANS** _____ 50 _____

    CHILD SUPPORT/ALIMONY _____ —0— _____

    OTHER _____ —0— _____

    TOTAL MONTHLY DEBTS _____ 1798 _____ D.

Gross income (A.) × 33% = the allowable
debts. Total debts (D.) must not
exceed Line (E.). _____ 1320 – NOT QUALIFIED _____ E.

* private mortgage insurance is computed as ¼% of the loan amount divided by 12.

** you need only count debts that will extend beyond 10 months. However, if any obligation is greater than $100 per month, it may count against the buyer even if it has less than 10 months remaining.

CONVENTIONAL BUYER QUALIFICATION WORKSHEET

NAME:_____ MORTGAGE AMOUNT_____

GROSS MONTHLY INCOME _____A.

MORTGAGE PAYMENT

    PRINCIPAL AND INTEREST _____

    TAXES _____

    INSURANCE _____

    PRIVATE MORTGAGE INSUR.* _____

    TOTAL MORTGAGE PAYMENT _____B.

INCOME QUALIFICATION. TAKE 25% of the total mortgage payment (A.) to compute (C.). Line (B.) must not exceed (C.). _____C.

DEBT QUALIFICATION

    TOTAL MORTGAGE PAYMENT (B.) _____

    AUTO PAYMENTS** _____

    INSTALLMENT CHARGES** _____

    LOANS** _____

    CHILD SUPPORT/ALIMONY _____

    OTHER _____

    TOTAL MONTHLY DEBTS _____D.

Gross income (A.) × 33% = the allowable debts. Total debts (D.) must not exceed Line (E.). _____E.

* private mortgage insurance is computed as ¼% of the loan amount divided by 12.

** you need only count debts that will extend beyond 10 months. However, if any obligation is greater than $100 per month, it may count against the buyer even if it has less than 10 months remaining.

SAMPLE FHA BUYER QUALIFICATION WORKSHEET

NAME _Joseph L. Prospect_   MORTGAGE AMOUNT _69,500 (MAXIMUM AMT.)_

GROSS MONTHLY INCOME   + _4,000_

MINUS FEDERAL TAXES (USE TABLE)   − _983_

NET INCOME   = _3,017_   A.

TOTAL MORTGAGE PAYMENT OF PRINC., IN-
TEREST, TAXES, INSUR. AND P.M.I.*   + _1,122.00_

MAINTENANCE AND UTILITIES   + _100_

TOTAL HOUSING EXPENSE   = _1,222_   B.

Take the NET INCOME (A.) AND multiply by
35% to figure the allowable housing expense
(C.). Line (C.) must be greater than Line (B.)
to qualify.   = _1,056 NOT QUALIFIED_   C.

DEBT QUALIFICATION

TOTAL HOUSING EXPENSE (B.)   + _1,222_

SOCIAL SECURITY (6.65 × gross income with
a maximum of $165)   + _165_

MONTHLY DEBTS OVER 12 MONTHS   + _400_

TOTAL DEBTS   = _1,787_   D.

Net income (A.) × 50% = the allowable debts.
Line (E.) must be greater than line (D.) to qual-
ify.   = _1,509 NOT QUALIFIED_ E.

* FHA PMI is ½% × mortgage divided by 12.

Caution: These figures are only guidelines. Other factors such as job stability, creditworthiness, and cash reserves will be considered.

FHA BUYER QUALIFICATION WORKSHEET

NAME_____ MORTGAGE AMOUNT_____

GROSS MONTHLY INCOME   +_____

MINUS FEDERAL TAXES (USE TABLE)   −_____

NET INCOME   =_____A.

TOTAL MORTGAGE PAYMENT OF PRINC., IN-
TEREST, TAXES, INSUR. AND P.M.I.*   +_____

MAINTENANCE AND UTILITIES   +_____

TOTAL HOUSING EXPENSE   =_____B.
Take the NET INCOME (A.) AND multiply by
35% to figure the allowable housing expense
(C.). Line (C.) must be greater than Line (B.)
to qualify.   =_____C.

DEBT QUALIFICATION

TOTAL HOUSING EXPENSE (B.)   +_____

SOCIAL SECURITY (6.65 × gross income with
a maximum of $165)   +_____

MONTHLY DEBTS OVER 12 MONTHS   +_____

TOTAL DEBTS   =_____D.

Net income (A.) × 50% = the allowable debts.
Line (E.) must be greater than line (D.) to qualify.   =_____E.

* FHA PMI is ½% × mortgage divided by 12.

Caution: These figures are only guidelines. Other factors such as job stability, creditworthiness, and cash reserves will be considered.

SAMPLE VA BUYER QUALIFICATION WORKSHEET

NAME Joseph L. Prospect MORTGAGE AMOUNT 93,550 GROSS MONTHLY INCOME 4,000

SUBTRACT MONTHLY PAYMENTS FOR:

FEDERAL TAXES (USE TAX TABLE) 983

SOCIAL SECURITY (6.65 × gross inc.) .... 165 (MAX)

MONTHLY OBLIGATIONS (over six months) 50

CHILD CARE EXPENSE (if any) 0

MAINTENANCE AND UTILITIES 100

COMMUTING EXPENSE 50

LIFE AND HEALTH INSURANCE 0

TOTAL MORTGAGE PYMT (P.I.T.I.) 1,378

TOTAL DEDUCTIONS 2,726   B.

NET INCOME (SUBTRACT B FROM A) 1,274   A.

The following net income should be left over after subtracting the total deductions from the veteran's gross monthly income in order to qualify him based on income. But he must also have a decent credit rating and a stable source of income. If the veteran does not qualify on the following schedule a down payment will be needed. If a down payment is made, the VA may not require as much net income as shown on the scale below.

VETERAN ONLY	$230
FAMILY OF TWO	$460
FAMILY OF THREE	$575
FAMILY OF FOUR	$690 QUALIFIES!
FAMILY OF FIVE	$805
FAMILY OF SIX	$920
FAMILY OF SEVEN	$1,035
FAMILY OF EIGHT	$1,150

CAUTION: THESE FIGURES ARE ONLY GUIDELINES. OTHER FACTORS WILL BE CONSIDERED. VA QUALIFYING FORMULAS ARE CONSIDERED MORE LIBERAL THAN ANY OTHER.

VA BUYER QUALIFICATION WORKSHEET

NAME_____ MORTGAGE AMOUNT_____ GROSS MONTHLY INCOME_____

SUBTRACT MONTHLY PAYMENTS FOR:

FEDERAL TAXES (USE TAX TABLE) _____

SOCIAL SECURITY (6.65 × gross inc.) _____

MONTHLY OBLIGATIONS (over six months) _____

CHILD CARE EXPENSE (if any) _____

MAINTENANCE AND UTILITIES _____

COMMUTING EXPENSE _____

LIFE AND HEALTH INSURANCE _____

TOTAL MORTGAGE PYMT (P.I.T.I.) _____

TOTAL DEDUCTIONS _____B.

NET INCOME (SUBTRACT B FROM A) _____A.

The following net income should be left over after subtracting the total deductions from the veteran's gross monthly income in order to qualify him based on income. But he must also have a decent credit rating and a stable source of income. If the veteran does not qualify on the following schedule a down payment will be needed. If a down payment is made, the VA may not require as much net income as shown on the scale below.

VETERAN ONLY	$230
FAMILY OF TWO	$460
FAMILY OF THREE	$575
FAMILY OF FOUR	$690
FAMILY OF FIVE	$805
FAMILY OF SIX	$920
FAMILY OF SEVEN	$1,035
FAMILY OF EIGHT	$1,150

CAUTION: THESE FIGURES ARE ONLY GUIDELINES. OTHER FACTORS WILL BE CONSIDERED. VA QUALIFYING FORMULAS ARE CONSIDERED MORE LIBERAL THAN ANY OTHER.

SINGLE Persons—MONTHLY Payroll Period

And the wages are—		And the number of withholding allowances claimed is—										
		0	1	2	3	4	5	6	7	8	9	10 or more
At least	But less than	The amount of income tax to be withheld shall be—										
$580	$600	$80.90	$65.20	$50.20	$35.20	$20.80	$8.30	$0	$0	$0	$0	$0
600	640	87.20	70.60	55.60	40.60	25.60	12.80	.30	0	0	0	0
640	680	95.60	78.10	62.80	47.80	32.80	18.80	6.30	0	0	0	0
680	720	104.00	86.50	70.00	55.00	40.00	25.00	12.30	0	0	0	0
720	760	112.40	94.90	77.40	62.20	47.20	32.20	18.30	5.80	0	0	0
760	800	120.80	103.30	85.80	69.40	54.40	39.40	24.40	11.80	0	0	0
800	840	129.20	111.70	94.20	76.70	61.60	46.60	31.60	17.80	5.30	0	0
840	880	138.10	120.10	102.60	85.10	68.80	53.80	38.80	23.80	11.30	0	0
880	920	148.50	128.50	111.00	93.50	76.00	61.00	46.00	31.00	17.30	4.80	0
920	960	158.90	137.20	119.40	101.90	84.40	68.20	53.20	38.20	23.30	10.80	0
960	1,000	169.30	147.60	127.80	110.30	92.80	75.40	60.40	45.40	30.40	16.80	4.30
1,000	1,040	179.70	158.00	136.40	118.70	101.20	83.70	67.60	52.60	37.60	22.80	10.30
1,040	1,080	190.10	168.40	146.80	127.10	109.60	92.10	74.80	59.80	44.80	29.80	16.30
1,080	1,120	200.50	178.80	157.20	135.50	118.00	100.50	83.00	67.00	52.00	37.00	22.30
1,120	1,160	210.90	189.20	167.60	145.90	126.40	108.90	91.40	74.20	59.20	44.20	29.20
1,160	1,200	221.30	199.60	178.00	156.30	134.80	117.30	99.80	82.30	66.40	51.40	36.40
1,200	1,240	233.20	210.00	188.40	166.70	145.00	125.70	108.20	90.70	73.60	58.60	43.60
1,240	1,280	245.20	220.40	198.80	177.10	155.40	134.10	116.60	99.10	81.60	65.80	50.80
1,280	1,320	257.20	232.20	209.20	187.50	165.80	144.20	125.00	107.50	90.00	73.00	58.00
1,320	1,360	269.20	244.20	219.60	197.90	176.20	154.60	133.40	115.90	98.40	80.90	65.20
1,360	1,400	281.20	256.20	231.20	208.30	186.60	165.00	143.30	124.30	106.80	89.30	72.40
1,400	1,440	293.20	268.20	243.20	218.70	197.00	175.40	153.70	132.70	115.20	97.70	80.20
1,440	1,480	306.20	280.20	255.20	230.20	207.40	185.80	164.10	142.40	123.60	106.10	88.60
1,480	1,520	319.80	292.20	267.20	242.20	217.80	196.20	174.50	152.80	132.00	114.50	97.00
1,520	1,560	333.40	305.10	279.20	254.20	229.20	206.60	184.90	163.20	141.60	122.90	105.40
1,560	1,600	347.00	318.70	291.20	266.20	241.20	217.00	195.30	173.60	152.00	131.30	113.80
1,600	1,640	360.60	332.30	304.00	278.20	253.20	228.20	205.70	184.00	162.40	140.70	122.20
1,640	1,680	374.20	345.90	317.60	290.20	265.20	240.20	216.10	194.40	172.80	151.10	130.60
1,680	1,720	387.80	359.50	331.20	302.80	277.20	252.20	227.20	204.80	183.20	161.50	139.80
1,720	1,760	401.40	373.10	344.80	316.40	289.20	264.20	239.20	215.20	193.60	171.90	150.20
1,760	1,800	415.00	386.70	358.40	330.00	301.70	276.20	251.20	226.20	204.00	182.30	160.60
1,800	1,840	428.60	400.30	372.00	343.60	315.30	288.20	263.20	238.20	214.40	192.70	171.00
1,840	1,880	442.20	413.90	385.60	357.20	328.90	300.60	275.20	250.20	225.20	203.10	181.40
1,880	1,920	457.10	427.50	399.20	370.80	342.50	314.20	287.20	262.20	237.20	213.50	191.80
1,920	1,960	472.70	441.10	412.80	384.40	356.10	327.80	299.40	274.20	249.20	224.20	202.20
1,960	2,000	488.30	455.80	426.40	398.00	369.70	341.40	313.00	286.20	261.20	236.20	212.60
2,000	2,040	503.90	471.40	440.00	411.60	383.30	355.00	326.60	298.30	273.20	248.20	223.20
2,040	2,080	519.50	487.00	454.50	425.20	396.90	368.60	340.20	311.90	285.20	260.20	235.20
2,080	2,120	535.10	502.60	470.10	438.80	410.50	382.20	353.80	325.50	297.20	272.20	247.20
2,120	2,160	550.70	518.20	485.70	453.20	424.10	395.80	367.40	339.10	310.80	284.20	259.20
2,160	2,200	566.30	533.80	501.30	468.80	437.70	409.40	381.00	352.70	324.40	296.20	271.20
2,200	2,240	581.90	549.40	516.90	484.40	451.90	423.00	394.60	366.30	338.00	309.60	283.20
2,240	2,280	597.50	565.00	532.50	500.00	467.50	436.60	408.20	379.90	351.60	323.20	295.20
2,280	2,320	613.10	580.60	548.10	515.60	483.10	450.60	421.80	393.50	365.20	336.80	308.50
2,320	2,360	628.70	596.20	563.70	531.20	498.70	466.20	435.40	407.10	378.80	350.40	322.10
2,360	2,400	644.30	611.80	579.30	546.80	514.30	481.80	449.30	420.70	392.40	364.00	335.70
2,400	2,440	659.90	627.40	594.90	562.40	529.90	497.40	464.90	434.30	406.00	377.60	349.30
2,440	2,480	675.50	643.00	610.50	578.00	545.50	513.00	480.50	448.00	419.60	391.20	362.90
2,480	2,520	691.10	658.60	626.10	593.60	561.10	528.60	496.10	463.60	433.20	404.80	376.50
2,520	2,560	706.70	674.20	641.70	609.20	576.70	544.20	511.70	479.20	446.80	418.40	390.10
2,560	2,600	722.30	689.80	657.30	624.80	592.30	559.80	527.30	494.80	462.30	432.00	403.70
2,600	2,640	737.90	705.40	672.90	640.40	607.90	575.40	542.90	510.40	477.90	445.60	417.30
2,640	2,680	753.50	721.00	688.50	656.00	623.50	591.00	558.50	526.00	493.50	461.00	430.90
2,680	2,720	769.10	736.60	704.10	671.60	639.10	606.60	574.10	541.60	509.10	476.60	444.50
2,720	2,760	784.70	752.20	719.70	687.20	654.70	622.20	589.70	557.20	524.70	492.20	459.70

39% of the excess over $2760.00 plus —												
$2,760 and over		792.50	760.00	727.50	695.00	662.50	630.00	597.50	565.00	532.50	500.00	467.50

MARRIED Persons—MONTHLY Payroll Period

And the wages are—		And the number of withholding allowances claimed is—										
		0	1	2	3	4	5	6	7	8	9	10 or more
At least	But less than	The amount of income tax to be withheld shall be—										
$0	$200	$0	$0	$0	$0	$0	$0	$0	$0	$0	$0	$0
200	204	.30	0	0	0	0	0	0	0	0	0	0
204	208	.90	0	0	0	0	0	0	0	0	0	0
208	212	1.50	0	0	0	0	0	0	0	0	0	0
212	216	2.10	0	0	0	0	0	0	0	0	0	0
216	220	2.70	0	0	0	0	0	0	0	0	0	0
220	224	3.30	0	0	0	0	0	0	0	0	0	0
224	228	3.90	0	0	0	0	0	0	0	0	0	0
228	232	4.50	0	0	0	0	0	0	0	0	0	0
232	236	5.10	0	0	0	0	0	0	0	0	0	0
236	240	5.70	0	0	0	0	0	0	0	0	0	0
240	248	6.60	0	0	0	0	0	0	0	0	0	0
248	256	7.80	0	0	0	0	0	0	0	0	0	0
256	264	9.00	0	0	0	0	0	0	0	0	0	0
264	272	10.20	0	0	0	0	0	0	0	0	0	0
272	280	11.40	0	0	0	0	0	0	0	0	0	0
280	288	12.60	.10	0	0	0	0	0	0	0	0	0
288	296	13.80	1.30	0	0	0	0	0	0	0	0	0
296	304	15.00	2.50	0	0	0	0	0	0	0	0	0
304	312	16.20	3.70	0	0	0	0	0	0	0	0	0
312	320	17.40	4.90	0	0	0	0	0	0	0	0	0
320	328	18.60	6.10	0	0	0	0	0	0	0	0	0
328	336	19.80	7.30	0	0	0	0	0	0	0	0	0
336	344	21.00	8.50	0	0	0	0	0	0	0	0	0
344	352	22.20	9.70	0	0	0	0	0	0	0	0	0
352	360	23.40	10.90	0	0	0	0	0	0	0	0	0
360	368	24.60	12.10	0	0	0	0	0	0	0	0	0
368	376	25.80	13.30	.80	0	0	0	0	0	0	0	0
376	384	27.00	14.50	2.00	0	0	0	0	0	0	0	0
384	392	28.20	15.70	3.20	0	0	0	0	0	0	0	0
392	400	29.40	16.90	4.40	0	0	0	0	0	0	0	0
400	420	31.50	19.00	6.50	0	0	0	0	0	0	0	0
420	440	34.50	22.00	9.50	0	0	0	0	0	0	0	0
440	460	37.50	25.00	12.50	0	0	0	0	0	0	0	0
460	480	40.50	28.00	15.50	3.00	0	0	0	0	0	0	0
480	500	43.50	31.00	18.50	6.00	0	0	0	0	0	0	0
500	520	46.50	34.00	21.50	9.00	0	0	0	0	0	0	0
520	540	49.50	37.00	24.50	12.00	0	0	0	0	0	0	0
540	560	52.50	40.00	27.50	15.00	2.50	0	0	0	0	0	0
560	580	56.10	43.00	30.50	18.00	5.50	0	0	0	0	0	0
580	600	59.70	46.00	33.50	21.00	8.50	0	0	0	0	0	0
600	640	65.10	50.50	38.00	25.50	13.00	.50	0	0	0	0	0
640	680	72.30	57.30	44.00	31.50	19.00	6.50	0	0	0	0	0
680	720	79.50	64.50	50.00	37.50	25.00	12.50	0	0	0	0	0
720	760	86.70	71.70	56.70	43.50	31.00	18.50	6.00	0	0	0	0
760	800	93.90	78.90	63.90	49.50	37.00	24.50	12.00	0	0	0	0
800	840	101.10	86.10	71.10	56.10	43.00	30.50	18.00	5.50	0	0	0
840	880	108.30	93.30	78.30	63.30	49.00	36.50	24.00	11.50	0	0	0
880	920	115.50	100.50	85.50	70.50	55.50	42.50	30.00	17.50	5.00	0	0
920	960	123.70	107.70	92.70	77.70	62.70	48.50	36.00	23.50	11.00	0	0
960	1,000	132.10	114.90	99.90	84.90	69.90	54.90	42.00	29.50	17.00	4.50	0
1,000	1,040	140.50	123.00	107.10	92.10	77.10	62.10	48.00	35.50	23.00	10.50	0
1,040	1,080	148.90	131.40	114.30	99.30	84.30	69.30	54.30	41.50	29.00	16.50	4.00
1,080	1,120	157.30	139.80	122.30	106.50	91.50	76.50	61.50	47.50	35.00	22.50	10.00
1,120	1,160	165.70	148.20	130.70	113.70	98.70	83.70	68.70	53.70	41.00	28.50	16.00
1,160	1,200	174.10	156.60	139.10	121.60	105.90	90.90	75.90	60.90	47.00	34.50	22.00
1,200	1,240	182.50	165.00	147.50	130.00	113.10	98.10	83.10	68.10	53.10	40.50	28.00
1,240	1,280	191.20	173.40	155.90	138.40	120.90	105.30	90.30	75.30	60.30	46.50	34.00
1,280	1,320	200.80	181.80	164.30	146.80	129.30	112.50	97.50	82.50	67.50	52.50	40.00
1,320	1,360	210.40	190.40	172.70	155.20	137.70	120.20	104.70	89.70	74.70	59.70	46.00

At least	But less than	0	1	2	3	4	5	6	7	8	9	10 or more
							The amount of income tax to be withheld shall be—						
1,360	1,400	220.00	200.00	181.10	163.60	146.10	128.60	111.90	96.90	81.90	66.90	52.00
1,400	1,440	229.60	209.60	189.60	172.00	154.50	137.00	119.50	104.10	89.10	74.10	59.10
1,440	1,480	239.20	219.20	199.20	180.40	162.90	145.40	127.90	111.30	96.30	81.30	66.30
1,480	1,520	248.80	228.80	208.80	188.80	171.30	153.80	136.30	118.80	103.50	88.50	73.50
1,520	1,560	258.40	238.40	218.40	198.40	179.70	162.20	144.70	127.20	110.70	95.70	80.70
1,560	1,600	268.00	248.00	228.00	208.00	188.10	170.60	153.10	135.60	118.10	102.90	87.90
1,600	1,640	278.40	257.60	237.60	217.60	197.60	179.00	161.50	144.00	126.50	110.10	95.10
1,640	1,680	289.60	267.20	247.20	227.20	207.20	187.40	169.90	152.40	134.90	117.40	102.30
1,680	1,720	300.80	277.40	256.80	236.80	216.80	196.80	178.30	160.80	143.30	125.80	109.50
1,720	1,760	312.00	288.60	266.40	246.40	226.40	206.40	186.70	169.20	151.70	134.20	116.70
1,760	1,800	323.20	299.80	276.50	256.00	236.00	216.00	196.00	177.60	160.10	142.60	125.10
1,800	1,840	334.40	311.00	287.70	265.60	245.60	225.60	205.60	186.00	168.50	151.00	133.50
1,840	1,880	345.60	322.20	298.90	275.60	255.20	235.20	215.20	195.20	176.90	159.40	141.90
1,880	1,920	356.80	333.40	310.10	286.80	264.80	244.80	224.80	204.80	185.30	167.80	150.30
1,920	1,960	368.00	344.60	321.30	298.00	274.60	254.40	234.40	214.40	194.40	176.20	158.70
1,960	2,000	379.70	355.80	332.50	309.20	285.80	264.00	244.00	224.00	204.00	184.60	167.10
2,000	2,040	392.50	367.00	343.70	320.40	297.00	273.70	253.60	233.60	213.60	193.60	175.50
2,040	2,080	405.30	378.60	354.90	331.60	308.20	284.90	263.20	243.20	223.20	203.20	183.90
2,080	2,120	418.10	391.40	366.10	342.80	319.40	296.10	272.80	252.80	232.80	212.80	192.80
2,120	2,160	430.90	404.20	377.60	354.00	330.60	307.30	284.00	262.40	242.40	222.40	202.40
2,160	2,200	443.70	417.00	390.40	365.20	341.80	318.50	295.20	272.00	252.00	232.00	212.00
2,200	2,240	456.50	429.80	403.20	376.50	353.00	329.70	306.40	283.00	261.60	241.60	221.60
2,240	2,280	469.30	442.60	416.00	389.30	364.20	340.90	317.60	294.20	271.20	251.20	231.20
2,280	2,320	482.10	455.40	428.80	402.10	375.40	352.10	328.80	305.40	282.10	260.80	240.80
2,320	2,360	494.90	468.20	441.60	414.90	388.20	363.30	340.00	316.60	293.30	270.40	250.40
2,360	2,400	507.70	481.00	454.40	427.70	401.00	374.50	351.20	327.80	304.50	281.20	260.00
2,400	2,440	521.10	493.80	467.20	440.50	413.80	387.20	362.40	339.00	315.70	292.40	269.60
2,440	2,480	535.90	506.60	480.00	453.30	426.60	400.00	373.60	350.20	326.90	303.60	280.20
2,480	2,520	550.70	519.80	492.80	466.10	439.40	412.80	386.10	361.40	338.10	314.80	291.40
2,520	2,560	565.50	534.60	505.60	478.90	452.20	425.60	398.90	372.60	349.30	326.00	302.60
2,560	2,600	580.30	549.40	518.60	491.70	465.00	438.40	411.70	385.00	360.50	337.20	313.80
2,600	2,640	595.10	564.20	533.40	504.50	477.80	451.20	424.50	397.80	371.70	348.40	325.00
2,640	2,680	609.90	579.00	548.20	517.40	490.60	464.00	437.30	410.60	384.00	359.60	336.20
2,680	2,720	624.70	593.80	563.00	532.20	503.40	476.80	450.10	423.40	396.80	370.80	347.40
2,720	2,760	639.50	608.60	577.80	547.00	516.20	489.60	462.90	436.20	409.60	382.90	358.60
2,760	2,800	654.30	623.40	592.60	561.80	530.90	502.40	475.70	449.00	422.40	395.70	369.80
2,800	2,840	669.10	638.20	607.40	576.60	545.70	515.20	488.50	461.80	435.20	408.50	381.80
2,840	2,880	683.90	653.00	622.20	591.40	560.50	529.70	501.30	474.60	448.00	421.30	394.60
2,880	2,920	698.70	667.80	637.00	606.20	575.30	544.50	514.10	487.40	460.80	434.10	407.40
2,920	2,960	713.50	682.60	651.80	621.00	590.10	559.30	528.50	500.20	473.60	446.90	420.20
2,960	3,000	728.30	697.40	666.60	635.80	604.90	574.10	543.30	513.00	486.40	459.70	433.00
3,000	3,040	743.10	712.20	681.40	650.60	619.70	588.90	558.10	527.20	499.20	472.50	445.80
3,040	3,080	757.90	727.00	696.20	665.40	634.50	603.70	572.90	542.00	512.00	485.30	458.60
3,080	3,120	772.70	741.80	711.00	680.20	649.30	618.50	587.70	556.80	526.00	498.10	471.40
3,120	3,160	787.50	756.60	725.80	695.00	664.10	633.30	602.50	571.60	540.80	510.90	484.20
3,160	3,200	802.30	771.40	740.60	709.80	678.90	648.10	617.30	586.40	555.60	524.80	497.00
3,200	3,240	817.10	786.20	755.40	724.60	693.70	662.90	632.10	601.20	570.40	539.60	509.80
3,240	3,280	831.90	801.00	770.20	739.40	708.50	677.70	646.90	616.00	585.20	554.40	523.50
3,280	3,320	846.70	815.80	785.00	754.20	723.30	692.50	661.70	630.80	600.00	569.20	538.30
3,320	3,360	861.50	830.60	799.80	769.00	738.10	707.30	676.50	645.60	614.80	584.00	553.10
3,360	3,400	876.30	845.40	814.60	783.80	752.90	722.10	691.30	660.40	629.60	598.80	567.90
3,400	3,440	891.10	860.20	829.40	798.60	767.70	736.90	706.10	675.20	644.40	613.60	582.70
3,440	3,480	905.90	875.00	844.20	813.40	782.50	751.70	720.90	690.00	659.20	628.40	597.50
3,480	3,520	920.70	889.80	859.00	828.20	797.30	766.50	735.70	704.80	674.00	643.20	612.30
3,520	3,560	935.50	904.60	873.80	843.00	812.10	781.30	750.50	719.60	688.80	658.00	627.10

37% of the excess over $3,560 plus —

| $3,560 and over | | 942.90 | 912.00 | 881.20 | 850.40 | 819.50 | 788.70 | 757.90 | 727.00 | 696.20 | 665.40 | 634.50 |

THE EARNEST-MONEY CONTRACT— DOCUMENTING YOUR BUYER'S SERIOUS INTENT

You're ready to put your buyer's intent to buy and your intent to sell in writing. The fancy-sounding term used to describe this written agreement of sale is "earnest-money contract."

An earnest-money contract includes all the conditions under which you are selling your property to the buyer. The term "earnest money" refers to the cash deposit or security the buyer pays you as good-faith evidence of his intent to go through with the purchase. The amount of this cash deposit—usually a minimum of $1,000, although you can negotiate for a higher amount—is applied toward the down payment the buyer makes and should be deposited in an escrow account. The buyer should make the check out to the title company or your lawyer, depending upon who your escrow agent will be. In exchange for this cash deposit you will be removing your home from the market for other buyers. If the buyer fails to carry through the contract to completion, he or she may be required to forfeit this amount to you as seller.

Sample earnest-money contract forms for the various types of loans discussed in this book have been filled out and are included in this chapter. Read these forms *carefully* now, and again before signing. They cover every contingency pertaining to the sale of your home, including total purchase price, the amount of the cash deposit and down payment, the method of financing, the buyer's and seller's responsibility for closing costs, the dates of the closing and occupancy by the new owner, and any special provisions relevant to the sale. The earnest-money contract also specifies when the buyer shall apply for the needed financing and exactly how long the buyer has to obtain it. It is customary for the buyer to apply for financing within five working days from the date of this contract, so make sure your buyer applies for the loan without delay.

Blank copies of earnest-money contract forms for your personal use are located in Appendix G.

NOTE: Always have a lawyer review the agreement of sale *before* you sign it. This is important, especially as real-estate laws and customs vary greatly and are practiced differently in different parts of the country. (For more about what a lawyer can do for you, see Step Ten.)

THE PROPERTY CONDITION ADDENDUM

You should include a "property condition addendum" to every sales agreement. This brief form is quite important as it limits your liability as seller for repairs and protects the buyer from purchasing a home with major structural or mechanical problems. Ultimately it could save you from a lawsuit.

The property condition addendum covers the major structural items (foundation, roof, walls, etc.) and equipment and systems (plumbing, heating, etc.) in your home and provides for a termite inspection to be conducted at or prior to closing. Traditionally, the seller pays for the termite inspection while the buyer pays for all other charges and fees. The payment responsibilities are spelled out in the addendum. Fees for inspections vary depending upon the company you select, but average about $150. Consult the list of approved inspectors at your local Board of Realtors.

A filled-out sample of the property condition addendum is located at the end of this chapter and a blank copy for your personal use is in Appendix G.

THE CONTINGENCY CLAUSE ADDENDUM

If your prospective buyer makes the purchase of your home dependent upon the sale of his present residence, you should always protect yourself with a "contingency clause addendum." This addendum allows you to continue to show your home to other potential buyers. If you find another buyer before your original buyer is able to sell his or her home, the original buyer must proceed according to the conditions specified in the addendum.

A filled-out sample of the contingency clause addendum is located at the end of this chapter and a blank copy for your personal use is in Appendix G.

WHAT ABOUT BINDERS?

Many people reading this book live in states that will accept the use of a "binder" when selling your home. A binder is simply a paragraph or two, outlining in all too brief form your willingness to sell and a buyer's willingness to purchase your home.

It is strongly recommended that you avoid the use of this simplistic form. The earnest-money contract is a much better document. This strongly worded form is more comprehensive in scope than a binder and provides greater protection for both buyer and seller.

SAMPLE CONVENTIONAL LOAN—
RESIDENTIAL EARNEST-MONEY CONTRACT (RESALE)

1. PARTIES ___Joseph I. Homeseller & Mary Homeseller___ (Seller) agrees to sell and convey to ___James L. Prospect & Susan K. Prospect___ (Buyer) and Buyer agrees to buy from Seller the following property situated in ___Harris___ County, ___TX___ (State), known as ___8900 Lamar___ (Address).

2. PROPERTY: Lot ___1___, Block ___14___, ___River Oaks___ Addition, City of ___Houston___, or as described on attached exhibit, together with the following fixtures, if any; curtain rods, drapery rods, venetian blinds, window shades, screens and shutters, awnings, wall-to-wall carpeting, mirrors fixed in place, attic fans, permanently installed heating and air-conditioning units and equipment, lighting and plumbing fixtures, TV antennas, mailboxes, water softeners, shrubbery and all other property owned by Seller and attached to the above described real property. All property sold by this contract is called "Property."

3. CONTRACT SALES PRICE:

   A. Cash down payment payable at closing .... $___4,950___

   B. Note described in 4 below (the Note) in the amount of ... $___93,550___

   C. Any balance of Sales Price to be evidenced by a second lien note (the Second Note) to [check (1) or (2) below]:

   _____1. Seller, bearing interest at the rate of

   _____% per annum in

   _____ lump sum on or before _____

   _____ principal and interest installments of

   $_____, or more per _____ with first installment payable on

   _____

   _____2. Third Party in principal and interest installments not in excess of $_____ per month in the principal amount of .... $_____

   D. Sales Price payable to Seller on Loan funding after closing (Sum of A, B, & C) ....
   .... $___98,500___

4. FINANCING CONDITIONS: This contract is subject to approval for Buyer of a _____ Conventional or ___XX___ Conventional private mortgage insured third party loan (the Loan) of not less than the amount of the Note, amortizable monthly for not less than ___30___ years, with interest not to exceed ___13 7/8___ percent per annum, and approval of any third party Second Note. Buyer shall apply for all financing within ___5___ days from the effective date of this contract and shall make every reasonable effort to obtain approval. If all financing cannot be approved within

_____30_____ days from effective date of this contract, this contract shall terminate and Earnest Money shall be refunded to Buyer without delay.

5. EARNEST MONEY: $_____1,000.00_____ is herewith tendered and is to be deposited as Earnest Money with _____Stewart Title Company_____ as Escrow Agent, upon execution of the contract by both parties. Additional Earnest Money, if any, shall be deposited with the Escrow Agent on or before _____N/A_____, 19_____ in the amount of $_____N/A_____.

6. TITLE: Seller at Seller's expense shall furnish either:

_____X_____A. Owner's Policy of Title Insurance (the Title Policy) issued by _____Stewart Title Company_____ in the amount of the Sales Price and dated at or after closing:

OR

_____B. Complete Abstract of Title (the Abstract) certified by _____ _____ to current date.

NOTICE TO BUYER AS REQUIRED BY LAW, YOU should have the Abstract covering the Property examined by an attorney of YOUR selection, or YOU should be furnished with or obtain a Title Policy.

7. PROPERTY CONDITION [Check "A" or "B"]:

_____A. Buyer accepts the Property in its present condition, subject only to lender required repairs and _____.

_____X_____B. Buyer requires inspections and repairs required by the Property Condition Addendum (the Addendum) and any lender.

Upon Seller's receipt of all loan approvals and inspection reports Seller shall commence and complete prior to closing all required repairs at Seller's expense.

All inspections, reports and repairs required of Seller by this contract and the Addendum shall not exceed $_____50.00_____. If Seller fails to complete such requirements, Buyer may do so and Seller shall be liable up to the amount specified and the same paid from the proceeds of the sale. If such expenditures exceed the stated amount and Seller refuses to pay such excess, Buyer may pay the additional cost or accept the Property with limited repairs and this sale shall be closed as scheduled, or Buyer may terminate this contract and the Earnest Money shall be refunded to Buyer.

8. CLOSING: The closing of the sale (the Closing Date) shall be on or before _____May 1_____ 19_____81_____, or within 7 days after objections to title have been cured, whichever date is later; however, if necessary to complete Loan requirements, the Closing Date shall be extended daily up to 15 days.

9. POSSESSION: The possession of the Property shall be delivered to Buyer on _____May 1, 1981_____ in its present or required improved condition, ordinary wear and tear excepted. Any possession by Buyer prior to or by Seller after Closing Date shall establish a landlord tenant at sufferance relationship between the parties.

10. SPECIAL PROVISIONS:

[Insert terms and conditions of a factual nature applicable to this sale, e.g., personal property included in sale (curtains, draperies, valances, etc.), prior purchase or sale of other property, lessee's surrender of possession, and the like.]

11. SALES EXPENSES TO BE PAID IN CASH AT OR PRIOR TO CLOSING:

A. Loan appraisal fees shall be paid by ___Buyer___.

B. Seller's Expenses:

(1) Seller's Loan discount points not exceeding ___7___.

(2) Lender required repairs and any other inspections, reports, and repairs required of Seller herein, and in the Addendum.

(3) Prepayment penalties on any existing loans, plus cost of releasing such loans and recording releases, tax statements, ½ of any escrow fee, preparation of Deed, other expenses stipulated to be paid by Seller under other provisions of this contract.

C. Buyer's Expenses:

(1) Fees for loans (e.g., any private mortgage insurance premiums, loan and mortgage application, origination and commitment fees, Buyer's loan discount points not exceeding $_____.

(2) Expenses incident to loan(s) e.g., preparation of any Note, Deed of Trust and other loan documents, survey, recording fees, copies of restrictions and easements, Mortgagee's Title Policies, credit reports, photo(s), ½ of any escrow fee, any required premiums for flood and hazard insurance, any required reserve deposits for insurance premiums, ad valorem taxes and special assessments, interest on all monthly installment payment notes from date of disbursement to 1 month prior to dates of first monthly payments, expenses stipulated to be paid by Buyer under other provisions of this contract.

D. If any sales expenses exceed the maximum amount herein stipulated to be paid by either party, either party may terminate this contract unless the other party agrees to pay such excess.

12. PRORATIONS: Insurance (at Buyer's option), taxes and any rents and maintenance fees shall be prorated to the Closing Date.

13. TITLE APPROVAL: If Abstract is furnished, Seller shall deliver same to Buyer within 20 days from the effective date hereof. Buyer shall have 20 days from date of receipt of Abstract to deliver a copy of the title opinion to Seller, stating any objections to title, and only objections so stated shall be considered. If Title Policy is furnished, the Title shall guarantee Buyer's title to be good and indefeasible subject only to (i) restrictive covenants affecting the Property, (ii) any discrepancies, conflicts or shortages in area or boundary lines or any encroachments, or any overlapping of improvements, (iii) all taxes for the current and subsequent years, (iv) any existing building and zoning ordinances, (v) rights of parties in possession, (vi) any liens created as security for the sale consideration, and (vii) any reservations or exceptions contained in the Deed. In either instance, if title objections are disclosed, Seller shall have 30 days to cure the same. Exceptions permitted in the Deed and zoning ordinances shall not be valid objections to title. Seller shall furnish at Seller's expense tax statements showing no delinquent taxes and a General Warranty Deed conveying title subject only to liens securing debt created as part of the consideration, taxes for the current year, usual restrictive covenants and utility easements common to the platted subdivision of which the Property is a part and any other reservations or exceptions acceptable to Buyer. Each note herein provided shall be secured by Vendor's and Deed of Trust liens. In case of dispute as to the form of Deed, Note(s) or Deed(s) of Trust, such shall be upon a form prepared by the State Bar of _____TX_____ (State).

14. CASUALTY LOSS: If any part of Property is damaged or destroyed by fire or other casualty loss, Seller shall restore the same to its previous condition as soon as reasonably possible, but in any event by Closing Date, and if Seller is unable to do so without fault, this contract shall terminate and Earnest Money shall be refunded.

15. DEFAULT: If Buyer fails to comply herewith, Seller may either enforce specific performance or terminate this contract and receive the Earnest Money as liquidated damages.

    If Seller is unable without fault to deliver Abstract or Title Policy or to make any noncasualty repairs required herein within the time herein specified, Buyer may either terminate this contract and receive the Earnest Money as the sole remedy, or extend the time up to 30 days. If Seller fails to comply herewith for any other reason, Buyer may (i) terminate this contract and receive the Earnest Money, thereby releasing Seller from this contract, (ii) enforce specific performance hereof, or (iii) seek such other relief as may be provided by law.

16. ATTORNEY'S FEES: Any signatory to this contract who is the prevailing party in any legal proceeding against any other signatory brought under or with relation to this contract or transaction shall be additionally entitled to recover court costs and reasonable attorney fees from the nonprevailing party.

17. ESCROW: Earnest Money is deposited with Escrow Agent with the understanding that Escrow Agent (i) does not have any liability for performance or nonperformance of any party, (ii) has the right to require the receipt, release and authorization in writing of all parties before paying the deposit to any party, and (iii) is not liable for interest or other charge on the funds held. If any party unreasonably fails to agree in writing to an appropriate release of Earnest Money, then such party shall be liable to the other parties to the extent provided in paragraph 16. At closing, Earnest Money shall be applied to any cash down payment required, next to Buyer's closing costs and any excess refunded to Buyer. Before Buyer shall be entitled to refund of Earnest Money, any actual expenses incurred or paid on Buyer's behalf shall be deducted therefrom and paid to the creditors entitled thereto.

18. REPRESENTATIONS: Seller represents that unless securing payment of the Note there will be no Title I liens, unrecorded liens, or Uniform Commercial Code liens against any of the Property on Closing Date. If any representation above is untrue this contract may be terminated by Buyer and the Earnest Money shall be refunded without delay. Representations shall survive closing.

19. AGREEMENT OF PARTIES: This contract contains the entire agreement of the parties and cannot be changed except by their written consent.

20. CONSULT YOUR ATTORNEY: This is intended to be a legally binding contract. READ IT CAREFULLY. If you do not understand the effect of any part, consult your attorney BEFORE signing. Attorneys to represent parties may be designated below.

Seller's Atty: _____   Buyer's Atty: _____

EXECUTED in multiple originals effective the _____ day of _____, 19_____.

_____
Seller

_____
Seller

_____
Seller's Address

_____
Buyer

_____
Buyer

_____
Buyer's Address

SAMPLE FHA INSURED LOAN—
RESIDENTIAL EARNEST-MONEY CONTRACT (RESALE)

1. PARTIES _Joseph I. Homeseller & Mary Homeseller_ (Seller) agrees to

   sell and convey to _James L. Prospect & Susan K. Prospect_ (Buyer)

   and Buyer agrees to buy from Seller the following property situated in _Harris_

   County, _TX_ (State), known as _____

   8900 Lamar (Address).

2. PROPERTY: Lot _1_ , Block _14_ , _____ Addition, City of

   River Oaks , or as described on attached exhibit, together with the following

   fixtures, if any: curtain rods, drapery rods, venetian blinds, window shades, screens and shutters,

   awnings, wall-to-wall carpeting, mirrors fixed in place, attic fans, permanently installed heating and

   air-conditioning units and equipment, light and plumbing fixtures, TV antennas, mailboxes, water

   softeners, shrubbery and all other property owned by Seller and attached to the above described

   real property. All property sold by this contract is called "Property."

3. CONTRACT SALES PRICE:

   A. Cash down payment payable at closing .... $ _1,800.00_

   B. Amount of Note (the Note) described in 4-A below .... $ _63,200.00_

   C. Sales Price payable to Seller on Loan funding after closing (Sum of A plus B)......................

   .... $ _65,000.00_

4. FINANCING CONDITIONS:

   A. This contract is subject to approval for Buyer of a Section _203-B_ FHA Insured Loan
   (the Loan) of not less than the amount of the Note, amortizable monthly for not less than
   _30_ years, with interest at maximum rate allowable at time of Loan funding. Buyer shall
   apply for the Loan within _5_ days from the effective date of this contract and shall
   make every reasonable effort to obtain approval of the Loan. If the Loan has not been approved
   by the Closing Date, this contract shall terminate and Earnest Money shall be refunded to Buyer
   without delay.

   B. As required by HUD-FHA regulations, if FHA valuation is unknown, "It is expressly agreed that,
   notwithstanding any other provisions of this contract, the Purchaser (Buyer) shall not be obligated to complete the purchase of the Property described herein or to incur any penalty by forfeiture of Earnest Money deposits or otherwise unless the Seller has delivered to the Purchaser
   (Buyer) a written statement issued by the Federal Housing Commissioner setting forth the appraised value of the Property (excluding closing costs) of not less than $ _65,000.00_ ,
   which statement the Seller hereby agrees to deliver to the Purchaser (Buyer) promptly after

such appraised value statement is made available to the Seller. The Purchaser (Buyer) shall, however, have the privilege and option of proceeding with the consummation of this contract without regard to the amount of the appraised valuation made by the Federal Housing Commission. *The appraised valuation is arrived at to determine the maximum mortgage the Department of Housing and Urban Development will insure. HUD does not warrant the value or the condition of the property. The purchaser should satisfy himself/herself that the price and the condition of the property are acceptable.''*

5. EARNEST MONEY: $__1000.00__ is herewith tendered and is to be deposited as Earnest Money with __Stewart Title Company__ as Escrow Agent, upon execution of the contract by both parties. Additional Earnest Money, if any, shall be deposited with the Escrow Agent on or before __N/A__, 19____, in the amount of $__N/A__.

6. TITLE: Seller at Seller's expense shall furnish either:

__X__ A. Owner's Policy of Title Insurance (the Title Policy) issued by __Stewart Title Co.__ in the amount of the Sales Price and dated at or after closing;

OR

_____ B. Complete Abstract of Title (the Abstract) certified by _____ to current date.

NOTICE TO BUYER AS REQUIRED BY LAW, YOU should have the abstract covering the Property examined by an attorney of YOUR selection, or YOU should be furnished with or obtain a Title Policy.

7. PROPERTY CONDITION [Check ''A'' or ''B'']:

_____ A. Buyer accepts the Property in its present condition, subject only to required repairs and

_____

_____ .

__X__ B. Buyer requires inspections and repairs required by the Property Condition Addendum (the Addendum) and those required by FHA. Upon Seller's receipt of the Loan approval and inspection reports Seller shall commence and complete prior to closing all required repairs at Seller's expense.

All inspections, reports and repairs required of Seller by this contract and the Addendum shall not exceed $__50.__. If the Seller fails to complete such requirements, Buyer may do so and Seller shall be liable up to the amount specified and the same paid from the proceeds of the sale. If such expenditures exceed the stated amount and the Seller refuses to pay such excess, Buyer may pay the additional cost or accept the Property with the limited repairs and this sale shall be closed as scheduled, or Buyer may terminate this contract and the Earnest Money shall be refunded to Buyer.

8. CLOSING: The closing of the sale (the Closing Date) shall be on or before _____May 1,_____ 19 _81_ , or within 7 days after objections to title have been cured, whichever date is later; however, if necessary to complete Loan requirements, the Closing Date shall be extended daily up to 15 days.

9. POSSESSION: The possession of the Property shall be delivered to Buyer on _____May 1, 1981_____ in its present or required improved condition, ordinary wear and tear excepted. Any possession by Buyer prior to or by Seller after Closing Date shall establish a landlord tenant at sufferance relationship between the Parties.

10. SPECIAL PROVISIONS:

[Insert terms and conditions of a factual nature applicable to this sale, e.g., prior purchase or sale of other property, lessee surrender of possession and the like.]

11. SALES EXPENSES TO BE PAID IN CASH AT OR PRIOR TO CLOSING:

A. Loan appraisal fee (FHA application fee) shall be paid by _____Buyer_____ .

B. Seller's Expenses:

   (1) Seller's Loan discount points not exceeding _____7_____ .

   (2) FHA required repairs and any other inspections, reports, and repairs required of Seller herein, and in the Addendum.

   (3) Expenses incident to Loan (e.g., preparation of Loan documents, survey, recording fees, copies of restrictions and easements, amortization schedule, Mortgagee's Title Policy, Loan origination fee, credit reports, photographs).

   (4) Releases of existing loans, including prepayment penalties and recordation; tax statements, preparation of Deed; escrow fee; and other expenses stipulated to be paid by Seller under other provisions of this contract.

C. Buyer's Expenses: All prepaid items required by applicable HUD-FHA or other regulations (e.g., required premiums for flood and hazard insurance, required reserve deposits for FHA and other insurance, ad valorem taxes and special assessments); interest on the Note from date of disbursement to one month prior to date of first monthly payment; expenses stipulated to be paid by Buyer under other provisions of this contract.

D. If any sales expenses exceed the maximum amount herein stipulated to be paid by either party, either party may terminate this Contract unless other party agrees to pay such excess. In no event shall Buyer pay charges and fees other than those expressly permitted by FHA regulations.

12. PRORATIONS: Insurance (at Buyer's option), taxes, and any rents and maintenance fees shall be prorated to the Closing Date.

13. TITLE APPROVAL: If Abstract is furnished, Seller shall deliver same to Buyer within 20 days from the effective date hereof. Buyer shall have 20 days from date of receipt of Abstract to deliver a copy of the title opinion to Seller, stating any objections to title, and only objections so stated shall be considered. If Title Policy is furnished, the Title Policy shall guarantee Buyer's title to be good and indefeasible subject only to (i) restrictive covenants affecting the Property, (ii) any discrepancies, conflicts or shortages in area or boundary lines or any encroachments, or any overlapping of improvements, (iii) all taxes for the current and subsequent years, (iv) any existing building and zoning ordinances, (v) rights of parties in possession, (vi) any liens created as security for the sale consideration, and (vii) any reservations or exceptions contained in the Deed. In either instance, if title objections are disclosed, Seller shall have 30 days to cure the same. Exceptions permitted in the Deed and zoning ordinances shall not be valid objections to title. Seller shall furnish at Seller's expense tax statement showing no delinquent taxes and a General Warranty Deed conveying title subject only to liens securing debt created as part of the consideration, taxes for the current year, usual restrictive covenants and utility easements common to the platted subdivision of which the Property is a part and any other reservations or exceptions acceptable to Buyer. The Note shall be secured by Vendor's and Deed of Trust liens. In case of dispute as to the form of Deed, such shall be upon a form prepared by the State Bar of _____TX_____ (State).

14. CASUALTY LOSS: If any part of Property is damaged or destroyed by fire or other casualty loss, Seller shall restore the same to its previous condition as soon as reasonably possible, but in any event by Closing Date; and if the Seller is unable to do so without fault, this contract shall terminate and Earnest Money shall be refunded.

15. DEFAULT: If Buyer fails to comply herewith, Seller may either enforce specific performance or terminate this contract and receive the Earnest Money as liquidated damages.

If Seller is unable without fault to deliver Abstract or Title Policy or to make any noncasualty repairs required herein within the time herein specified, Buyer may either terminate this contract and receive the Earnest Money as the sole remedy, or extend the time up to 30 days. If Seller fails to comply herewith for any other reason, Buyer may (i) terminate this contract and receive the Earnest Money, thereby releasing Seller from this contract, (ii) enforce specific performance hereof, or (iii) seek such other relief as may be provided by law.

16. ATTORNEY'S FEES: Any signatory to this contract who is the prevailing party in any legal proceeding against any other signatory brought under or with relation to this contract or transaction shall be additionally entitled to recover court costs and reasonable attorney fees from the nonprevailing party.

17. ESCROW: Earnest Money is deposited with Escrow Agent with the understanding that Escrow Agent (i) does not assume or have any liability for performance or nonperformance of any party, (ii) has the right to require the receipt, release and authorization in writing of all parties before paying the deposit to any party, and (iii) is not liable for interest or other charge on the funds held. If any party unreasonably fails to agree in writing to an appropriate release of Earnest Money, then such party shall be liable to the other parties to the extent provided in paragraph 16. At closing, Earnest Money shall be applied to any cash down payment required, next to Buyer's closing costs and any excess refunded to Buyer. Before Buyer shall be entitled to refund of Earnest Money, any actual and FHA allowable expenses incurred or paid on Buyer's behalf shall be deducted therefrom and paid to the creditors entitled thereto.

18. REPRESENTATIONS: Seller represents that there will be no Title I liens, unrecorded liens or Uniform Commercial Code liens against any of the Property on Closing Date. If any representation above is untrue this contract may be terminated by Buyer and the Earnest Money shall be refunded without delay. Representations shall survive closing.

19. AGREEMENT OF PARTIES: This contract contains the entire agreement of the parties and cannot be changed except by their written consent.

20. CONSULT YOUR ATTORNEY: This is intended to be a legally binding contract. READ IT CAREFULLY. If you do not understand the effect of any part, consult your attorney BEFORE signing. Attorneys to represent parties may be designated below.

Seller's Atty: ———————————————   Buyer's Atty: ———————————————

EXECUTED in multiple originals effective the ——— day of ——————— , 19——— .

———————————————
Seller

———————————————
Seller

———————————————
Seller's Address

———————————————
Buyer

———————————————
Buyer

———————————————
Buyer's Address

SAMPLE VA GUARANTEED LOAN—
RESIDENTIAL EARNEST-MONEY CONTRACT (RESALE)

1. PARTIES _Joseph I. Homeseller and Mary Homeseller_ (Seller) agrees to sell and convey to _James L. Prospect and Susan K. Prospect_ (Buyer) and Buyer agrees to buy from Seller the following property situated in _Harris_ County, _TX_ (State), known as _8900 Lamar_ (Address).

2. PROPERTY: Lot _1_ Block _14_ _River Oaks_ Addition, City of _Houston_, or as described on attached exhibit, together with the following fixtures, if any: curtain rods, drapery rods, venetian blinds, window shades, screens and shutters, awnings, wall-to-wall carpeting, mirrors fixed in place, attic fans, permanently installed heating and air-conditioning units and equipment, light and plumbing fixtures, TV antennas, mailboxes, water softeners, shrubbery and all other property owned by Seller and attached to the above described real property. All property sold by this contract is called "Property."

3. CONTRACT SALES PRICE:

    A. Cash down payment payable at closing ....$ _-0-_

    B. Note described in 4 below (the Note) in the amount of ....$ _75,000.00_

    C. Sales Price payable to Seller on Loan funding after closing (Sum of A and B) ....
    ....$ _75,000.00_

4. FINANCING CONDITIONS: This contract is subject to approval for Buyer of a VA loan (the Loan) of not less than the amount of the Note, amortizable monthly for not less than _30_ years, with interest at maximum rate allowable at time of Loan funding. Buyer shall apply for the Loan within _5_ days from the effective date of this contract and shall make every reasonable effort to obtain approval. If the Loan has not been approved by the Closing Date, this contract shall terminate and the Earnest Money shall be refunded to Buyer without delay. VA NOTICE TO BUYER: "It is expressly agreed that, notwithstanding any other provisions of this contract, the Buyer shall not incur any penalty by forfeiture of earnest money or otherwise or be obligated to complete the purchase of the Property described herein, if the contract purchase price or cost exceeds the reasonable value of the Property established by the Veterans Administration. The Buyer shall, however, have the privilege and option of proceeding with the consummation of this contract without regard to the amount of the reasonable value established by the Veterans Administration." Buyer agrees that should Buyer elect to complete the purchase at an amount in excess of the reasonable value established by VA, Buyer shall pay such excess amount in cash from a source which Buyer agrees to disclose to the VA and which Buyer represents will not be from borrowed funds except as approved by VA. If VA reasonable value of the Property is less than the Sales Price (3C above), Seller

may reduce the Sales Price to an amount equal to the VA reasonable value and both parties agree to close the sale at such lower Sales Price with appropriate adjustments to 3A and 3B above.

5. EARNEST MONEY: $_____1,000.00_____ is herewith tendered and is to be deposited as Earnest Money with _____Stewart Title Company_____, as Escrow Agent, upon execution of the contract by both parties. Additional Earnest Money, if any, shall be deposited with the Escrow Agent on or before _____N/A_____, 19_____, in the amount of $____N/A____.

6. TITLE: Seller at Seller's expense shall furnish either:

____X____A. Owner's Policy of Title Insurance (the Title Policy) issued by _____
_____ in the amount of the Sales Price and dated at or after closing: OR

_____B. Complete Abstract of Title (the Abstract) certified by _____
to current date.

NOTICE TO BUYER AS REQUIRED BY LAW, YOU should have the Abstract covering the Property examined by an attorney of YOUR selection, or YOU should be furnished with or obtain a Title Policy.

7. PROPERTY CONDITION [Check "A" or "B"]:

_____A. Buyer accepts the Property in its present condition, subject only to VA required repairs and _____
_____ .

____X____B. Buyer requires inspections and repairs required by the Property Condition Addendum (the Addendum) and those required by VA. Upon Seller's receipt of the Loan approval and inspection reports Seller shall commence and complete prior to closing all required repairs at Seller's expense.

All inspections, reports and repairs required of Seller by this contract and the Addendum shall not exceed $____50.00____. If Seller fails to complete such requirements, Buyer may do so and Seller shall be liable up to the amount specified and the same paid from the proceeds of the sale. If such expenditures exceed the stated amount and Seller refuses to pay such excess, Buyer may pay the additional cost or accept the Property with the limited repairs and this sale shall be closed as scheduled, or Buyer may terminate this contract and the Earnest Money shall be refunded to Buyer.

8. CLOSING: The closing of the sale (the Closing Date) shall be on or before ____May 1st____, 19__81__, or within 7 days after objections to title have been cured, whichever date is later; however, if necessary to complete Loan requirements, the Closing Date shall be extended daily up to 15 days.

9. POSSESSION: The possession of the Property shall be delivered to Buyer on ____May 1st, 1981____ in its present or required improved condition, ordinary wear and

tear excepted. Any possession by Buyer prior to or by Seller after Closing Date shall establish a landlord tenant at sufferance relationship between the parties.

10. SPECIAL PROVISIONS:

[Insert terms and conditions of a factual nature applicable to this sale, e.g., prior purchase or sale of other property, lessee surrender of possession and the like.]

11. SALES EXPENSES TO BE PAID IN CASH AT OR PRIOR TO CLOSING:

    A. Loan appraisal fees shall be paid by _____Buyer_____ .

    B. Seller's Expenses:

        (1) Seller's Loan discount points not exceeding _____7_____ .

        (2) VA required repairs and other inspections, reports and repairs required of Seller herein, and in the Addendum.

        (3) Releases of existing loans, including prepayment penalties and recordation; escrow fee, tax statement, preparation of Deed, Note and Deed of Trust, expenses VA prohibits Buyer to pay (e.g., copies of restrictions, photos, excess cost of survey of Property), other expenses stipulated to be paid by Seller under other provisions of this contract.

    C. Buyer's Expenses: Expenses incident to Loan (e.g., credit reports, recording fees, Mortgagee's Title Policy; Loan origination fee, that portion of survey cost Buyer can pay by VA regulation, Loan related inspection fees, premiums for 1 year's hazard insurance and any flood insurance, required reserve deposits for insurance premiums, ad valorem taxes and special assessments, interest from date of disbursement to 1 month prior to date of first monthly payment on the Note; premiums on nonrequired insurance, expenses stipulated to be paid by Buyer under other provisions of this contract.

    D. If any sales expenses exceed the maximum amount herein stipulated to be paid by either party, either party may terminate this contract unless the other party agrees to pay such expenses. In no event shall Buyer pay charges and fees other than those expressly permitted by VA Regulations.

12. PRORATIONS: Insurance (at Buyer's option), taxes and any rents and maintenance fees shall be prorated to the Closing Date.

13. TITLE APPROVAL: If Abstract is furnished, Seller shall deliver same to Buyer within 20 days from the effective date hereof. Buyer shall have 20 days from date of receipt of Abstract to deliver a copy of the title opinion to Seller, stating any objections to title, and only objections so stated shall be considered. If Title Policy is furnished, the Title shall guarantee Buyer's title to be good and inde-feasible subject only to (i) restrictive covenants affecting the Property, (ii) any discrepancies, con-flicts or shortages in area or boundary lines or any encroachments, or any overlapping of improve-ments, (iii) all taxes for the current and subsequent years, (iv) any existing building and zoning ordinances, (v) rights of parties in possession, (vi) any liens created as security for the sale consid-eration, and (vii) any reservations or exceptions contained in the Deed. In either instance, if title objections are disclosed, Seller shall have 30 days to cure the same. Exceptions permitted in the Deed and zoning ordinances shall not be valid objections to title. Seller shall furnish at Seller's ex-pense tax statements showing no delinquent taxes and a General Warranty Deed conveying title subject only to liens securing debt created as part of the consideration, taxes for the current year, usual restrictive covenants and utility easements common to the platted subdivision of which the Property is a part and any other reservations or exceptions acceptable to Buyer. The Note shall be secured by Vendor's and Deed of Trust liens. In case of dispute as to the form of Deed, such shall be upon a form prepared by the State Bar of _____TX_____ (State).

14. CASUALTY LOSS: If any part of Property is damaged or destroyed by fire or other casualty loss, Seller shall restore the same to its previous condition as soon as reasonably possible, but in any event by Closing Date, and if Seller is unable to do so without fault, this contract shall terminate and Earnest Money shall be refunded.

15. DEFAULT: If Buyer fails to comply herewith, Seller may either enforce specific performance or ter-minate this contract and receive the Earnest Money as liquidated damages.

    If Seller is unable without fault to deliver Abstract or Title Policy or to make any noncasualty re-pairs required herein within the time herein specified, Buyer may either terminate this contract and receive the Earnest Money as the sole remedy, or extend the time up to 30 days. If Seller fails to comply herewith for any other reason, Buyer may (i) terminate this contract and receive the Ear-nest Money, thereby releasing Seller from this contract, (ii) enforce specific performance hereof, or (iii) seek such other relief as may be provided by law.

16. ATTORNEY'S FEES: Any signatory to this contract who is the prevailing party in any legal proceed-ing against any other signatory brought under or with relation to this contract or transaction shall be additionally entitled to recover court costs and reasonable attorney fees from the nonprevailing party.

17. ESCROW: Earnest Money is deposited with Escrow Agent with the understanding that Escrow Agent (i) does not have any liability for performance or nonperformance of any party, (ii) has the right to require the receipt, release and authorization in writing of all parties before paying the deposit to any party, and (iii) is not liable for interest or other charge on the funds held. If any party unreasonably fails to agree in writing to an appropriate release of Earnest Money, then such party shall be liable to the other parties to the extent provided in paragraph 16. At closing, Earnest Money shall be applied to any cash down payment required, next to Buyer's closing costs and any excess refunded to Buyer. Before Buyer shall be entitled to refund of Earnest Money, any actual and VA allowable expenses incurred or paid on Buyer's behalf shall be deducted therefrom and paid to the creditors entitled thereto.

18. REPRESENTATIONS: Seller represents that there will be no Title I liens, unrecorded liens or Uniform Commercial Code liens against any of the Property on Closing Date. If any representation above is untrue this contract may be terminated by Buyer and the Earnest Money shall be refunded without delay. Representations shall survive closing.

19. AGREEMENT OF PARTIES: This contract contains the entire agreement of the parties and cannot be changed except by their written consent.

20. CONSULT YOUR ATTORNEY: This is intended to be a legally binding contract. READ IT CAREFULLY. If you do not understand the effect of any part, consult your attorney BEFORE signing. Attorneys to represent parties may be designated below.

Seller's Atty: _____   Buyer's Atty: _____

EXECUTED in multiple originals effective the _____ day of _____ , 19_____ .

_____
Seller

_____
Buyer

_____
Seller

_____
Buyer

_____
Seller's Address

_____
Buyer's Address

SAMPLE ASSUMPTION OF LOAN—
RESIDENTIAL EARNEST-MONEY CONTRACT (RESALE)

1. PARTIES _Joseph I. Homeseller & Mary Homeseller_ (Seller) agrees to
sell and convey to _James L. Prospect & Susan K. Prospect_ (Buyer)
and Buyer agrees to buy from Seller the following property situated in _Harris_
County, _TX_ (State), known as _8900 Lamar_ (Address).

2. PROPERTY: Lot _1_, Block _14_, _River Oaks_ Addition, City of
Houston, or as described on attached exhibit, together with the following
fixtures, if any; curtain rods, drapery rods, venetian blinds, window shades, screens and shutters,
awnings, wall-to-wall carpeting, mirrors fixed in place, attic fans, permanently installed heating and
air-conditioning units and equipment, lighting and plumbing fixtures, TV antennas, mailboxes,
water softener, shrubbery and all other property owned by Seller and attached to the above described real property. All property sold by this contract is called "Property."

3. CONTRACT SALES PRICE:

A. _____ Exact _X_ Approximate Cash down payment payable at closing...........................
.... $ _30,000.00_

B. Buyer's assumption of the unpaid balance of a promissory note (the Note) payable in present
monthly installments of $_400.00_, including principal and interest and any reserve de-
posits, with Buyer's first installment payable to _Haskell Mortgage_
_____ on _July 1_, 19 _81_, in the assumed principal balance of
which at closing (allowing for an agreed $250.00 variance) will be............$ _40,000.00_

C. Any balance of Sales Price to be evidenced by a second lien note payable to [check (1) or (2)
below]:

    _____(1) Seller bearing interest at the rate of _____% per annum, in
        _____lump sum on or before _____
        _____principal and interest installments of $_____, or more per
        _____, with first installment payable on _____.

    _____(2) Third Party in principal and interest installments not in excess of
        $_____ per month, and in the _____ Exact _____ Approximate
        (check "Approximate" only if A above and D below are "Exact") amount of ....
        ....$ _N/A_

D. The _XX_ Exact _____ Approximate total Sales Price (Sum of A, B, and C above ....
.... $ _70,000.00_

4. FINANCING CONDITIONS: If a Noteholder on assumption (i) requires Buyer to pay an assumption fee in excess of $ 50.00 and Seller declines to pay such excess, (ii) raises the existing interest rate above _____%, or (iii) requires approval of Buyer or can accelerate the Note and Buyer does not receive from the Noteholder written approval and acceleration waiver prior to the Closing Date, Buyer may terminate this contract and the Earnest Money shall be refunded. Buyer shall apply for the approval and waiver under (iii) above within 7 days from the effective date hereof and shall make every reasonable effort to obtain the same.

5. EARNEST MONEY: $ 1,000.00 is herewith tendered and is to be deposited as Earnest Money with Stewart Title Company as Escrow Agent, upon execution of the contract by both parties. Additional Earnest Money, if any, shall be deposited with the Escrow Agent on or before June 15 , 19 81 in the amount of $ N/A .

6. TITLE: Seller at Seller's expense shall furnish either:

   X   A. Owner's Policy of Title Insurance (the Title Policy) issued by Stewart Title Company in the amount of the Sales Price and dated at or after closing:

         OR

        B. Complete Abstract of Title (the Abstract) certified by _____ _____ to current date.

NOTICE TO BUYER AS REQUIRED BY LAW, YOU should have the Abstract covering the Property examined by an attorney of YOUR selection, or YOU should be furnished with or obtain a Title Policy.

7. PROPERTY CONDITION [Check "A" or "B"]:

   X   A. Buyer accepts the Property in its present condition, subject only to _____ Replacement of broken window glass in rear of house.

        B. Buyer requires inspections and repairs required by the Property Condition Addendum (the Addendum). Upon Seller's receipt of all loan approvals and inspection reports Seller shall commence and complete prior to closing all required repairs at Seller's expense.

All inspections, reports and repairs required of Seller by this contract and the Addendum shall not exceed $ 300.00 . If Seller fails to complete such requirements, Buyer may do so and Seller shall be liable up to the amount specified and the same paid from the proceeds of the sale. If such expenditures exceed the stated amount and Seller refuses to pay such excess, Buyer may pay the additional cost or accept the Property with limited repairs and this sale shall be closed as scheduled, or Buyer may terminate this contract and the Earnest Money shall be refunded.

8. CLOSING: The closing of the sale (the Closing Date) shall be on or before June 25 19 81 , or within 7 days after objections to title have been cured, whichever date is later.

9. POSSESSION: The possession of the Property shall be delivered to Buyer on _____ June 27, 1981 _____ in its present or required improved condition, ordinary wear and tear excepted. Any possession by Buyer prior to or by Seller after Closing Date shall establish a landlord tenant at sufferance relationship between the parties.

10. SPECIAL PROVISIONS:

[Insert terms and conditions of a factual nature applicable to this sale, e.g., personal property included in sale (curtains, draperies, valances, etc.), prior purchase or sale of other property, lessee's surrender of possession, and the like.]

11. PRORATION: Taxes, insurance, rents, interest and maintenance fees, if any, ___X___ SHALL _____ SHALL NOT be prorated to the Closing Date. If these are not prorated, all funds held in reserve for payment of taxes, maintenance fees and insurance and the insurance policy shall be transferred to the Buyer by Seller without cost to Buyer.

12. SALES EXPENSES TO BE PAID IN CASH AT OR PRIOR TO CLOSING: Preparing Deed, preparing and recording Deed of Trust to Secure Assumption, all inspections, reports and repairs required of Seller herein and in the Addendum and ½ of escrow fee shall be Seller's expense. All other costs and expenses incurred in connection with this contract which are not recited herein to be the obligation of Seller, shall be the obligation of Buyer. Unless otherwise paid, before Buyer shall be entitled to refund of Earnest Money, any such costs and expenses shall be deducted therefrom and paid to the creditors entitled thereto. If any sales expenses exceed the maximum amount herein stipulated to be paid by either party, either party may terminate this contract unless the other party agrees to pay such excess.

13. TITLE APPROVAL: If Abstract is furnished, Seller shall deliver same to Buyer within 20 days from the effective date hereof. Buyer shall have 20 days from date of receipt of Abstract to deliver a copy of the title opinion to Seller, stating any objections to title, and only objections so stated shall be considered. If Title Policy is furnished, the Title shall guarantee Buyer's title to be good and indefeasible subject only to (i) restrictive covenants affecting the Property, (ii) any discrepancies, conflicts or shortages in area or boundary lines or any encroachments, or any overlapping of improvements, (iii) all taxes for the current and subsequent years, (iv) any existing building and zoning ordinances, (v) rights of parties in possession, (vi) any liens created as security for the sale consideration, and (vii) any reservations or exceptions contained in the Deed. In either instance, if title objections are disclosed, Seller shall have 30 days to cure the same. Exceptions permitted in the

Deed and zoning ordinances shall not be valid objections to title. Seller shall furnish at Seller's expense tax statements showing no delinquent taxes and a General Warranty Deed conveying title subject only to liens securing debt created as part of the consideration, taxes for the current year, usual restrictive covenants and utility easements common to the platted subdivision of which the Property is a part and any other reservations or exceptions acceptable to Buyer. Each note herein provided shall be secured by Vendor's and Deed of Trust liens. A Vendor's lien shall be retained and a Deed of Trust to Secure Assumption required, which shall be automatically released on execution and delivery of a release by Noteholder. In the case of dispute as to the form of Deed, Note(s) or Deed(s) of Trust, such shall be upon a form prepared by the State Bar of _____TX_____ (State).

14. CASUALTY LOSS: If any part of Property is damaged or destroyed by fire or other casualty loss, Seller shall restore the same to its previous condition as soon as reasonably possible, but in any event by Closing Date, and if Seller is unable to do so without fault, this contract shall terminate and Earnest Money shall be refunded.

15. DEFAULT: If Buyer fails to comply herewith, Seller may either enforce specific performance or terminate this contract and receive the Earnest Money as liquidated damages.

     If Seller is unable without fault to deliver Abstract or Title Policy or to make any noncasualty repairs required herein within the time herein specified, Buyer may either terminate this contract and receive the Earnest Money as the sole remedy, or extend the time up to 30 days. If Seller fails to comply herewith for any other reason, Buyer may (i) terminate this contract and receive the Earnest Money, thereby releasing Seller from this contract, (ii) enforce specific performance hereof, or (iii) seek such other relief as may be provided by law.

16. ATTORNEY'S FEES: Any signatory to this contract who is the prevailing party in any legal proceeding against any other signatory brought under or with relation to this contract or transaction shall be additionally entitled to recover court costs and reasonable attorney fees from the nonprevailing party.

17. ESCROW: Earnest Money is deposited with Escrow Agent with the understanding that Escrow Agent (i) does not have any liability for performance or nonperformance of any party, (ii) has the right to require the receipt, release and authorization in writing of all parties before paying the deposit to any party, and (iii) is not liable for interest or other charge on the funds held. If any party unreasonably fails to agree in writing to an appropriate release of Earnest Money, then such party shall be liable to the other parties to the extent provided in paragraph 16. At closing, Earnest Money shall be applied to any cash down payment required, next to Buyer's closing costs and any excess refunded to Buyer. Before Buyer shall be entitled to refund of Earnest Money, any actual expenses incurred or paid on Buyer's behalf shall be deducted therefrom and paid to the creditors entitled thereto.

18. REPRESENTATIONS: Seller represents that unless securing payment of the Note there will be no Title I liens, unrecorded liens or Uniform Commercial Code liens against any of the Property on Closing Date, that loan(s) will be without default, and reserve deposits will not be deficient. If any representation above is untrue this contract may be terminated by Buyer and the Earnest Money shall be refunded without delay. Representations shall survive closing.

19. THIRD PARTY FINANCING: If financing by Third Party under 3C(2) above is required herein, Buyer shall have 15 days from effective date hereof to obtain the same, and failure to secure the same after reasonable effort shall render this contract null and void, and the Earnest Money refunded without delay.

20. AGREEMENT OF PARTIES: This contract contains the entire agreement of the parties and cannot be changed except by their written consent.

21. CONSULT YOUR ATTORNEY: This is intended to be a legally binding contract. READ IT CARE-FULLY. If you do not understand the effect of any part, consult your attorney BEFORE signing. Attorneys to represent parties may be designated below.

_____   _____
Seller's Atty: Buyer's Atty:

EXECUTED in multiple originals effective the ——— day of ———, 19 ——.

_____   _____
Seller   Buyer

_____   _____
Seller   Buyer

_____   _____
Seller's Address   Buyer's Address

SAMPLE CONTRACT FOR DEED
ALL CASH OR OWNER FINANCED—RESIDENTIAL EARNEST-MONEY CONTRACT
(RESALE)

1. PARTIES ___Joseph I. Homeseller & Mary Homeseller___ (Seller) agrees to
sell and convey to ___James L. Prospect & Susan K. Prospect___ (Buyer)
and Buyer agrees to buy from Seller the following property situated in ___Harris___
County, ___TX___ (State), known as ___8900 Lamar___
_____ (Address).

2. PROPERTY: Lot ___1___, Block ___14___, ___River Oaks___ Addition, City
of ___Houston___, or as described on attached exhibit, together with the following fixtures, if any; curtain rods, drapery rods, venetian blinds, window shades, screens and shutters, awnings, wall-to-wall carpeting, mirrors fixed in place, attic fans, permanently installed heating and air-conditioning units and equipment, lighting and plumbing fixtures, TV antennas,
mailboxes, water softeners, shrubbery and all other property owned by Seller and attached to the
above described real property. All property sold by this contract is called "Property."

3. CONTRACT SALES PRICE:
   A. Cash down payment payable at closing ....$ ___10,000.00___
   B. Note described in 4B below (the Note) ....$ ___60,000.00___
   C. Sales Price payable to Seller (Sum of A and B) ....$ ___70,000.00___

4. FINANCING CONDITIONS:
   _____ A. This is an all cash sale; no financing is involved.
   ___X___ B. The Note in the principal sum shown in 3B above, dated as of the Closing Date, to be
   executed and delivered by Buyer and payable to the order of Seller, bearing interest at
   the rate of ___ten___ percent per annum from date thereof until maturity, matured unpaid principal and interest to bear interest at the rate of 10% per annum, principal and
   interest to be due and payable

       ___X___ (1) In ___sixty___ installments of $___526.80___ or more each, be-
       ginning on or before ___July 1, 1981___ after date of the Note, and
       [Check "a" or "b"]

           _____ a. continuing regularly and at the same intervals thereafter until
               fully paid.

           ___X___ b. continuing regularly and at the same intervals thereafter until
           ___July 1___ 19___86___, when the entire balance of princi-
           pal and accrued interest shall be due and payable.

_____ (2) In a lump sum on or before _____ after date of the Note.

_____ C. This contract is subject to Buyer furnishing Seller evidence that Buyer has a history of good credit.

5. EARNEST MONEY: $ __1,000.00__ is herewith tendered and is to be deposited as Earnest Money with __Stewart Title Company__ as Escrow Agent, upon execution of the contract by both parties. Additional Earnest Money, if any, shall be deposited with the Escrow Agent on or before __N/A__, 19____ in the amount of $ __N/A__.

6. TITLE: Seller at Seller's expense shall furnish either:

__X__ A. Owner's Policy of Title Insurance (the Title Policy) issued by __See special provisions__ in the amount of the Sales Price and dated at or after closing:

OR

_____ B. Complete Abstract of Title (the Abstract) certified by _____ to current date.

NOTICE TO BUYER AS REQUIRED BY LAW, YOU should have the Abstract covering the Property examined by an attorney of YOUR selection, or YOU should be furnished with or obtain a Title Policy.

7. PROPERTY CONDITION [Check ''A'' or ''B'']:

__X__ A. Buyer accepts the Property in its present condition, subject only to __Replace broken window in rear of house.__

_____ B. Buyer requires inspections and repairs required by the Property Condition Addendum (the Addendum). Seller shall commence and complete prior to closing all required repairs at Seller's expense.

All inspections, reports and repairs required of Seller by this contract and the Addendum shall not exceed $ __300.00__. If Seller fails to complete such requirements, Buyer may do so and Seller shall be liable up to the amount specified and the same paid from the proceeds of the sale. If such expenditures exceed the stated amount and Seller refuses to pay such excess, Buyer may pay the additional cost or accept the Property with limited repairs and this sale shall be closed as scheduled, or Buyer may terminate this contract and the Earnest Money shall be refunded to Buyer.

8. CLOSING: The closing of the sale (the Closing Date) shall be on or before __June 15__ 19__81__, or within 7 days after objections to title have been cured, whichever date is later.

9. POSSESSION: The possession of the Property shall be delivered to Buyer on __June 16, 1981__ in its present or required improved condition, ordinary wear and tear excepted. Any possession by Buyer prior to or by Seller after Closing Date shall establish a landlord tenant at sufferance relationship between the parties.

10. SPECIAL PROVISIONS:

[Insert terms and conditions of a factual nature applicable to this sale, e.g., personal property included in sale (curtains, draperies, valances, etc.), prior purchase or sale of other property, lessee's surrender of possession and the like.]

11. SALES EXPENSES TO BE PAID IN CASH AT OR PRIOR TO CLOSING:

   A. Seller's Expenses:

      (1) Any inspections, reports and repairs required of Seller herein, and in the Addendum.

      (2) All cost of releasing existing loans and recording the releases; tax statements, ½ of any escrow fees, preparation of Deed, copies of restrictions and easements, other expenses to be paid by Seller under other provisions of this contract.

   B. Buyer's Expenses: All expenses incident to any loan (e.g., preparation of Note, Deed of Trust and other loan documents, recording fees, Mortgagee's Title Policy, credit reports, ½ of any escrow fee, one year premium for hazard insurance unless insurance is prorated, and expenses stipulated to be paid by Buyer under other provisions of this contract.

   C. If any sales expenses exceed the maximum amount herein stipulated to be paid by either party, either party may terminate this contract unless the other party agrees to pay such excess.

12. PRORATIONS: Insurance (at Buyer's option), taxes and any rents and maintenance fees shall be prorated to the Closing Date.

13. TITLE APPROVAL: If Abstract is furnished, Seller shall deliver same to Buyer within 20 days from the effective date hereof. Buyer shall have 20 days from date of receipt of Abstract to deliver a copy of the title opinion to Seller, stating any objections to title, and only objections so stated shall be considered. If Title Policy is furnished, the Title shall guarantee Buyer's title to be good and indefeasible subject only to (i) restrictive covenants affecting the Property, (ii) any discrepancies, conflicts or shortages in area or boundary lines or any encroachments, or any overlapping of improvements, (iii) all taxes for the current and subsequent years, (iv) any existing building and zoning ordinances, (v) rights of parties in possession, (vi) any liens created as security for the sale consid-

eration, and (vii) any reservations or exceptions contained in the Deed. In either instance, if title objections are disclosed, Seller shall have 30 days to cure the same. Exceptions permitted in the Deed and zoning ordinances shall not be valid objections to title. Seller shall furnish at Seller's expense tax statements showing no delinquent taxes and a General Warranty Deed conveying title subject only to liens securing debt created as part of the consideration, taxes for the current year, usual restrictive covenants and utility easements common to the platted subdivision of which the Property is a part and any other reservations or exceptions acceptable to Buyer. The Note shall be secured by Vendor's and Deed of Trust liens. In case of dispute as to the form of Deed, Deed of Trust or Note, such shall be upon a form prepared by the State Bar of _____TX_____ (State).

14. CASUALTY LOSS: If any part of Property is damaged or destroyed by fire or other casualty loss, Seller shall restore the same to its previous condition as soon as reasonably possible, but in any event by Closing Date, and if Seller is unable to do so without fault, this contract shall terminate and Earnest Money shall be refunded.

15. DEFAULT: If Buyer fails to comply herewith, Seller may either enforce specific performance or terminate this contract and receive the Earnest Money as liquidated damages.

   If Seller is unable without fault to deliver Abstract or Title Policy or to make any noncasualty repairs required herein within the time herein specified, Buyer may either terminate this contract and receive the Earnest Money as the sole remedy, or extend the time up to 30 days. If Seller fails to comply herewith for any other reason, Buyer may (i) terminate this contract and receive the Earnest Money, thereby releasing Seller from this contract, (ii) enforce specific performance hereof, or (iii) seek such other relief as may be provided by law.

16. ATTORNEY'S FEES: Any signatory to this contract who is the prevailing party in any legal proceeding against any other signatory brought under or with relation to this contract or transaction shall be additionally entitled to recover court costs and reasonable attorney fees from the nonprevailing party.

17. ESCROW: Earnest Money is deposited with Escrow Agent with the understanding that Escrow Agent (i) does not have any liability for performance or nonperformance of any party, (ii) has the right to require the receipt, release and authorization in writing of all parties before paying the deposit to any party, and (iii) is not liable for interest or other charge on the funds held. If any party unreasonably fails to agree in writing to an appropriate release of Earnest Money, then such party shall be liable to the other parties to the extent provided in paragraph 16. At closing, Earnest Money shall be applied to any cash down payment required, next to Buyer's closing costs and any excess refunded to Buyer. Before Buyer shall be entitled to refund of Earnest Money, any actual expenses incurred or paid on Buyer's behalf shall be deducted therefrom and paid to the creditors entitled thereto.

18. REPRESENTATIONS: Seller represents that there will be no Title I liens, unrecorded liens or Uniform Commercial Code liens against any of the Property on Closing Date. If any representation above is untrue this contract may be terminated by Buyer and the Earnest Money shall be refunded without delay. Representations shall survive closing.

19. AGREEMENT OF PARTIES: This contract contains the entire agreement of the parties and cannot be changed except by their written consent.

20. CONSULT YOUR ATTORNEY: This is intended to be a legally binding contract. READ IT CAREFULLY. If you do not understand the effect of any part, consult your attorney BEFORE signing. Attorneys to represent parties may be designated below.

Seller's Atty: _____   Buyer's Atty: _____

EXECUTED in multiple originals effective the _____ day of _____, 19_____.

_____   _____
Seller   Buyer

_____   _____
Seller   Buyer

_____   _____
Seller's Address   Buyer's Address

SAMPLE SECOND MORTGAGE IN CONTRACT—
RESIDENTIAL EARNEST-MONEY CONTRACT (RESALE)

1. PARTIES __Joseph I. Homeseller & Mary Homeseller__ (Seller) agrees to

   sell and convey to __James L. Prospect & Susan K. Prospect__ (Buyer)

   and Buyer agrees to buy from Seller the following property situated in __Harris__

   County, __TX__ (State), known as __8900 Lamar__

   _____ (Address).

2. PROPERTY: Lot __1__, Block __14__, __River Oaks__ Addition, City of

   __Houston__, or as described on attached exhibit, together with the following

   fixtures, if any; curtain rods, drapery rods, venetian blinds, window shades, screens and shutters,
   awnings, wall-to-wall carpeting, mirrors fixed in place, attic fans, permanently installed heating and
   air-conditioning units and equipment, lighting and plumbing fixtures, TV antennas, mailboxes,
   water softener, shrubbery and all other property owned by Seller and attached to the above described real property. All property sold by this contract is called "Property."

3. CONTRACT SALES PRICE:

   A. __XX__ Exact _____ Approximate Cash down payment payable at closing ....

   .... $ __20,000.00__

   B. Buyer's assumption of the unpaid balance of a promissory note (the Note) payable in present

   monthly installments of $__400.00__, including principal and interest and any reserve

   deposits, with Buyer's first installment payable to __Haskell Mortgage__

   on __July 1,__, 19__81__, in the assumed principal balance

   of which at closing (allowing for an agreed $250 variance) will be ....$ __40,000.00__

   C. Any balance of Sales Price to be evidenced by a second lien note payable to [check (1) or (2)
   below]:

   _____(1) Seller bearing interest at the rate of _____% per annum, in

   _____lump sum on or before _____

   _____principal and interest installments of $_____, or more per

   _____, with first installment payable on

   _____.

   __X__(2) Third Party in principal and interest installments not in excess of

   $__150.00__ per month and in the __XX__ Exact _____ Approximate

   (check "Approximate" only if A above and D below are "Exact") amount of ....

   .... $ __10,000.00__

   D. The __XX__ Exact _____ Approximate total Sales Price (Sum of A, B, and C above) ....

   .... $ __70,000.00__

4. FINANCING CONDITIONS: If a Noteholder on assumption (i) requires Buyer to pay an assumption fee in excess of $_____100.00_____ and Seller declines to pay such excess, (ii) raises the existing interest rate above _____12___%, or (iii) requires approval of Buyer or can accelerate the Note and Buyer does not receive from the Noteholder written approval and acceleration waiver prior to the Closing Date, Buyer may terminate this contract and the Earnest Money shall be refunded. Buyer shall apply for the approval and waiver under (iii) above within 7 days from the effective date hereof and shall make every reasonable effort to obtain the same.

5. EARNEST MONEY: $_____1,000.00_____ is herewith tendered and is to be deposited as Earnest Money with _____Stewart Title Company_____ as Escrow Agent, upon execution of the contract by both parties. Additional Earnest Money, if any, shall be deposited with the Escrow Agent on or before _____N/A_____, 19_____ in the amount of $_____N/A_____.

6. TITLE: Seller at Seller's expense shall furnish either:

____X____ A. Owner's Policy of Title Insurance (the Title Policy) issued by _____Stewart Title Co._____ in the amount of the Sales Price and dated at or after closing:

OR

_____ B. Complete Abstract of Title (the Abstract) certified by _____ to current date.

NOTICE TO BUYER AS REQUIRED BY LAW, YOU should have the Abstract covering the Property examined by an attorney of YOUR selection, or YOU should be furnished with or obtain a Title Policy.

7. PROPERTY CONDITION [Check "A" or "B"]:

____X____ A. Buyer accepts the Property in its present condition, subject only to _____Replace broken window glass in rear of house._____

_____ B. Buyer requires inspections and repairs required by the Property Condition Addendum (the Addendum). Upon Seller's receipt of all loan approvals and inspection reports Seller shall commence and complete prior to closing all required repairs at Seller's expense.

All inspections, reports and repairs required of Seller by this contract and the Addendum shall not exceed $_____100.00_____. If Seller fails to complete such requirements, Buyer may do so and Seller shall be liable up to the amount specified and the same paid from the proceeds of the sale. If such expenditures exceed the stated amount and Seller refuses to pay such excess, Buyer may pay the additional cost or accept the Property with limited repairs and this sale shall be closed as scheduled, or Buyer may terminate this contract and the Earnest Money shall be refunded.

8. CLOSING: The closing of the sale (the Closing Date) shall be on or before _____June 20,_____ 19_81___, or within 7 days after objections to title have been cured, whichever date is later.

9. POSSESSION: The possession of the Property shall be delivered to Buyer on _____
   __June 21, 1981__ in its present or required improved condition, ordinary wear and tear
   excepted. Any possession by Buyer prior to or by Seller after Closing Date shall establish a landlord
   tenant at sufferance relationship between the parties.

10. SPECIAL PROVISIONS:

   [Insert terms and conditions of a factual nature applicable to this sale, e.g., personal property included in sale (curtains, draperies, valances, etc.), prior purchase or sale of other property, lessee's
   surrender of possession, and the like.]

11. PRORATION: Taxes, insurance, rents, interest and maintenance fees, if any, ___X___SHALL
   _____SHALL NOT be prorated to the Closing Date. If these are not prorated, all funds held in re-
   serve for payment of taxes, maintenance fees and insurance and the insurance policy shall be
   transferred to the Buyer by Seller without cost to Buyer.

12. SALES EXPENSES TO BE PAID IN CASH AT OR PRIOR TO CLOSING: Preparing Deed, preparing and
   recording Deed of Trust to Secure Assumption, all inspections, reports and repairs required of
   Seller herein and in the Addendum and ½ of escrow fee shall be Seller's expense. All other costs
   and expenses incurred in connection with this contract which are not recited herein to be the obligation of Seller, shall be the obligation of Buyer. Unless otherwise paid, before Buyer shall be entitled to refund of Earnest Money, any such costs and expenses shall be deducted therefrom and
   paid to the creditors entitled thereto. If any sales expenses exceed the maximum amount herein
   stipulated to be paid by either party, either party may terminate this contract unless the other party
   agrees to pay such excess.

13. TITLE APPROVAL: If Abstract is furnished, Seller shall deliver same to Buyer within 20 days from
   the effective date hereof. Buyer shall have 20 days from date of receipt of Abstract to deliver a copy
   of the title opinion to Seller, stating any objections to title, and only objections so stated shall be
   considered. If Title Policy is furnished, the Title shall guarantee Buyer's title to be good and indefeasible subject only to (i) restrictive covenants affecting the Property, (ii) any discrepancies, conflicts or shortages in area or boundary lines or any encroachments, or any overlapping of improve-

ments, (iii) all taxes for the current and subsequent years, (iv) any existing building and zoning ordinances, (v) rights of parties in possession, (vi) any liens created as security for the sale consideration, and (vii) any reservations or exceptions contained in the Deed. In either instance, if title objections are disclosed, Seller shall have 30 days to cure the same. Exceptions permitted in the Deed and zoning ordinances shall not be valid objections to title. Seller shall furnish at Seller's expense tax statements showing no delinquent taxes and a General Warranty Deed conveying title subject only to liens securing debt created as part of the consideration, taxes for the current year, usual restrictive covenants and utility easements common to the platted subdivision of which the Property is a part and any other reservations or exceptions acceptable to Buyer. Each note herein provided shall be secured by Vendor's and Deed of Trust liens. A Vendor's lien shall be retained and a Deed of Trust to Secure Assumption required, which shall be automatically released on execution and delivery of a release by Noteholder. In the case of dispute as to the form of Deed, Note(s) or Deed(s) of Trust, such shall be upon a form prepared by the State Bar of _____ TX _____ (State).

14. CASUALTY LOSS: If any part of Property is damaged or destroyed by fire or other casualty loss, Seller shall restore the same to its previous condition as soon as reasonably possible, but in any event by Closing Date, and if Seller is unable to do so without fault, this contract shall terminate and Earnest Money shall be refunded.

15. DEFAULT: If Buyer fails to comply herewith, Seller may either enforce specific performance or terminate this contract and receive the Earnest Money as liquidated damages.

   If Seller is unable without fault to deliver Abstract or Title Policy or to make any noncasualty repairs required herein within the time herein specified, Buyer may either terminate this contract and receive the Earnest Money as the sole remedy, or extend the time up to 30 days. If Seller fails to comply herewith for any other reason, Buyer may (i) terminate this contract and receive the Earnest Money, thereby releasing Seller from this contract, (ii) enforce specific performance hereof, or (iii) seek such other relief as may be provided by law.

16. ATTORNEY'S FEES: Any signatory to this contract who is the prevailing party in any legal proceeding against any other signatory brought under or with relation to this contract or transaction shall be additionally entitled to recover court costs and reasonable attorney fees from the nonprevailing party.

17. ESCROW: Earnest Money is deposited with Escrow Agent with the understanding that Escrow Agent (i) does not have any liability for performance or nonperformance of any party, (ii) has the right to require the receipt, release and authorization in writing of all parties before paying the deposit to any party, and (iii) is not liable for interest or other charge on the funds held. If any party unreasonably fails to agree in writing to an appropriate release of Earnest Money, then such party shall be liable to the other parties to the extent provided in paragraph 16. At closing, Earnest Money shall

be applied to any cash down payment required, next to Buyer's closing costs and any excess refunded to Buyer. Before Buyer shall be entitled to refund of Earnest Money, any actual expenses incurred or paid on Buyer's behalf shall be deducted therefrom and paid to the creditors entitled thereto.

18. REPRESENTATIONS: Seller represents that unless securing payment of the Note there will be no Title I liens, unrecorded liens or Uniform Commercial Code liens against any of the Property on Closing Date, that loan(s) will be without default, and reserve deposits will not be deficient. If any representation above is untrue this contract may be terminated by Buyer and the Earnest Money shall be refunded without delay. Representations shall survive closing.

19. THIRD PARTY FINANCING: If financing by Third Party under 3C(2) above is required herein, Buyer shall have 15 days from effective date hereof to obtain the same, and failure to secure the same after reasonable effort shall render this contract null and void, and the Earnest Money refunded without delay.

20. AGREEMENT OF PARTIES: This contract contains the entire agreement of the parties and cannot be changed except by their written consent.

21. CONSULT YOUR ATTORNEY: This is intended to be a legally binding contract. READ IT CAREFULLY. If you do not understand the effect of any part, consult your attorney BEFORE signing.
    Attorneys to represent parties may be designated below.

Seller's Atty: _____   Buyer's Atty: _____

EXECUTED in multiple originals effective the _____ day of _____, 19_____.

_____   _____
Seller   Buyer

_____   _____
Seller   Buyer

_____   _____
Seller's Address   Buyer's Address

SAMPLE ALL CASH OR OWNER FINANCED—
RESIDENTIAL EARNEST-MONEY CONTRACT
(RESALE)

1. PARTIES ___Joseph I. Homeseller & Mary Homeseller___ (Seller) agrees to

   sell and convey to ___James L. Prospect & Susan K. Prospect___ (Buyer)

   and Buyer agrees to buy from Seller the following property situated in ___Harris___

   County, ___TX___ (State), known as ___8900 Lamar___

   _____ (Address).

2. PROPERTY: Lot ___1___, Block ___14___, ___River Oaks___ Addition, City of

   ___Houston___, or as described on attached exhibit, together with the following

   fixtures, if any; curtain rods, drapery rods, venetian blinds, window shades, screens and shutters,

   awnings, wall-to-wall carpeting, mirrors fixed in place, attic fans, permanently installed heating and

   air-conditioning units and equipment, lighting and plumbing fixtures, TV antennas, mailboxes,

   water softeners, shrubbery and all other property owned by Seller and attached to the above de-

   scribed real property. All property sold by this contract is called "Property."

3. CONTRACT SALES PRICE:

   A. Cash down payment payable at closing .... $ ___20,000.00___

   B. Note described in 4B below (the Note) .... $ ___50,000.00___

   C. Sales Price payable to Seller (Sum of A and B) .... $ ___70,000.00___

4. FINANCING CONDITIONS:

   _____A. This is an all cash sale; no financing is involved.

   __X__B. The Note in the principal sum shown in 3B above, dated as of the Closing Date, to be

   executed and delivered by Buyer and payable to the order of Seller, bearing interest at

   the rate of ___12___ percent per annum from date thereof until maturity, matured un-

   paid principal and interest to bear interest at the rate of 10% per annum, principal and

   interest to be due and payable

   ___XX___ (1) In ___monthly___ installments of $ ___514.50___ or more each, be-

   ginning on or before ___July 1, 1981___ after date of the Note, and

   [Check "a" or "b"]

   _____a. continuing regularly and at the same intervals thereafter until

   fully paid.

   __X__b. continuing regularly and at the same intervals thereafter until

   ___June 1___ 19 ___91___, when the entire balance of princi-

   pal and accrued interest shall be due and payable.

_____ (2) In a lump sum on or before _____ after date of the

Note.

___X___ C. This contract is subject to Buyer furnishing Seller evidence that Buyer has a history of

good credit.

5. EARNEST MONEY: $___1,000.00___ is herewith tendered and is to be deposited as Earnest

Money with _____Stewart Title Co._____ as Escrow Agent, upon execution of the con-

tract by both parties. Additional Earnest Money, if any, shall be deposited with the Escrow Agent on

or before _____N/A_____ , 19_____ in the amount of $_____N/A_____ .

6. TITLE: Seller at Seller's expense shall furnish either:

___XX___ A. Owner's Policy of Title Insurance (the Title Policy) issued by _____Stewart_____

_____Title Co._____ in the amount of the Sales Price and dated at or after closing:

OR

_____ B. Complete Abstract of Title (the Abstract) certified by _____

_____ to current date.

NOTICE TO BUYER AS REQUIRED BY LAW, YOU should have the Abstract covering the Property

examined by an attorney of YOUR selection, or YOU should be furnished with or obtain a Title Pol-

icy.

7. PROPERTY CONDITION [Check "A" or "B"]:

___X___ A. Buyer accepts the Property in its present condition, subject only to ___Replacement___
of broken window glass at rear of house.

_____ B. Buyer requires inspections and repairs required by the Property Condition Addendum

(the Addendum). Seller shall commence and complete prior to closing all required re-

pairs at Seller's expense.

All inspections, reports and repairs required of Seller by this contract and the Addendum shall not

exceed $_____100.00_____ . If Seller fails to complete such requirements, Buyer may do so and

Seller shall be liable up to the amount specified and the same paid from the proceeds of the sale. If

such expenditures exceed the stated amount and Seller refuses to pay such excess, Buyer may pay

the additional cost or accept the Property with limited repairs and this sale shall be closed as sched-

uled, or Buyer may terminate this contract and the Earnest Money shall be refunded to Buyer.

8. CLOSING: The closing of the sale (the Closing Date) shall be on or before ___June 15___

19__81__ , or within 7 days after objections to title have been cured, whichever date is later.

9. POSSESSION: The possession of the Property shall be delivered to Buyer on

___June 16, 1981___ in its present or required improved condition, ordinary wear and tear

excepted. Any possession by Buyer prior to or by Seller after Closing Date shall establish a landlord

tenant at sufferance relationship between the parties.

10. SPECIAL PROVISIONS:

[Insert terms and conditions of a factual nature applicable to this sale, e.g., personal property included in sale (curtains, draperies, valances, etc.), prior purchases or sale of other property, lessee's surrender of possession and the like.]

11. SALES EXPENSES TO BE PAID IN CASH AT OR PRIOR TO CLOSING:

    A. Seller's Expenses:

        (1) Any inspections, reports and repairs required of Seller herein, and in the Addendum.

        (2) All cost of releasing existing loans and recording the releases; tax statements, ½ of any escrow fees, preparation of Deed, copies of restrictions and easements, other expenses to be paid by Seller under other provisions of this contract.

    B. Buyer's Expenses: All expenses incident to any loan (e.g., preparation of Note, Deed of Trust and other loan documents, recording fees, Mortgagee's Title Policy, credit reports, ½ of any escrow fee, one year premium for hazard insurance unless insurance is prorated, and expenses stipulated to be paid by Buyer under other provisions of this contract.

    C. If any sales expenses exceed the maximum amount herein stipulated to be paid by either party, either party may terminate this contract unless the other party agrees to pay such excess.

12. PRORATIONS: Insurance (at Buyer's option), taxes and any rents and maintenance fees shall be prorated to the Closing Date.

13. TITLE APPROVAL: If Abstract is furnished, Seller shall deliver same to Buyer within 20 days from the effective date hereof. Buyer shall have 20 days from date of receipt of Abstract to deliver a copy of the title opinion to Seller, stating any objections to title, and only objections so stated shall be considered. If Title Policy is furnished, the Title shall guarantee Buyer's title to be good and indefeasible subject only to (i) restrictive covenants affecting the Property, (ii) any discrepancies, conflicts or shortages in area or boundary lines or any encroachments, or any overlapping of improvements, (iii) all taxes for the current and subsequent years, (iv) any existing building and zoning

ordinances, (v) rights of parties in possession, (vi) any liens created as security for the sale consideration, and (vii) any reservations or exceptions contained in the Deed. In either instance, if title objections are disclosed, Seller shall have 30 days to cure the same. Exceptions permitted in the Deed and zoning ordinances shall not be valid objections to title. Seller shall furnish at Seller's expense tax statements showing no delinquent taxes and a General Warranty Deed conveying title subject only to liens securing debt created as part of the consideration, taxes for the current year, usual restrictive covenants and utility easements common to the platted subdivision of which the Property is a part and any other reservations or exceptions acceptable to Buyer. The Note shall be secured by Vendor's and Deed of Trust liens. In case of dispute as to the form of Deed, Deed of Trust or Note, such shall be upon a form prepared by the State Bar of _____TX_____ (State).

14. CASUALTY LOSS: If any part of Property is damaged or destroyed by fire or other casualty loss, Seller shall restore the same to its previous condition as soon as reasonably possible, but in any event by Closing Date, and if Seller is unable to do so without fault, this contract shall terminate and Earnest Money shall be refunded.

15. DEFAULT: If Buyer fails to comply herewith, Seller may either enforce specific performance or terminate this contract and receive the Earnest Money as liquidated damages.

    If Seller is unable without fault to deliver Abstract or Title Policy or to make any noncasualty repairs required herein within the time herein specified, Buyer may either terminate this contract and receive the Earnest Money as the sole remedy, or extend the time up to 30 days. If Seller fails to comply herewith for any other reason, Buyer may (i) terminate this contract and receive the Earnest Money, thereby releasing Seller from this contract, (ii) enforce specific performance hereof, or (iii) seek such other relief as may be provided by law.

16. ATTORNEY'S FEES: Any signatory to this contract who is the prevailing party in any legal proceeding against any other signatory brought under or with relation to this contract or transaction shall be additionally entitled to recover court costs and reasonable attorney fees from the nonprevailing party.

17. ESCROW: Earnest Money is deposited with Escrow Agent with the understanding that Escrow Agent (i) does not have any liability for performance or nonperformance of any party, (ii) has the right to require the receipt, release and authorization in writing of all parties before paying the deposit to any party, and (iii) is not liable for interest or other charge on the funds held. If any party unreasonably fails to agree in writing to an appropriate release of Earnest Money, then such party shall be liable to the other parties to the extent provided in paragraph 16. At closing, Earnest Money shall be applied to any cash down payment required, next to Buyer's closing costs and any excess refunded to Buyer. Before Buyer shall be entitled to refund of Earnest Money, any actual expenses incurred or paid on Buyer's behalf shall be deducted therefrom and paid to the creditors entitled thereto.

18. REPRESENTATIONS: Seller represents that there will be no Title I liens, unrecorded liens or Uniform Commercial Code liens against any of the Property on Closing Date. If any representation above is untrue this contract may be terminated by Buyer and the Earnest Money shall be refunded without delay. Representations shall survive closing.

19. AGREEMENT OF PARTIES: This contract contains the entire agreement of the parties and cannot be changed except by their written consent.

20. CONSULT YOUR ATTORNEY: This is intended to be a legally binding contract. READ IT CAREFULLY. If you do not understand the effect of any part, consult your attorney BEFORE signing. Attorneys to represent parties may be designated below.

Seller's Atty: _____   Buyer's Atty: _____

EXECUTED in multiple originals effective the _____ day of _____ , 19_____ .

_____   _____
Seller   Buyer

_____   _____
Seller   Buyer

_____   _____
Seller's Address   Buyer's Address

SAMPLE WRAPAROUND MORTGAGE
ALL CASH OR OWNER FINANCED—RESIDENTIAL EARNEST-MONEY CONTRACT
(RESALE)

1. PARTIES __Joseph I. Homeseller & Mary Homeseller__ (Seller) agrees to

   sell and convey to __James L. Prospect & Susan K. Prospect__ (Buyer)

   and Buyer agrees to buy from Seller the following property situated in __Harris__

   County, __TX__ (State), known as _____

   __8900 Lamar__ (Address).

2. PROPERTY: Lot __1__ , Block __14__ , __River Oaks__ Addition, City of

   __Houston__ , or as described on attached exhibit, together with the following

   fixtures, if any; curtain rods, drapery rods, venetian blinds, window shades, screens and shutters,
   awnings, wall-to-wall carpeting, mirrors fixed in place, attic fans, permanently installed heating and
   air-conditioning units and equipment, lighting and plumbing fixtures, TV antennas, mailboxes,
   water softeners, shrubbery and all other property owned by Seller and attached to the above described real property. All property sold by this contract is called "Property."

3. CONTRACT SALES PRICE:

   A. Cash down payment payable at closing .... $ 10,000.00

   B. Note described in 4B below (the Note) .... $ 60,000.00

   C. Sales Price payable to Seller (Sum of A and B) .... $ 70,000.00

4. FINANCING CONDITIONS:

   _____ A. This is an all cash sale; no financing is involved.

   __XX__ B. The Note in the principal sum shown in 3B above, dated as of the Closing Date, to be
   executed and delivered by Buyer and payable to the order of Seller, bearing interest at
   the rate of __12%__ percent per annum from date thereof until maturity, matured unpaid principal and interest to bear interest at the rate of 10% per annum, principal and
   interest to be due and payable

   __X__ (1) In __360 monthly__ installments of $ __600.00__ or more
   each, beginning on or before __July 1, 1981__ after date of the
   Note, and [Check "a" or "b"]

   __X__ a. continuing regularly and at the same intervals thereafter until
   fully paid.

   _____ b. continuing regularly and at the same intervals thereafter until
   _____ 19_____ , when the entire balance of princi-
   pal and accrued interest shall be due and payable.

_____(2) In a lump sum on or before _____ after date of the Note.

___X___C. This contract is subject to Buyer furnishing Seller evidence that Buyer has a history of good credit.

5. EARNEST MONEY: $___1,000.00___ is herewith tendered and is to be deposited as Earnest Money with ___Stewart Title Company___ as Escrow Agent, upon execution of the contract by both parties. Additional Earnest Money, if any, shall be deposited with the Escrow Agent on or before ___N/A___ , 19_____ in the amount of $___N/A___ .

6. TITLE: Seller at Seller's expense shall furnish either:

___X___A. Owner's Policy of Title Insurance (the Title Policy) issued by ___Stewart Title Company___ in the amount of the Sales Price and dated at or after closing:

OR

_____B. Complete Abstract of Title (the Abstract) certified by _____ _____ to current date.

NOTICE TO BUYER AS REQUIRED BY LAW, YOU should have the Abstract covering the Property examined by an attorney of YOUR selection, or YOU should be furnished with or obtain a Title Policy.

7. PROPERTY CONDITION [Check "A" or "B"]:

___X___A. Buyer accepts the Property in its present condition, subject only to _____ Repair broken window glass at rear of house

_____B. Buyer requires inspections and repairs required by the Property Condition Addendum (the Addendum). Seller shall commence and complete prior to closing all required repairs at Seller's expense.

All inspections, reports and repairs required of Seller by this contract and the Addendum shall not exceed $___100.00___ . If Seller fails to complete such requirements, Buyer may do so and Seller shall be liable up to the amount specified and the same paid from the proceeds of the sale. If such expenditures exceed the stated amount and Seller refuses to pay such excess, Buyer may pay the additional cost or accept the Property with limited repairs and this sale shall be closed as scheduled, or Buyer may terminate this contract and the Earnest Money shall be refunded to Buyer.

8. CLOSING: The closing of the sale (the Closing Date) shall be on or before ___June 15___ 19__81__ , or within 7 days after objections to title have been cured, whichever date is later.

9. POSSESSION: The possession of the Property shall be delivered to Buyer on ___June 17, 1981___ in its present or required improved condition, ordinary wear and tear excepted. Any possession by Buyer prior to or by Seller after Closing Date shall establish a landlord tenant at sufferance relationship between the parties.

10. SPECIAL PROVISIONS:

[Insert terms and conditions of a factual nature applicable to this sale, e.g., personal property included in sale (curtains, draperies, valances, etc.), prior purchase or sale of other property, lessee's surrender of possession and the like.]

11. SALES EXPENSES TO BE PAID IN CASH AT OR PRIOR TO CLOSING:

   A. Seller's Expenses:

   (1) Any inspections, reports and repairs required of Seller herein, and in the Addendum.

   (2) All cost of releasing existing loans and recording the releases; tax statements, ½ of any escrow fees, preparation of Deed, copies of restrictions and easements, other expenses to be paid by Seller under other provisions of this contract.

   B. Buyer's Expenses: All expenses incident to any loan (e.g., preparation of Note, Deed of Trust and other loan documents, recording fees, Mortgagee's Title Policy, credit reports, ½ of any escrow fee, one year premium for hazard insurance unless insurance is prorated, and expenses stipulated to be paid by Buyer under other provisions of this contract.

   C. If any sales expenses exceed the maximum amount herein stipulated to be paid by either party, either party may terminate this contract unless the other party agrees to pay such excess.

12. PRORATIONS: Insurance (at Buyer's option), taxes and any rents and maintenance fees shall be prorated to the Closing Date.

13. TITLE APPROVAL: If Abstract is furnished, Seller shall deliver same to Buyer within 20 days from the effective date hereof. Buyer shall have 20 days from date of receipt of Abstract to deliver a copy of the title opinion to Seller, stating any objections to title, and only objections so stated shall be considered. If Title Policy is furnished, the Title shall guarantee Buyer's title to be good and indefeasible subject only to (i) restrictive covenants affecting the Property, (ii) any discrepancies, conflicts or shortages in area or boundary lines or any encroachments, or any overlapping of improvements, (iii) all taxes for the current and subsequent years, (iv) any existing building and zoning

ordinances, (v) rights of parties in possession, (vi) any liens created as security for the sale consideration, and (vii) any reservations or exceptions contained in the Deed. In either instance, if title objections are disclosed, Seller shall have 30 days to cure the same. Exceptions permitted in the Deed and zoning ordinances shall not be valid objections to title. Seller shall furnish at Seller's expense tax statements showing no delinquent taxes and a General Warranty Deed conveying title subject only to liens securing debt created as part of the consideration, taxes for the current year, usual restrictive covenants and utility easements common to the platted subdivision of which the Property is a part and any other reservations or exceptions acceptable to Buyer. The Note shall be secured by Vendor's and Deed of Trust liens. In case of dispute as to the form of Deed, Deed of Trust or Note, such shall be upon a form prepared by the State Bar of _____TX_____ (State).

14. CASUALTY LOSS: If any part of Property is damaged or destroyed by fire or other casualty loss, Seller shall restore the same to its previous condition as soon as reasonably possible, but in any event by Closing Date, and if Seller is unable to do so without fault, this contract shall terminate and Earnest Money shall be refunded.

15. DEFAULT: If Buyer fails to comply herewith, Seller may either enforce specific performance or terminate this contract and receive the Earnest Money as liquidated damages.

    If Seller is unable without fault to deliver Abstract or Title Policy or to make any noncasualty repairs required herein within the time herein specified, Buyer may either terminate this contract and receive the Earnest Money as the sole remedy, or extend the time up to 30 days. If Seller fails to comply herewith for any other reason, Buyer may (i) terminate this contract and receive the Earnest Money, thereby releasing Seller from this contract, (ii) enforce specific performance hereof, or (iii) seek such other relief as may be provided by law.

16. ATTORNEY'S FEES: Any signatory to this contract who is the prevailing party in any legal proceeding against any other signatory brought under or with relation to this contract or transaction shall be additionally entitled to recover court costs and reasonable attorney fees from the nonprevailing party.

17. ESCROW: Earnest Money is deposited with Escrow Agent with the understanding that Escrow Agent (i) does not have any liability for performance or nonperformance of any party, (ii) has the right to require the receipt, release and authorization in writing of all parties before paying the deposit to any party, and (iii) is not liable for interest or other charge on the funds held. If any party unreasonably fails to agree in writing to an appropriate release of Earnest Money, then such party shall be liable to the other parties to the extent provided in paragraph 16. At closing, Earnest Money shall be applied to any cash down payment required, next to Buyer's closing costs and any excess refunded to Buyer. Before Buyer shall be entitled to refund of Earnest Money, any actual expenses incurred or paid on Buyer's behalf shall be deducted therefrom and paid to the creditors entitled thereto.

18. REPRESENTATIONS: Seller represents that there will be no Title I liens, unrecorded liens or Uniform Commercial Code liens against any of the Property on Closing Date. If any representation above is untrue this contract may be terminated by Buyer and the Earnest Money shall be refunded without delay. Representations shall survive closing.

19. AGREEMENT OF PARTIES: This contract contains the entire agreement of the parties and cannot be changed except by their written consent.

20. CONSULT YOUR ATTORNEY: This is intended to be a legally binding contract. READ IT CARE-FULLY. If you do not understand the effect of any part, consult your attorney BEFORE signing. Attorneys to represent parties may be designated below.

Seller's Atty: _____   Buyer's Atty: _____

EXECUTED in multiple originals effective the _____ day of _____ , 19_____ .

_____   _____
Seller   Buyer

_____   _____
Seller   Buyer

_____   _____
Seller's Address   Buyer's Address

SAMPLE VA GUARANTEED LOAN WITH SECOND MORTGAGE—RESIDENTIAL EARNEST-MONEY CONTRACT (RESALE)

1. PARTIES ___Joseph I. Homeseller & Mary Homeseller___ (Seller) agrees to sell and convey to ___James L. Prospect & Susan K. Prospect___ (Buyer) and Buyer agrees to buy from Seller the following property situated in ___Harris___ County, ___TX___ (State), known as ___8900 Lamar___ (Address).

2. PROPERTY: Lot ___1___ Block ___14___, ___River Oaks___ Addition, City of ___Houston___, or as described on attached exhibit, together with the following fixtures, if any: curtain rods, drapery rods, venetian blinds, window shades, screens and shutters, awnings, wall-to-wall carpeting, mirrors fixed in place, attic fans, permanently installed heating and air-conditioning units and equipment, lighting and plumbing fixtures, TV antennas, mailboxes, water softeners, shrubbery and all other property owned by Seller and attached to the above described real property. All property sold by this contract is called "Property."

3. CONTRACT SALES PRICE:
   A. Cash down payment payable at closing ....$ 40,000.00
   B. Note described in 4 below (the Note) in the amount of ....*15,000.00 $ 125,000.00
   C. Sales price payable to Seller on Loan funding after closing (Sum of A and B). 180,000.00
   ....$

4. FINANCING CONDITIONS: This contract is subject to approval for Buyer of a VA loan (the Loan) of not less than the amount of the Note, amortizable monthly for not less than ___30___ years, with interest at maximum rate allowable at time of Loan funding. Buyer shall apply for the Loan within ___3___ days from the effective date of this contract and shall make every reasonable effort to obtain approval. If the Loan has not been approved by the Closing Date, this contract shall terminate and the Earnest Money shall be refunded to Buyer without delay. VA NOTICE TO BUYER: "It is expressly agreed that, notwithstanding any other provisions of this contract, the Buyer shall not incur any penalty by forfeiture of earnest money or otherwise or be obligated to complete the purchase of the Property described herein, if the contract purchase price or cost exceeds the reasonable value of the Property established by the Veterans Administration. The Buyer shall, however, have the privilege and option of proceeding with the consummation of this contract without regard to the amount of the reasonable value established by the Veterans Administration." Buyer agrees that should Buyer elect to complete the purchase at an amount in excess of the reasonable value established by VA, Buyer shall pay such excess amount in cash from a source which Buyer agrees to disclose to the VA and which Buyer represents will not be from borrowed funds except as approved by VA. If VA reasonable value of the Property is less than the Sales Price (3C above), Seller

may reduce the Sales Price to an amount equal to the VA reasonable value and both parties agree to close the sale at such lower Sales Price with appropriate adjustments to 3A and 3B above.

5. EARNEST MONEY: $____1,000____ is herewith tendered and is to be deposited as Earnest Money with ____Stewart Title Company____, as Escrow Agent, upon execution of the contract by both parties. Additional Earnest Money, if any, shall be deposited with the Escrow Agent on or before ____N/A____, 19____, in the amount of $____N/A____.

6. TITLE: Seller at Seller's expense shall furnish either:

____X____A. Owner's Policy of Title Insurance (the Title Policy) issued by ____Stewart Title Company____ in the amount of the Sales Price and dated at or after closing:

OR

_____B. Complete Abstract of Title (the Abstract) certified by _____ to current date.

NOTICE TO BUYER AS REQUIRED BY LAW, YOU should have the Abstract covering the Property examined by an attorney of YOUR selection, or YOU should be furnished with or obtain a Title Policy.

7. PROPERTY CONDITION [Check "A" OR "B"]:

____X____A. Buyer accepts the Property in its present condition, subject only to VA required repairs and ____Repair of broken window glass in rear of house____
_____

_____B. Buyer requires inspections and repairs required by the Property Condition Addendum (the Addendum) and those required by VA. Upon Seller's receipt of the Loan approval and inspection reports Seller shall commence and complete prior to closing all required repairs at Seller's expense.

All inspections, reports and repairs required of Seller by this contract and the Addendum shall not exceed $____100.00____. If Seller fails to complete such requirements, Buyer may do so and Seller shall be liable up to the amount specified and the same paid from the proceeds of the sale. If such expenditures exceed the stated amount and Seller refuses to pay such excess, Buyer may pay the additional cost or accept the Property with the limited repairs and this sale shall be closed as scheduled, or Buyer may terminate this contract and the Earnest Money shall be refunded to Buyer.

8. CLOSING: The closing of the sale (the Closing Date) shall be on or before ____June 30____ 19__81__, or within 7 days after objections to title have been cured, whichever date is later; however, if necessary to complete Loan requirements, the Closing Date shall be extended daily up to 15 days.

9. POSSESSION: The possession of the Property shall be delivered to Buyer on ____July 1, 1981____ in

its present or required improved condition, ordinary wear and tear excepted. Any possession by Buyer prior to or by Seller after Closing Date shall establish a landlord tenant at sufferance relationship between the parties.

10. SPECIAL PROVISIONS:

[Insert terms and conditions of a factual nature applicable to this sale, e.g., prior purchase or sale of other property, lessee surrender of possession and the like.]

11. SALES EXPENSES TO BE PAID IN CASH AT OR PRIOR TO CLOSING:

   A. Loan appraisal fees shall be paid by ___Buyer___ .

   B. Seller's Expenses:

      (1) Seller's Loan discount points not exceeding ___7___ .

      (2) VA required repairs and any other inspections, reports and repairs required of Seller herein, and in the Addendum.

      (3) Releases of existing loans, including prepayment penalties and recordation: escrow fee, tax statement, preparation of Deed, Note and Deed of Trust, expenses VA prohibits Buyer to pay (e.g., copies of restrictions, photos, excess cost of survey of Property), other expenses stipulated to be paid by Seller under other provisions of this contract.

   C. Buyer's Expenses: Expenses incident to Loan (e.g., credit reports, recording fees, Mortgagee's Title Policy; Loan origination fee, that portion of survey cost Buyer can pay by VA regulation, Loan related inspection fees, premiums for 1 year's hazard insurance and any flood insurance, required reserve deposits for insurance premiums, ad valorem taxes and special assessments, interest from date of disbursement to 1 month prior to date of first monthly payment on the Note; premiums on non-required insurance, expenses stipulated to be paid by Buyer under other provisions of this contract.

   D. If any sales expenses exceed the maximum amount herein stipulated to be paid by either party, either party may terminate this contract unless the other party agrees to pay such excess. In no event shall Buyer pay charges and fees other than those expressly permitted by VA Regulations.

12. PRORATIONS: Insurance (at Buyer's option), taxes and any rents and maintenance fees shall be prorated to the Closing Date.

13. TITLE APPROVAL: If Abstract is furnished, Seller shall deliver same to Buyer within 20 days from the effective date hereof. Buyer shall have 20 days from date of receipt of Abstract to deliver a copy of the title opinion to Seller, stating any objections to title, and only objections so stated shall be considered. If Title Policy is furnished, the Title shall guarantee Buyer's title to be good and indefeasible subject only to (i) restrictive covenants affecting the Property, (ii) any discrepancies, conflicts or shortages in area or boundary lines or any encroachments, or any overlapping of improvements, (iii) all taxes for the current and subsequent years, (iv) any existing building and zoning ordinances, (v) rights of parties in possession, (vi) any liens created as security for the sale consideration, and (vii) any reservations or exceptions contained in the Deed. In either instance, if title objections are disclosed, Seller shall have 30 days to cure the same. Exceptions permitted in the Deed and zoning ordinances shall not be valid objections to title. Seller shall furnish at Seller's expense tax statements showing no delinquent taxes and a General Warranty Deed conveying title subject only to liens securing debt created as part of the consideration, taxes for the current year, usual restrictive covenants and utility easements common to the platted subdivision of which the Property is a part and any other reservations or exceptions acceptable to Buyer. The Note shall be secured by Vendor's and Deed of Trust liens. In case of dispute as to the form of Deed, such shall be upon a form prepared by the State Bar of _____TX_____ (State).

14. CASUALTY LOSS: If any part of Property is damaged or destroyed by fire or other casualty loss, Seller shall restore the same to its previous condition as soon as reasonably possible, but in any event by Closing Date, and if Seller is unable to do so without fault, this contract shall terminate and Earnest Money shall be refunded.

15. DEFAULT: If Buyer fails to comply herewith, Seller may either enforce specific performance or terminate this contract and receive the Earnest Money as liquidated damages.

    If Seller is unable without fault to deliver Abstract or Title Policy or to make any noncasualty repairs required herein within the time herein specified, Buyer may either terminate this contract and receive the Earnest Money as the sole remedy, or extend the time up to 30 days. If Seller fails to comply herewith for any other reason, Buyer may (i) terminate this contract and receive the Earnest Money, thereby releasing Seller from this contract, (ii) enforce specific performance hereof, or (iii) seek such other relief as may be provided by law.

16. ATTORNEY'S FEES: Any signatory to this contract who is the prevailing party in any legal proceeding against any other signatory brought under or with relation to this contract or transaction shall be additionally entitled to recover court costs and reasonable attorney fees from the nonprevailing party.

17. ESCROW: Earnest Money is deposited with Escrow Agent with the understanding that Escrow Agent (i) does not have any liability for performance or nonperformance of any party, (ii) has the right to

require the receipt, release and authorization in writing of all parties before paying the deposit to any party, and (iii) is not liable for interest or other charge on the funds held. If any party unreasonably fails to agree in writing to an appropriate release of Earnest Money, then such party shall be liable to the other parties to the extent provided in paragraph 16. At closing, Earnest Money shall be applied to any cash down payment required, next to Buyer's closing costs and any excess refunded to Buyer. Before Buyer shall be entitled to refund of Earnest Money, any actual and VA allowable expenses incurred or paid on Buyer's behalf shall be deducted therefrom and paid to the creditors entitled thereto.

18. REPRESENTATIONS: Seller represents that there will be no Title I liens, unrecorded liens or Uniform Commercial Code liens against any of the Property on Closing Date. If any representation above is untrue this contract may be terminated by Buyer and the Earnest Money shall be refunded without delay. Representations shall survive closing.

19. AGREEMENT OF PARTIES: This contract contains the entire agreement of the parties and cannot be changed except by their written consent.

20. CONSULT YOUR ATTORNEY: This is intended to be a legally binding contract. READ IT CAREFULLY. If you do not understand the effect of any part, consult your attorney BEFORE signing. Attorneys to represent parties may be designated below.

Seller's Atty: _____   Buyer's Atty: _____

EXECUTED in multiple originals effective the _____ day of _____, 19_____.

_____   _____
Seller   Buyer

_____   _____
Seller   Buyer

_____   _____
Seller's Address   Buyer's Address

SAMPLE PROPERTY CONDITION ADDENDUM
ADDENDUM TO EARNEST-MONEY CONTRACT BETWEEN THE UNDERSIGNED PARTIES CONCERNING THE PROPERTY AT

8900 Lamar

Houston, Texas
(Street Address and City)

CHECK APPLICABLE BOXES:

___X___ A. TERMITES: Seller, at Seller's expense, shall furnish to Buyer at or prior to closing a written report by a Structural Pest Control Business Licensee, dated within 30 days before Closing Date and stating that there is no visible evidence of active termites or visible damage to the improvements from the same in need of repair. Such report shall not cover fences, trees, and shrubs.

___X___ B. CONDITION OF PROPERTY:

Buyer shall have the right at Buyer's expense (i) within ___5___ days from the effective date of this contract to have any of the STRUCTURAL items indicated below, and (ii) within ___5___ days from the effective date of this contract to have any of the EQUIPMENT AND SYSTEMS items indicated below, inspected by inspectors of Buyer's choice and to give Seller within such time periods a written report of required repairs to any of the items checked below which are not performing the function for which intended or which are in need of immediate repair. Failure to do so shall be deemed a waiver of Buyer's inspection and repair rights and Buyer agrees to accept Property in its present condition.

ITEMS THAT BUYER MAY REQUIRE TO BE INSPECTED (check applicable boxes):

STRUCTURAL:

___X___ foundation ___X___ roof ___X___ load bearing walls ___X___ floors ___X___ ceilings _____ basement ___X___ water penetration _____ and _____

_____

EQUIPMENT AND SYSTEMS:

___X___ plumbing system (including any water heaters, wells and septic system), ___X___ central heating and air conditioning, ___X___ electrical system, ___X___ heating and cooling units in the walls, floor, ceilings, roof or windows, ___X___ any built-in range, oven, dishwasher, disposer, kitchen exhaust fan, trash compactor, ___X___ swimming pool and related mechanical equipment, ___X___ sprinkler systems _____ and _____

_____

Repairs required by inspections and reports shall be at Seller's expense.

_____C. Seller shall make the following repairs in addition to those required above: _____

_____

_____

_____

All inspections shall be made by trained and qualified persons who regularly provide such service and all repairs shall be by trained and qualified persons who are, whenever possible, manufacturer-approved service persons or are licensed or bonded whenever such license or bond is required by law. For these purposes and for reinspections after repairs have been completed, Seller shall permit access to the Property at any reasonable time.

___X___D. Where gas supplier, regulations or ordinances require inspection on transfer of gas service, Seller consents to transfer gas service to Buyer's name within 7 days prior to closing. Seller shall arrange and pay at closing for any repairs necessary if gas leak is discovered. Buyer's failure to request such transfer in time to complete the inspection prior to closing shall release the Seller of liability for repair of gas leaks.

_____   _____
Seller   Buyer

_____   _____
Seller   Buyer

SAMPLE CONTINGENCY CLAUSE ADDENDUM—SALE OF BUYER'S HOME

ADDENDUM TO EARNEST-MONEY CONTRACT BETWEEN THE UNDERSIGNED PARTIES DATED __April 15, 1981__ AND CONCERNING THE PROPERTY LOCATED AT __8900 Lamar__.

1. This Contract is contingent upon the closing and funding of Buyer's home located at __6900 Twin Lake__ __Houston__, __Texas__ (State), on or before 6:00 p.m. on the __15th__ day of __May__, 19__81__. If such sale and funding does not occur within such time period this Contract shall be null and void and the Earnest Money returned to Buyer.

2. It is further agreed Seller's home will continue to be shown and offered for sale and should Seller receive a written offer to purchase such home from a third party purchaser which is acceptable to Seller, Seller or his agent will notify Buyer in writing by certified mail, telegram, or personal delivery, that Seller requires removal of said contingency. Buyer will have __48__ hours following receipt of such notice to deliver in writing, by personal delivery or telegram, to Seller's agent (designated below) notice of Buyer's election to (i) waive this contingency, immediately deposit with Escrow Agent $__1,000.00__ as additional Earnest Money and close the sale under the terms of this Contract, or (ii) declare this contract null and void and receive a refund of the Earnest Money.

3. If Buyer fails to elect and notify Seller's agent within such time period, Seller shall receive the Earnest Money and this contract shall be null and void.

4. If Buyer waives this contingency and is then unable to secure funding of a new loan or assumption approval of an existing loan, as the case may be, for this purchase because of ownership of the above referred to home, Seller shall receive the entire amount of the Earnest Money as increased.

SELLER _____

SELLER _____

BUYER _____

BUYER _____

BUYER'S ADDRESS & TELEPHONE #

HIRING A LAWYER TO REVIEW YOUR SALES AGREEMENT

A good real-estate attorney can be an invaluable ally in selling your home. The few hundred dollars you'll probably spend to hire a lawyer well versed in real estate to help you review your agreement of sale (earnest-money contract) and any other legal documents and to preside over the actual closing can save you *thousands* of dollars.

WHY DO YOU NEED A LAWYER?

One very good reason is that real-estate law is a highly complex specialty. And, like any specialty, it requires expertise to use it to your best advantage. Real-estate laws in the United States are not uniform; they differ widely from state to state and even from county to county. Local customs and practices, the accepted legal interpretation of certain words and phrases used in real-estate transactions, and the particular state laws—governing joint ownership of a home, to use just one example—are important considerations that a real-estate attorney will be familiar with and can handle properly and with dispatch. Hiring a real-estate attorney will save you an enormous amount of time that you would otherwise have to spend researching the law yourself.

Another reason why hiring a real-estate lawyer is a wise idea is that he or she will be knowledgeable about any additional wording or documents needed for the particular method of financing being used (wraparound mortgage, contract for deed, and so on). Your attorney can also inform you of the current status of any method of finance in your particular state. For example, the use of a wraparound mortgage in some states may trigger the mortgage company to enforce what is known as a "due on sale" clause. This simply means that when the mortgage company discovers you have sold your home by any method other than those the *mortgage company* approves of, it is possible for them to call the entire balance of the note due and payable immediately. "Due on sale" clauses are legal in some states and illegal in others.

Or, you may discover that the title to your property which *you* thought was in good order is not acceptable to your buyer—in which case, depending upon the reason, he or she may have the right to withdraw from the deal and recover the earnest money. A lawyer can help you prepare for such situations, thus eliminating any surprises as you get down to the wire.

Another good reason is that if unforeseen problems should arise between you and your buyer, your lawyer can help you negotiate in a calm, professional manner. Even if your relationship with the buyer has been amicable all along, things can sometimes change when it gets right down to the actual exchange of money. It's best to be prepared.

A real-estate attorney may also be knowledgeable about the tax implications of your transaction. This kind of knowledge can save you money—lots of it.

Finally, the best reason to hire a lawyer to help you is that he or she will *protect* you. It is almost certain that your buyer will ask a lawyer to review the sales agreement. As a novice, don't be caught in the position of trying to negotiate with an expert! If you retain a lawyer, you will have a professional acting as your advocate. And, because your lawyer is working for you, he will try to facilitate the closing in every way possible. After all, it's in your lawyer's interest that the deal go through. The peace of mind that comes with having an expert represent you in this process is worth it. *Get a lawyer.*

WHEN SHOULD YOU SEE A LAWYER?

Before you finally decide upon a particular method of financing and *before* you sign any agreements. If you know that the sale of your home will be complicated because of liens against your property, a recent divorce settlement, or any other reason, see a lawyer at the time you first decide to sell.

WHAT WILL A LAWYER DO FOR YOU?

Just as every home is unique—with its own history of ownership, mortgage, and so on—every real-estate transaction is unique. In general, however, here are some of the things you can expect a lawyer to do for you:

1. Review the sales agreement (earnest-money contract) and make any adjustments or additions necessary.
2. Make sure that the sales agreement accurately reflects all the terms of the sale (if not, you can expect big trouble ahead).
3. Negotiate on your behalf to resolve any outstanding financial or property differences between you and your buyer.
4. Advise you on special clauses or provisions to add to the sales agreement for your protection.
5. Advise you of the necessary documents and forms you may need to complete the sale (certificate of title, affidavit of title, bill of sale, tax transfer notices, zoning or building certificates, survey plat, etc.).
6. Advise you on the tax consequences of your sale.
7. Apportion any tax or other local or municipal assessments due you.
8. Obtain a title policy.
9. Deposit the earnest money in an escrow account.
10. Preside over the actual closing of the transaction.

HOW TO FIND A REAL-ESTATE LAWYER

There are a number of ways to locate a qualified, competent real-estate attorney to help you with the sale and closing. First, ask friends who have sold their homes and were pleased with the results for referrals.

Another way to find a qualified attorney is to call the mortgage department of your local bank or savings and loan association and ask them for referrals. Banks hire real-estate lawyers to handle their own mortgages and it's likely that a lawyer referred by a bank will have considerable experience. Having a lawyer who has represented clients on both sides of the fence can come in handy if any negotiations with your buyer's lawyer are likely to be involved.

Your local Board of Realtors and Bar Association are also good sources of names. And don't forget to ask your own lawyer for recommendations.

Once you have a list of names, call up each lawyer, briefly state that you are selling your home without a broker, and explain what you'll want him or her to do. Does the person sound responsive or is he too busy to talk with you? Do you detect confidence and reliability in the voice you hear? Energy? You can tell a lot from this conversation. If it sounds promising to you, inquire about fees, then set up a preliminary interview. Most reputable lawyers will agree to see a potential client for a short exploratory interview (about fifteen minutes) without charge. Remember, though, a good lawyer is a skilled professional. Don't take up his or her time with needless questions. If you prepare a list of the questions you want the lawyer to answer beforehand (fees, time involved, any special expertise that would be useful to you), the interview should proceed smoothly and you will know if this is the person whom you want to retain.

The thing to keep in mind when hiring a lawyer is that this person should be someone you feel you can trust. After all, he or she is representing *you.*

WHAT SHOULD YOU EXPECT TO PAY?

Surprisingly little, considering the value of the service you are getting. Most real-estate lawyers charge fees based on a percentage of the total purchase price of the property. Generally the fee is in the neighborhood of from one-half to one percent of the total sales price. So, for example, if you are selling your home for $75,000, a typical fee might range from $375 to $750; for a $50,000 home, from $250 to $500.

Some lawyers charge a flat fee for their services, usually about $200 to $400. This might be to your advantage if your sale is a relatively uncomplicated one.

If a lawyer tells you that he or she charges by the hour, make sure you find out what the hourly rate is. Alternatively, with a complex sales transaction where special documents, title searches, or extended negotiations are involved, the lawyer may charge one fee (based on a percentage) for reviewing the sales agreement and presiding at the closing and another fee (at an hourly rate) for the extra work required.

Paying for a lawyer's services is not the place to stint. The amount you pay is a tax-deductible expense from the profit on the sale of your home. Just be sure to find out exactly what the fee will be before you agree to hire the lawyer.

SET UP AN ESCROW ACCOUNT

Once your lawyer and your buyer's lawyer have reviewed the sales agreement, you and the buyer each sign the agreement (make sure you give the buyer his copy), and the buyer gives you a check for the amount of earnest money due you. Now you're ready to set up an escrow account to handle the closing. You can do this yourself by going to your local title company and telling them to set up an account, or your lawyer can do it for you. In some areas, depending on local custom, your lawyer may set up an escrow account himself, thus acting as your escrow agent.

"Escrow" is the term for the neutral third party which retains, processes, and records all documents and paperwork involved in the sale and handles (collects and pays out) the exchange of money as it becomes due. Escrow holds any documents and deposit money until all conditions of the agreement have been met and all documents signed.

One of the things escrow does in preparation for the closing is to order a policy of title insurance. Title insurance is the fee paid to a title company to conduct a title search (usually at the county courthouse) to verify that the seller's ownership of the property is valid and as claimed. Title insurance protects the buyer and lender against any legal defects in the title. Any liens (outstanding claims against your property for debts owed) will be uncovered in a title search. Escrow makes certain all such debts are resolved before the closing.

Escrow performs a number of other necessary functions as well. Escrow collects the remainder of the down payment from the buyer and any money due from the lender, prorates any taxes or special assessments as appropriate, pays out any money due for inspection fees, title insurance, points, etc., prepares the deed—the written document transferring ownership of the property from you to the buyer—and sets the closing date.

Escrow can take anywhere from three days (for owner-financed sales where a bank is not involved) to two months (for sales where bank financing is required). Escrow fees average about $200 to $500 and are part of the closing costs for the transaction. They are usually split between buyer and seller.

A title company officer, an official from your bank or savings and loan association, or your attorney may serve as escrow agent.

THE CLOSING

This is the moment you've worked and waited for, when you and your buyer sign and exchange documents and you officially transfer the deed to the property to the buyer. Your attorney and your buyer's attorney should both be present. The closing usually takes place in the office of either attorney or at the bank where your buyer received his loan.

The costs involved in this transaction are called "closing costs." Closing costs consist of all the expenses involved in the final transfer of property from you to your buyer, apart from the actual price of the property, and are paid only once, on the day of closing.

Closing costs vary, depending upon where you live and the method of financing used to purchase your home. Some closing costs may be negotiable, so be sure to check with your lawyer. Closing costs usually average about 3% of the total purchase price. Ask your escrow agent for an estimate of what closing costs typically run in your area.

The earnest-money contract (agreement of sale) which you and your buyer negotiated earlier usually spells out which closing costs are your responsibility as seller and which are the responsibility of the buyer. The following list gives you an idea of the charges to expect:

Buyer's Expenses
1. documentary stamps on notes
2. fee for recording deed and mortgage
3. escrow fees
4. attorney's fees
5. title insurance
6. appraisal and inspection fees
7. survey charge

Seller's Expenses
1. cost of abstract of title, title insurance
2. documentary stamps on deed
3. fee for recording mortgage
4. survey charge
5. escrow fees
6. attorney's fees
7. real-estate commission

APPENDIXES

A. SUMMARY OF THE NEW TAX ADVANTAGES FOR HOMEOWNERS

FLASH FOR HOMEOWNERS!

At last, your favorite uncle—Uncle Sam, that is—has come through in a big way for you as a homeowner. The massive new tax legislation passed in 1981 has dramatically improved the ways in which you, as an owner or seller, can save or shelter money that otherwise would go straight into the coffers of the IRS.

Not only has this new legislation instituted a tremendous across-the-board reduction in individual tax rates and lowered the maximum tax bracket, it has also *improved the home sale tax exemption, lowered the ceiling on maximum long-term capital gains from sales, extended the rules governing home sales and replacements* (thus *delaying payment of capital gains taxes* due on the sale), and completely *overhauled the depreciation rules on real property in homeowners' favor.*

Here's a summary of the critical tax-saving features for homeowners in the new law:

1. A 23% across-the-board cut in individual tax rates that will become effective in stages through 1984.
2. A lowering of the maximum tax bracket from 70% to 50% effective beginning in 1982.
3. A reduction from 28% to 20% of the maximum long-term capital gains from sales and exchanges on sales after June 9, 1981, and on installment sale payments received after 1981.
4. A 25% increase in the home sale tax exemption allowed for homeowners over age 55. These homeowners can now exempt from taxes profits of up to $125,000 on home sales of principal residences. This inflation-indexed rule is a substantial improvement over the previous $100,000 exemption allowed. This is a once-in-a-lifetime exemption and to be eligible the homeowner must have lived in the home for three of the previous five years.
5. An extension of 6 months, from 18 months to 24 months, for selling a principal residence and replacing it with a home of an equivalent or greater value in order to take advantage of delayed capital gains tax payments, effective July 20, 1981. This extension also applies to homes sold before July 20, 1981, provided that the previous replacement deadline of 18 months had not yet expired. In other words, if you had sold your home any time in the year and a half prior to July 20, 1981, but had not yet bought a new home under the specified conditions, you could add another six months to the deadline and still qualify for the postponement of capital gains taxes due on the sale.
6. A new, accelerated schedule for writing off depreciable personal property. Under this law, called the "Accelerated Cost Recovery System" (ACRS), personal property items have new three-, five-, and ten-year depreciation schedules, and most personal property can be depreciated in five years. This law is effective retroactively, applying to depreciable items placed in service after 1980.
7. A vastly accelerated schedule for depreciating most real property from the old useful-life tables of up to 50 years to as little as 15 years. This law also allows you to choose between straight line or accelerated methods of depreciation. It applies to real property acquired after January 1, 1981.

Consult your accountant or tax advisor for more information about the new tax legislation and to find out the best ways of using it to your advantage.

B. TAX BENEFITS OF OWNER FINANCING

You can make it easier to sell your home if you take back a mortgage. And you will receive special tax breaks for doing so. In fact, you can get a double tax break—combining the sale-and-replacement break with the tax-deferred installment sale, now simpler than ever.

Let's say you sell your home and buy another one within 24 months. You pay no tax on your profit, as long as the new home costs at least as much as what you got for the old home. That's the home sale-and-replacement break. But if your new home cost less than the sale price of the old, there's going to be a tax. But here is the good news: if you take back a purchase-money mortgage you can take advantage of a unique tax-saving combination—teaming up the sale-and-replacement break with an installment sale. Part of your gain on the home sale is deferred with the sale-and-replacement break. The remaining gain is taxable, but is reported on the installment method. Result: you defer tax on a good part of your gain.

Example

Mr. Nathan bought his home many years ago for $25,000 and now sells it for $100,000. The buyer gives him a $40,000 down payment, but can't get conventional financing for the balance. So Mr. Nathan takes back a ten-year, interest-bearing mortgage for the $60,000 balance. A few months after the sale, Mr. Nathan buys a $65,000 condominium.

- Sale and replacement: $40,000 of his $75,000 gain is not currently taxed. But the $35,000 remaining gain is subject to tax. Reason: the $100,000 sale price of Mr. Nathan's old home exceeds the purchase price of the new home by $35,000.
- Installment sale: Mr. Nathan can report that $35,000 taxable gain on the installment method. Only 35% ($35,000 gain not sheltered by the sale-and-replacement break, divided by $100,000 sales price) of each of the buyer's payments is taxable capital gain.

Without installment reporting, Mr. Nathan would have had a $35,000 capital gain in the year of the sale. Using installment reporting, he has capital gain of only $14,000 in the year he sells (35% of the $40,000 down-payment). The balance of his taxable gain is deferred and is payable only as the buyer makes mortgage payments to Mr. Nathan.

The installment sale break can also be combined with the $125,000 exclusion. (According to the new tax law, homesellers aged 55 or over get a once-in-a-lifetime break—the first $125,000 of profit escapes tax completely.)

Example

The Smiths bought their home many years ago for $50,000. They are now over age 55 and sell their home for $200,000. They intend to rent an apartment. Their buyer gives them an $80,000 down payment, and they take back a ten-year mortgage for the $120,000 balance. The buyer is to pay them $12,000 a year, plus interest. The amount of each payment that is taxable is the portion that bears the same relationship to the whole payment as the profit (minus the $125,000 exclusion) bears to the sale price. The sale price here is $200,000, and the Smiths' profit, less the exclusion, is $25,000. So only one eighth of each principal payment is taxable ($25,000 is one eighth of $200,000). The interest that the buyer pays the Smiths is, of course, fully taxable income.

C. HELP YOUR BUYER MAKE THE MOST OF MOVING-EXPENSE DEDUCTIONS

The hundreds of thousands of prospective real-estate buyers who make job-connected moves each year—whether they have to move in their present job or for a new job—are entitled to a number of moving-expense deductions.

These deductions can mean more completed sales to homeowners who know the moving-expense rules and show their buyers how to make the most of them.

Here's a look at what families on the move can deduct:

1. the cost of moving household goods and personal effects
2. the reasonable travel costs of the taxpayer and his family
3. the expenses of premove house-hunting trips, provided the taxpayer is already employed at the new location

4. food and lodging while waiting to move into a new home—with a 30-day limit
5. certain expenses (attorney's fees, points, etc.) connected with the sale of the old house and the purchase of the new

There's an overall limit of $3,000 for the last three expenses, but the amount of house-hunting and temporary living expenses can't exceed $1,500. Buyers qualify for the moving-expense deduction if their new job is at least 35 miles farther from their old home than their old job was from their old home.

Tell your prospective buyer what I've told you. He can get a deduction for all direct costs plus up to $3,000 in indirect moving expenses. That could be enough to persuade him to buy your home right away.

Give a copy of a record book like the one reprinted below to your prospective buyer, and be sure to keep one for yourself. Keep it up-to-date every time you sell and replace. This form will enable you to trace your tax basis back to your original home. And that's important, because the bigger your tax basis, the smaller your gain when you sell. Thanks to this record, and your receipts and bills, you'll have a much easier time supplying needed proof if you are ever called in for an audit.

Eventually you will sell a home and not replace it with another. And when that happens, all the tax you've been postponing will come due at once. Then it will be essential that you have proof to show that your bigger tax basis, and smaller gain, are justified. That's why I've included this money-saving form in my book.

Example

Mr. and Mrs. Johnson bought their first home in 1955 for $20,000. They added a patio and finished off the basement for $3,000. They sold the home in 1960 for $30,000. Result: a gain of $7,000—the difference between the selling price ($30,000) and the adjusted basis ($23,000, the $20,000 cost plus the $3,000 capital improvement). The Johnsons buy a new home for $30,000—the same amount they received for the old one—so the tax on the gain is postponed. However, the tax basis for the new home is not $30,000, but the $23,000 adjusted basis of the old one.

Year	Transaction	Adjusted basis
1960	New home ($30,000)	$23,000
1961	Landscaping ($2,000)	$25,000
1962	Swimming pool ($4,000)	$29,000
1965	Home sold ($45,000)	$29,000
		($16,000 capital gain)
1965	New home ($50,000)	$34,000
	tax deferred	(cost less $16,000)
1967	Added room ($10,000)	$44,000
1970	Home sold ($70,000)	$44,000
		($26,000 capital gain)
1970	New home ($75,000)	$49,000
	tax deferred	(cost less $26,000)
1972	Tennis court ($9,000)	$58,000

Now let's see what happens if Mr. Johnson sells this last home for $100,000. If they kept records, the computation will not be all that difficult. Mr. Johnson merely subtracts the adjusted basis ($58,000) from the selling price ($100,000). Result: a taxable gain of $42,000. If they didn't keep records, the government can assign an approximate basis to the home—possibly resulting in a much higher tax bill. Mr. Johnson will have a hard time reconstructing the costs of improvements, and that can mean an additional taxable gain of $25,000. Also, the government can question the amounts the Johnsons received when they sold their homes and the amounts spent on the purchases.

HOME EXPENDITURE RECORD BOOK

YEAR	TRANSACTION	ADJUSTED BASIS

E. TAX WORKSHEETS

WORKSHEET 1—COMPUTING THE ADJUSTED BASIS OF YOUR OLD HOUSE

1. Enter the original cost of your old house. Be sure to include closing costs incurred when you purchased the house. $_____

2. Now enter the cost of all improvements you added to the property. $_____

3. Total lines 1 and 2. $_____

4. When you bought this house, did you postpone any gain on the house you sold before? If you did, record it here. $_____

5. Did you ever deduct depreciation on the house—for example, as rental property or use as a home office? If you did, record it here. $_____

6. Did you ever deduct a casualty loss to your old house? If you did, record the total taken here. $_____

7. Total lines 4, 5, 6. $_____

8. Now subtract the total in line 7 from line 3. The difference is your adjusted basis. $_____

WORKSHEET 2—COMPUTING THE GAIN ON SALE

1. Enter the sale price—the total consideration you are receiving for the property. This price includes cash, notes assumed, and notes taken back. Date sold _____

   $_____

2. Now enter the total selling expenses, which include sales commissions if any, recording fees, title policy fees, escrow fees, and all other expenses of this nature directly related to the sale of the old house. Do not include interest or real-estate taxes paid; these are itemized deductions. Do not include personal items like insurance or impound account money. $_____

3. Subtract line 2 from line 1. This figure is the amount realized. $_____

4. Now enter the adjusted basis from Worksheet 1, Item 8. $_____

5. The difference is the gain or loss on the sale of your old house. $_____

If the amount realized is more than the adjusted basis, the difference is a gain; if the amount realized is less than your adjusted basis, you have suffered a loss on the sale. And a loss on the sale of your personal residence is not deductible. But today, almost all sales result in a gain. It is necessary for effective tax planning that you know how much gain you are realizing.

A word about the "date sold" recorded in Worksheet 2. The replacement time period starts 24 months before that date and ends 24 months after that date. If you build your own replacement residence, you qualify for a 6-month extension at the end of that period.

WORKSHEET 3—COMPUTING THE ADJUSTED SALES PRICE AND THE POSTPONED GAIN.

1. Enter the amount realized (Worksheet 2, Item 3). $_____

2. Enter the total of any fixing-up expenses you had that qualify. $_____

3. Deduct line 2 from line 1. This is your adjusted sales price. $_____

4. Write here the purchase cost of your new house. $_____
   Is the cost of your new house more than the adjusted sales price?
   YES_____ NO_____ If the answer is yes, stop here. You have a tax-free exchange, and the entire gain (see Worksheet 2) is postponed. If no, continue below.

5. Enter the amount by which your adjusted sales price (line 3) exceeds the cost of your new house (line 4). $_____

6. Now enter the amount of your gain on the sale (Worksheet 2, Item 5). $_____

7. The amount of gain not postponed and recognized this year for income-tax purposes is the smaller of amounts at 5 and 6 above. Enter it here. $_____

Remember, it's the total replacement cost that counts, not just the purchase cost of the new house. The amount at Item 7 above is the amount by which you might want to increase the replacement cost during the original replacement time period. You can do this by adding improvements.

You now have an opportunity to sell your home and escape all tax on the first $125,000 of gain. Here are the key provisions:

1. The seller must be at least 55 years old at the time of sale. If Mr. Homeseller is married, then the age of his spouse can make a big difference. Mr. Homeseller can get the break if three conditions are met: a) Mrs. Homeseller is 55 years or over at the time of the sale, b) Mr. and Mrs. Homeseller jointly own the home, and c) they file a joint tax return.
2. The home that's sold must be a "principal residence."
3. The break is a permanent exclusion—any tax on up to $125,000 gain is completely wiped out, not merely postponed.
4. The homeseller can get this break whether he buys a replacement home or not.

What must homesellers do? They have to keep track of their gain from each sale over the years up until the election of the $125,000 exclusion. That's why the *Home Expenditure Record Book* is so important—it provides an accurate running total of the accumulating gain. This record book will not only clinch a homeseller's right to his tax break, but it will signal the proper time to sell. According to law, the $125,000 tax-free exclusion applies only to sales made after July 21, 1981, but in actual practice the break can wipe out the tax on gain made from sales years before that by eligible homesellers. Let's go back to the Johnsons, who had built up a $42,000 gain by the time they sold in the early '70s. That gain, on which they've paid no tax up until now, was built up from sales in 1965 and 1970. However, if the Johnsons elect to exclude now—and let's assume they are over 55—they get all this pre-1981 build-up tax-free. Should the Johnsons elect the exclusion at this point? Homesellers can't split up the $125,000 and use it to shelter two sales. If the Johnsons elect this break now, they shelter only $42,000 in gain—not the full $125,000 they could protect. And that means $83,000 of tax shelter is lost! There's no getting around this once-in-a-lifetime provision by carrying over that unused $83,000 to another home sale.

Sellers can roll over their gain into the purchase of a replacement home. If these new homes cost more than the selling price of the old ones, they'll continue putting off payment of the current tax. No changes were made in the rules allowing homesellers to defer paying current tax on any gain by buying a replacement home, except for one liberalization. Owners can get the break twice now if a job-related move forces them to sell more than once during the 24-month period; and they also qualify for the moving-expense deduction.

G. CALCULATING MORTGAGE INTEREST PAYMENTS

Principal and Interest Payment Per $1,000 of Loan

Interest Rate	30 Year	25 Year	20 Year	15 Year	10 Year
10.00	8.78	9.09	9.66	10.75	13.22
10.125	8.87	9.18	9.73	10.82	13.30
10.25	8.97	9.27	9.82	10.90	13.36
10.375	9.05	9.35	9.90	10.98	13.42
10.50	9.15	9.45	9.99	11.06	13.50
10.625	9.24	9.53	10.07	11.13	13.56
10.75	9.34	9.63	·10.16	11.21	13.64
10.875	9.45	9.71	10.24	11.29	13.70
11.00	9.53	9.81	10.33	11.37	13.78
11.125	9.62	9.89	10.41	11.44	13.85
11.25	9.72	9.99	10.50	11.53	13.92
11.375	9.81	10.07	10.58	11.60	13.99
11.50	9.91	10.17	10.67	11.69	14.06
11.625	10.00	10.26	10.75	11.76	14.13
11.75	10.10	10.35	10.84	11.85	14.21
11.875	10.19	10.44	10.92	11.92	14.27
12.00	10.29	10.53	11.01	12.00	14.35
12.125	10.38	10.62	11.10	12.08	14.42
12.25	10.48	10.72	11.19	12.16	14.49
12.375	10.58	10.81	11.27	12.24	14.56
12.50	10.67	10.90	11.36	12.33	14.64
12.625	10.77	11.00	11.45	12.41	14.71
12.75	10.87	11.09	11.54	12.49	14.78
12.875	10.96	11.18	11.63	12.57	14.86
13.00	11.06	11.28	11.73	12.65	14.93
13.125	11.16	11.37	11.80	12.73	15.00
13.25	11.26	11.47	11.89	12.82	15.08
13.375	11.36	11.56	11.98	12.90	15.15
13.50	11.45	11.66	12.07	12.98	15.23
13.625	11.55	11.75	12.16	13.07	15.30
13.75	11.65	11.85	12.25	13.15	15.38
13.875	11.75	11.94	12.34	13.23	15.45
14.00	11.85	12.04	12.44	13.32	15.53
14.125	11.95	12.13	12.53	13.40	15.60
14.25	12.05	12.23	12.62	13.49	15.68
14.378	12.15	12.33	12.71	13:57	15.75
14.50	12.25	12.42	12.80	13.66	15.83
14.625	12.35	12.52	12.89	13.74	15.90
14.75	12.44	12.61	12.98	13.83	15.98
14.875	12.54	12.71	13.08	13.91	16.06
15.00	12.65	12.81	13.17	14.00	16.14
15.125	12.75	12.91	13.27	14.09	16.22
15.25	12.85	13.01	13.36	14.17	16.29
15.375	12.95	13.10	13.46	14.26	16.37
15.50	13.05	13.20	13.54	14.34	16.45
15.625	13.15	13.30	13.64	14.43	16.52
15.75	13.25	13.40	13.73	14.52	16.60
15.875	13.35	13.50	13.82	14.60	16.68
16.00	13.45	13.59	13.92	14.69	16.76
16.125	13.55	13.69	14.01	14.78	16.83
16.250	13.65	13.79	14.11	14.87	16.91
16.375	13.76	13.89	14.20	14.95	16.99
16.50	13.86	13.99	14.29	15.04	17.07
16.625	13.96	14.09	14.39	15.13	17.15
16.75	14.06	14.18	14.48	15.22	17.23
16.875	14.16	14.28	14.58	15.30	17.31
17.00	14.26	14.38	14.67	15.40	17.38
17.125	14.36	14.48	14.76	15.48	17.54
17.250	14.46	14.58	14.86	15.57	17.54
17.375	14.56	14.68	14.95	15.66	17.62
17.50	14.67	14.78	15.05	15.75	17.70
17.625	14.77	14.88	15.15	15.84	17.79
17.75	14.87	14.98	15.25	15.93	17.86
17.875	14.97	15.08	15.34	16.02	17.94
18.00	15.08	15.18	15.44	16.11	18.02

To calculate payment for principal and interest: Multiply factor from above times the thousands of loan amount. *Example:* 30-year loan for $50,000 at 11% interest equals $476.50. 9.53 × 50 = $476.50 payment for principal and mortgage.

H. PREMIUM PAYMENTS FOR HOMEOWNERS' AND TITLE INSURANCE

HOMEOWNERS INSURANCE (Buyer's Cost)			TITLE INSURANCE (Seller's Cost)	
Loan Amount	Annual Premium	Monthly Premium	Sales Price	Lifetime Premium
$40,000	$230.00	$19.20	$40,000	$284.00
41,000	236.00	19.70	41,000	288.00
42,000	242.00	20.20	42,000	292.00
43,000	248.00	20.65	43,000	297.00
44,000	253.00	21.10	44,000	301.00
45,000	259.00	21.60	45,000	306.00
46,000	265.00	22.10	46,000	310.00
47,000	270.00	22.50	47.000	315.00
48,000	276.00	23.00	48,000	319.00
49,000	282.00	23.50	49,000	324.00
50,000	288.00	24.00	50,000	328.00
51,000	294.00	24.50	51,000	332.00
52,000	299.00	25.00	52,000	337.00
53,000	305.00	25.50	53,000	341.00
54,000	311.00	26.00	54,000	346.00
55,000	317.00	26.50	55,000	350.00
56,000	322.00	26.85	56,000	355.00
57,000	328.00	27.40	57,000	359.00
58,000	334.00	27.85	58,000	363.00
59,000	339.00	28.25	59,000	368.00
60,000	340.00	28.25	60,000	372.00
61,000	345.00	28.75	61,000	377.00
62,000	349.00	29.05	62,000	381.00
63,000	350.00	29.15	63,000	386.00
64,000	352.00	29.35	64,000	390.00
65,000	357.00	29.75	65,000	395.00
66,000	363.00	30.25	66,000	399.00
67,000	368.00	30.65	67,000	403.00
68,000	374.00	31.00	68,000	408.00
69,000	375.00	31.25	69,000	412.00
70,000	378.00	31.50	70,000	417.00
71,000	380.00	31.70	71,000	421.00
72,000	385.00	32.10	72,000	426.00
73,000	390.00	32.50	73,000	430.00
74,000	396.00	33.00	74,000	435.00
75,000	401.00	33.45	75,000	439.00
80,000	417.00	34.75	80,000	461.00
85,000	455.00	37.90	85,000	483.00
90,000	458.00	38.15	90,000	506.00
95,000	478.00	39.85	95,000	528.00
100,000	498.00	41.50	100,000	550.00
105,000	518.00	43.15	105,000	577.00
110,000	538.00	44.85	110,000	605.00
115,000	558.00	46.50	115,000	633.00
120,000	578.00	48.15	120,000	660.00
125,000	598.00	49.85	125,000	687.00
130,000	618.00	51.50	130,000	715.00
135,000	638.00	53.15	135,000	742.00
140,000	658.00	54.85	140,000	770.00

The above figures are estimates. Some insurance companies may be higher or lower.

The title insurance premium is paid only one time, usually at closing. It is normally a seller's expense. The buyer must purchase a rider to protect the mortgage company (if one is involved) for approximately $30 extra.

I. HOUSE-SALE CONTRACT FORMS

On the following pages are all the blank contract forms and tabular data you need to sell your house. These forms may be duplicated only for your personal use in selling your house and may not be sold or used for any other purpose.

CONVENTIONAL LOAN—
RESIDENTIAL EARNEST-MONEY CONTRACT (RESALE)

1. PARTIES _____ (Seller) agrees to

   sell and convey to _____ (Buyer)

   and Buyer agrees to buy from Seller the following property situated in _____

   County, _____ (State), known as _____ (Address).

2. PROPERTY: Lot _____, Block _____, _____

   Addition, City of _____, or as described on attached exhibit, together

   with the following fixtures, if any; curtain rods, drapery rods, venetian blinds, window shades,

   screens and shutters, awnings, wall-to-wall carpeting, mirrors fixed in place, attic fans, perma-

   nently installed heating and air-conditioning units and equipment, lighting and plumbing fixtures,

   TV antennas, mailboxes, water softeners, shrubbery and all other property owned by Seller and at-

   tached to the above described real property. All property sold by this contract is called "Property."

3. CONTRACT SALES PRICE:

   A. Cash down payment payable at closing .... $ _____

   B. Note described in 4 below (the Note) in the amount of ... $ _____

   C. Any balance of Sales Price to be evidenced by a second lien note (the Second Note) to [check (1)

   or (2) below]:

   _____ 1. Seller, bearing interest at the rate of

          _____% per annum in

          _____ lump sum on or before _____

          _____ principal and interest installments of

          $ _____, or more per _____ with first installment payable on

          _____

   _____ 2. Third Party in principal and interest installments not in excess of $ _____ per

          month in the principal amount of .... $ _____

   D. Sales Price payable to Seller on Loan funding after closing (Sum of A, B, & C) ....

   .... $ _____

4. FINANCING CONDITIONS: This contract is subject to approval for Buyer of a _____ Conven-

   tional or _____ Conventional private mortgage insured third party loan (the Loan) of not less

   than the amount of the Note, amortizable monthly for not less than _____ years, with interest

   not to exceed _____ percent per annum, and approval of any third party Second Note. Buyer

   shall apply for all financing within _____ days from the effective date of this contract and shall

   make every reasonable effort to obtain approval. If all financing cannot be approved within

_____ days from effective date of this contract, this contract shall terminate and Earnest Money shall be refunded to Buyer without delay.

5. EARNEST MONEY: $_____ is herewith tendered and is to be deposited as Earnest Money with _____ as Escrow Agent, upon execution of the contract by both parties. Additional Earnest Money, if any, shall be deposited with the Escrow Agent on or before _____, 19_____ in the amount of $_____.

6. TITLE: Seller at Seller's expense shall furnish either:

_____A. Owner's Policy of Title Insurance (the Title Policy) issued by _____ _____ in the amount of the Sales Price and dated at or after closing:

OR

_____B. Complete Abstract of Title (the Abstract) certified by _____ _____ to current date.

NOTICE TO BUYER AS REQUIRED BY LAW, YOU should have the Abstract covering the Property examined by an attorney of YOUR selection, or YOU should be furnished with or obtain a Title Policy.

7. PROPERTY CONDITION [Check "A" or "B"]:

_____A. Buyer accepts the Property in its present condition, subject only to lender required repairs and _____.

_____B. Buyer requires inspections and repairs required by the Property Condition Addendum (the Addendum) and any lender.

Upon Seller's receipt of all loan approvals and inspection reports Seller shall commence and complete prior to closing all required repairs at Seller's expense.

All inspections, reports and repairs required of Seller by this contract and the Addendum shall not exceed $_____. If Seller fails to complete such requirements, Buyer may do so and Seller shall be liable up to the amount specified and the same paid from the proceeds of the sale. If such expenditures exceed the stated amount and Seller refuses to pay such excess, Buyer may pay the additional cost or accept the Property with limited repairs and this sale shall be closed as scheduled, or Buyer may terminate this contract and the Earnest Money shall be refunded to Buyer.

8. CLOSING: The closing of the sale (the Closing Date) shall be on or before _____ 19_____, or within 7 days after objections to title have been cured, whichever date is later; however, if necessary to complete Loan requirements, the Closing Date shall be extended daily up to 15 days.

9. POSSESSION: The possession of the Property shall be delivered to Buyer on _____ in its present or required improved condition, ordinary wear and tear excepted. Any possession by Buyer prior to or by Seller after Closing Date shall establish a landlord tenant at sufferance relationship between the parties.

10. SPECIAL PROVISIONS:

[Insert terms and conditions of a factual nature applicable to this sale, e.g., personal property included in sale (curtains, draperies, valances, etc.), prior purchase or sale of other property, lessee's surrender of possession, and the like.]

11. SALES EXPENSES TO BE PAID IN CASH AT OR PRIOR TO CLOSING:

    A. Loan appraisal fees shall be paid by _____ .

    B. Seller's Expenses:

        (1) Seller's Loan discount points not exceeding _____ .

        (2) Lender required repairs and any other inspections, reports, and repairs required of Seller herein, and in the Addendum.

        (3) Prepayment penalties on any existing loans, plus cost of releasing such loans and recording releases, tax statements, ½ of any escrow fee, preparation of Deed, other expenses stipulated to be paid by Seller under other provisions of this contract.

    C. Buyer's Expenses:

        (1) Fees for loans (e.g., any private mortgage insurance premiums, loan and mortgage application, origination and commitment fees, Buyer's loan discount points not exceeding $_____ .

        (2) Expenses incident to loan(s) e.g., preparation of any Note, Deed of Trust and other loan documents, survey, recording fees, copies of restrictions and easements, Mortgagee's Title Policies, credit reports, photo(s), ½ of any escrow fee, any required premiums for flood and hazard insurance, any required reserve deposits for insurance premiums, ad valorem taxes and special assessments, interest on all monthly installment payment notes from date of disbursement to 1 month prior to dates of first monthly payments, expenses stipulated to be paid by Buyer under other provisions of this contract.

    D. If any sales expenses exceed the maximum amount herein stipulated to be paid by either party, either party may terminate this contract unless the other party agrees to pay such excess.

12. PRORATIONS: Insurance (at Buyer's option), taxes and any rents and maintenance fees shall be prorated to the Closing Date.

13. TITLE APPROVAL: If Abstract is furnished, Seller shall deliver same to Buyer within 20 days from the effective date hereof. Buyer shall have 20 days from date of receipt of Abstract to deliver a copy of the title opinion to Seller, stating any objections to title, and only objections so stated shall be considered. If Title Policy is furnished, the Title shall guarantee Buyer's title to be good and indefeasible subject only to (i) restrictive covenants affecting the Property, (ii) any discrepancies, conflicts or shortages in area or boundary lines or any encroachments, or any overlapping of improvements, (iii) all taxes for the current and subsequent years, (iv) any existing building and zoning ordinances, (v) rights of parties in possession, (vi) any liens created as security for the sale consideration, and (vii) any reservations or exceptions contained in the Deed. In either instance, if title objections are disclosed, Seller shall have 30 days to cure the same. Exceptions permitted in the Deed and zoning ordinances shall not be valid objections to title. Seller shall furnish at Seller's expense tax statements showing no delinquent taxes and a General Warranty Deed conveying title subject only to liens securing debt created as part of the consideration, taxes for the current year, usual restrictive covenants and utility easements common to the platted subdivision of which the Property is a part and any other reservations or exceptions acceptable to Buyer. Each note herein provided shall be secured by Vendor's and Deed of Trust liens. In case of dispute as to the form of Deed, Note(s) or Deed(s) of Trust, such shall be upon a form prepared by the State Bar of _____ (State).

14. CASUALTY LOSS: If any part of Property is damaged or destroyed by fire or other casualty loss, Seller shall restore the same to its previous condition as soon as reasonably possible, but in any event by Closing Date, and if Seller is unable to do so without fault, this contract shall terminate and Earnest Money shall be refunded.

15. DEFAULT: If Buyer fails to comply herewith, Seller may either enforce specific performance or terminate this contract and receive the Earnest Money as liquidated damages.

    If Seller is unable without fault to deliver Abstract or Title Policy or to make any noncasualty repairs required herein within the time herein specified, Buyer may either terminate this contract and receive the Earnest Money as the sole remedy, or extend the time up to 30 days. If Seller fails to comply herewith for any other reason, Buyer may (i) terminate this contract and receive the Earnest Money, thereby releasing Seller from this contract, (ii) enforce specific performance hereof, or (iii) seek such other relief as may be provided by law.

16. ATTORNEY'S FEES: Any signatory to this contract who is the prevailing party in any legal proceeding against any other signatory brought under or with relation to this contract or transaction shall be additionally entitled to recover court costs and reasonable attorney fees from the nonprevailing party.

17. ESCROW: Earnest Money is deposited with Escrow Agent with the understanding that Escrow Agent (i) does not have any liability for performance or nonperformance of any party, (ii) has the right to require the receipt, release and authorization in writing of all parties before paying the deposit to any party, and (iii) is not liable for interest or other charge on the funds held. If any party unreasonably fails to agree in writing to an appropriate release of Earnest Money, then such party shall be liable to the other parties to the extent provided in paragraph 16. At closing, Earnest Money shall be applied to any cash down payment required, next to Buyer's closing costs and any excess refunded to Buyer. Before Buyer shall be entitled to refund of Earnest Money, any actual expenses incurred or paid on Buyer's behalf shall be deducted therefrom and paid to the creditors entitled thereto.

18. REPRESENTATIONS: Seller represents that unless securing payment of the Note there will be no Title I liens, unrecorded liens, or Uniform Commercial Code liens against any of the Property on Closing Date. If any representation above is untrue this contract may be terminated by Buyer and the Earnest Money shall be refunded without delay. Representations shall survive closing.

19. AGREEMENT OF PARTIES: This contract contains the entire agreement of the parties and cannot be changed except by their written consent.

20. CONSULT YOUR ATTORNEY: This is intended to be a legally binding contract. READ IT CAREFULLY. If you do not understand the effect of any part, consult your attorney BEFORE signing. Attorneys to represent parties may be designated below.

Seller's Atty: _____   Buyer's Atty: _____

EXECUTED in multiple originals effective the _____ day of _____, 19_____.

_____   _____
Seller   Buyer

_____   _____
Seller   Buyer

_____   _____
Seller's Address   Buyer's Address

FHA INSURED LOAN—
RESIDENTIAL EARNEST-MONEY CONTRACT (RESALE)

1. PARTIES _____ (Seller) agrees to

   sell and convey to _____ (Buyer)

   and Buyer agrees to buy from Seller the following property situated in _____

   County, _____ (State), known as _____

   _____ (Address).

2. PROPERTY: Lot _____, Block _____, _____ Addition, City of

   _____ , or as described on attached exhibit, together with the following

   fixtures, if any: curtain rods, drapery rods, venetian blinds, window shades, screens and shutters,

   awnings, wall-to-wall carpeting, mirrors fixed in place, attic fans, permanently installed heating and

   air-conditioning units and equipment, light and plumbing fixtures, TV antennas, mailboxes, water

   softeners, shrubbery and all other property owned by Seller and attached to the above described

   real property. All property sold by this contract is called "Property."

3. CONTRACT SALES PRICE:

   A. Cash down payment payable at closing ....$_____

   B. Amount of Note (the Note) described in 4-A below ....$_____

   C. Sales Price payable to Seller on Loan funding after closing (Sum of A plus B)........................

   ....$_____

4. FINANCING CONDITIONS:

   A. This contract is subject to approval for Buyer of a Section _____ FHA Insured Loan

      (the Loan) of not less than the amount of the Note, amortizable monthly for not less than

      _____ years, with interest at maximum rate allowable at time of Loan funding. Buyer shall

      apply for the Loan within _____ days from the effective date of this contract and shall

      make every reasonable effort to obtain approval of the Loan. If the Loan has not been approved

      by the Closing Date, this contract shall terminate and Earnest Money shall be refunded to Buyer

      without delay.

   B. As required by HUD-FHA regulations, if FHA valuation is unknown, "It is expressly agreed that,

      notwithstanding any other provisions of this contract, the Purchaser (Buyer) shall not be obli-

      gated to complete the purchase of the Property described herein or to incur any penalty by for-

      feiture of Earnest Money deposits or otherwise unless the Seller has delivered to the Purchaser

      (Buyer) a written statement issued by the Federal Housing Commissioner setting forth the ap-

      praised value of the Property (excluding closing costs) of not less than $_____ ,

      which statement the Seller hereby agrees to deliver to the Purchaser (Buyer) promptly after

such appraised value statement is made available to the Seller. The Purchaser (Buyer) shall, however, have the privilege and option of proceeding with the consummation of this contract without regard to the amount of the appraised valuation made by the Federal Housing Commission. *The appraised valuation is arrived at to determine the maximum mortgage the Department of Housing and Urban Development will insure. HUD does not warrant the value or the condition of the property. The purchaser should satisfy himself/herself that the price and the condition of the property are acceptable.''*

5. EARNEST MONEY: $——————— is herewith tendered and is to be deposited as Earnest Money with ————————————— as Escrow Agent, upon execution of the contract by both parties. Additional Earnest Money, if any, shall be deposited with the Escrow Agent on or before ——————— , 19——— , in the amount of $——————— .

6. TITLE: Seller at Seller's expense shall furnish either:

———A. Owner's Policy of Title Insurance (the Title Policy) issued by ——————— ——————— in the amount of the Sales Price and dated at or after closing;

OR

———B. Complete Abstract of Title (the Abstract) certified by ——————— to current date.

NOTICE TO BUYER AS REQUIRED BY LAW, YOU should have the abstract covering the Property examined by an attorney of YOUR selection, or YOU should be furnished with or obtain a Title Policy.

7. PROPERTY CONDITION [Check ''A'' or ''B'']:

———A. Buyer accepts the Property in its present condition, subject only to required repairs and

——————————————————————————————

—————————————————————————————— .

———B. Buyer requires inspections and repairs required by the Property Condition Addendum (the Addendum) and those required by FHA. Upon Seller's receipt of the Loan approval and inspection reports Seller shall commence and complete prior to closing all required repairs at Seller's expense.

All inspections, reports and repairs required of Seller by this contract and the Addendum shall not exceed $——————— . If the Seller fails to complete such requirements, Buyer may do so and Seller shall be liable up to the amount specified and the same paid from the proceeds of the sale. If such expenditures exceed the stated amount and the Seller refuses to pay such excess, Buyer may pay the additional cost or accept the Property with the limited repairs and this sale shall be closed as scheduled, or Buyer may terminate this contract and the Earnest Money shall be refunded to Buyer.

8. CLOSING: The closing of the sale (the Closing Date) shall be on or before _____ 19_____ , or within 7 days after objections to title have been cured, whichever date is later; however, if necessary to complete Loan requirements, the Closing Date shall be extended daily up to 15 days.

9. POSSESSION: The possession of the Property shall be delivered to Buyer on _____ in its present or required improved condition, ordinary wear and tear excepted. Any possession by Buyer prior to or by Seller after Closing Date shall establish a landlord tenant at sufferance relationship between the Parties.

10. SPECIAL PROVISIONS:

[Insert terms and conditions of a factual nature applicable to this sale, e.g., prior purchase or sale of other property, lessee surrender of possession and the like.]

11. SALES EXPENSES TO BE PAID IN CASH AT OR PRIOR TO CLOSING:

A. Loan appraisal fee (FHA application fee) shall be paid by _____ .

B. Seller's Expenses:

  (1) Seller's Loan discount points not exceeding _____ .

  (2) FHA required repairs and any other inspections, reports, and repairs required of Seller herein, and in the Addendum.

  (3) Expenses incident to Loan (e.g., preparation of Loan documents, survey, recording fees, copies of restrictions and easements, amortization schedule, Mortgagee's Title Policy, Loan origination fee, credit reports, photographs).

  (4) Releases of existing loans, including prepayment penalties and recordation; tax statements, preparation of Deed; escrow fee; and other expenses stipulated to be paid by Seller under other provisions of this contract.

C. Buyer's Expenses: All prepaid items required by applicable HUD-FHA or other regulations (e.g., required premiums for flood and hazard insurance, required reserve deposits for FHA and other insurance, ad valorem taxes and special assessments); interest on the Note from date of disbursement to one month prior to date of first monthly payment; expenses stipulated to be paid by Buyer under other provisions of this contract.

D. If any sales expenses exceed the maximum amount herein stipulated to be paid by either party, either party may terminate this Contract unless other party agrees to pay such excess. In no event shall Buyer pay charges and fees other than those expressly permitted by FHA regulations.

12. PRORATIONS: Insurance (at Buyer's option), taxes, and any rents and maintenance fees shall be prorated to the Closing Date.

13. TITLE APPROVAL: If Abstract is furnished, Seller shall deliver same to Buyer within 20 days from the effective date hereof. Buyer shall have 20 days from date of receipt of Abstract to deliver a copy of the title opinion to Seller, stating any objections to title, and only objections so stated shall be considered. If Title Policy is furnished, the Title Policy shall guarantee Buyer's title to be good and indefeasible subject only to (i) restrictive covenants affecting the Property, (ii) any discrepancies, conflicts or shortages in area or boundary lines or any encroachments, or any overlapping of improvements, (iii) all taxes for the current and subsequent years, (iv) any existing building and zoning ordinances, (v) rights of parties in possession, (vi) any liens created as security for the sale consideration, and (vii) any reservations or exceptions contained in the Deed. In either instance, if title objections are disclosed, Seller shall have 30 days to cure the same. Exceptions permitted in the Deed and zoning ordinances shall not be valid objections to title. Seller shall furnish at Seller's expense tax statement showing no delinquent taxes and a General Warranty Deed conveying title subject only to liens securing debt created as part of the consideration, taxes for the current year, usual restrictive covenants and utility easements common to the platted subdivision of which the Property is a part and any other reservations or exceptions acceptable to Buyer. The Note shall be secured by Vendor's and Deed of Trust liens. In case of dispute as to the form of Deed, such shall be upon a form prepared by the State Bar of _____ (State).

14. CASUALTY LOSS: If any part of Property is damaged or destroyed by fire or other casualty loss, Seller shall restore the same to its previous condition as soon as reasonably possible, but in any event by Closing Date; and if the Seller is unable to do so without fault, this contract shall terminate and Earnest Money shall be refunded.

15. DEFAULT: If Buyer fails to comply herewith, Seller may either enforce specific performance or terminate this contract and receive the Earnest Money as liquidated damages.

If Seller is unable without fault to deliver Abstract or Title Policy or to make any noncasualty repairs required herein within the time herein specified, Buyer may either terminate this contract and receive the Earnest Money as the sole remedy, or extend the time up to 30 days. If Seller fails to comply herewith for any other reason, Buyer may (i) terminate this contract and receive the Earnest Money, thereby releasing Seller from this contract, (ii) enforce specific performance hereof, or (iii) seek such other relief as may be provided by law.

16. ATTORNEY'S FEES: Any signatory to this contract who is the prevailing party in any legal proceeding against any other signatory brought under or with relation to this contract or transaction shall be additionally entitled to recover court costs and reasonable attorney fees from the nonprevailing party.

17. ESCROW: Earnest Money is deposited with Escrow Agent with the understanding that Escrow Agent (i) does not assume or have any liability for performance or nonperformance of any party, (ii) has the right to require the receipt, release and authorization in writing of all parties before paying the deposit to any party, and (iii) is not liable for interest or other charge on the funds held. If any party unreasonably fails to agree in writing to an appropriate release of Earnest Money, then such party shall be liable to the other parties to the extent provided in paragraph 16. At closing, Earnest Money shall be applied to any cash down payment required, next to Buyer's closing costs and any excess refunded to Buyer. Before Buyer shall be entitled to refund of Earnest Money, any actual and FHA allowable expenses incurred or paid on Buyer's behalf shall be deducted therefrom and paid to the creditors entitled thereto.

18. REPRESENTATIONS: Seller represents that there will be no Title I liens, unrecorded liens or Uniform Commercial Code liens against any of the Property on Closing Date. If any representation above is untrue this contract may be terminated by Buyer and the Earnest Money shall be refunded without delay. Representations shall survive closing.

19. AGREEMENT OF PARTIES: This contract contains the entire agreement of the parties and cannot be changed except by their written consent.

20. CONSULT YOUR ATTORNEY: This is intended to be a legally binding contract. READ IT CAREFULLY. If you do not understand the effect of any part, consult your attorney BEFORE signing. Attorneys to represent parties may be designated below.

Seller's Atty: _____   Buyer's Atty: _____

EXECUTED in multiple originals effective the _____ day of _____ , 19_____ .

_____   _____
Seller   Buyer

_____   _____
Seller   Buyer

_____   _____
Seller's Address   Buyer's Address

VA GUARANTEED LOAN—
RESIDENTIAL EARNEST-MONEY CONTRACT (RESALE)

1. PARTIES _____ (Seller) agrees to sell and convey to _____ (Buyer) and Buyer agrees to buy from Seller the following property situated in _____ County, _____ (State), known as _____ _____ (Address).

2. PROPERTY: Lot _____ Block _____ _____Addition, City of _____ , or as described on attached exhibit, together with the following fixtures, if any: curtain rods, drapery rods, venetian blinds, window shades, screens and shutters, awnings, wall-to-wall carpeting, mirrors fixed in place, attic fans, permanently installed heating and air-conditioning units and equipment, light and plumbing fixtures, TV antennas, mailboxes, water softeners, shrubbery and all other property owned by Seller and attached to the above described real property. All property sold by this contract is called "Property."

3. CONTRACT SALES PRICE:

   A. Cash down payment payable at closing ....$_____

   B. Note described in 4 below (the Note) in the amount of ....$_____

   C. Sales Price payable to Seller on Loan funding after closing (Sum of A and B) ....
   ....$_____

4. FINANCING CONDITIONS: This contract is subject to approval for Buyer of a VA loan (the Loan) of not less than the amount of the Note, amortizable monthly for not less than _____ years, with interest at maximum rate allowable at time of Loan funding. Buyer shall apply for the Loan within _____ days from the effective date of this contract and shall make every reasonable effort to obtain approval. If the Loan has not been approved by the Closing Date, this contract shall terminate and the Earnest Money shall be refunded to Buyer without delay. VA NOTICE TO BUYER: "It is expressly agreed that, notwithstanding any other provisions of this contract, the Buyer shall not incur any penalty by forfeiture of earnest money or otherwise or be obligated to complete the purchase of the Property described herein, if the contract purchase price or cost exceeds the reasonable value of the Property established by the Veterans Administration. The Buyer shall, however, have the privilege and option of proceeding with the consummation of this contract without regard to the amount of the reasonable value established by the Veterans Administration." Buyer agrees that should Buyer elect to complete the purchase at an amount in excess of the reasonable value established by VA, Buyer shall pay such excess amount in cash from a source which Buyer agrees to disclose to the VA and which Buyer represents will not be from borrowed funds except as approved by VA. If VA reasonable value of the Property is less than the Sales Price (3C above), Seller

may reduce the Sales Price to an amount equal to the VA reasonable value and both parties agree to close the sale at such lower Sales Price with appropriate adjustments to 3A and 3B above.

5. EARNEST MONEY: $—————————— is herewith tendered and is to be deposited as Earnest Money with ————————————————————— , as Escrow Agent, upon execution of the contract by both parties. Additional Earnest Money, if any, shall be deposited with the Escrow Agent on or before ————————————————— , 19———— , in the amount of $——————————.

6. TITLE: Seller at Seller's expense shall furnish either:

————A. Owner's Policy of Title Insurance (the Title Policy) issued by ——————————— ————————— in the amount of the Sales Price and dated at or after closing: OR

————B. Complete Abstract of Title (the Abstract) certified by ——————————— to current date.

NOTICE TO BUYER AS REQUIRED BY LAW, YOU should have the Abstract covering the Property examined by an attorney of YOUR selection, or YOU should be furnished with or obtain a Title Policy.

7. PROPERTY CONDITION [Check "A" or "B"]:

————A. Buyer accepts the Property in its present condition, subject only to VA required repairs and ——————————————————————————————————— —— .

————B. Buyer requires inspections and repairs required by the Property Condition Addendum (the Addendum) and those required by VA. Upon Seller's receipt of the Loan approval and inspection reports Seller shall commence and complete prior to closing all required repairs at Seller's expense.

All inspections, reports and repairs required of Seller by this contract and the Addendum shall not exceed $——————————— . If Seller fails to complete such requirements, Buyer may do so and Seller shall be liable up to the amount specified and the same paid from the proceeds of the sale. If such expenditures exceed the stated amount and Seller refuses to pay such excess, Buyer may pay the additional cost or accept the Property with the limited repairs and this sale shall be closed as scheduled, or Buyer may terminate this contract and the Earnest Money shall be refunded to Buyer.

8. CLOSING: The closing of the sale (the Closing Date) shall be on or before ——————————— , 19———— , or within 7 days after objections to title have been cured, whichever date is later; however, if necessary to complete Loan requirements, the Closing Date shall be extended daily up to 15 days.

9. POSSESSION: The possession of the Property shall be delivered to Buyer on ————————————————————— in its present or required improved condition, ordinary wear and

tear excepted. Any possession by Buyer prior to or by Seller after Closing Date shall establish a landlord tenant at sufferance relationship between the parties.

10. SPECIAL PROVISIONS:

[Insert terms and conditions of a factual nature applicable to this sale, e.g., prior purchase or sale of other property, lessee surrender of possession and the like.]

11. SALES EXPENSES TO BE PAID IN CASH AT OR PRIOR TO CLOSING:

A. Loan appraisal fees shall be paid by _____ .

B. Seller's Expenses:

(1) Seller's Loan discount points not exceeding _____ .

(2) VA required repairs and other inspections, reports and repairs required of Seller herein, and in the Addendum.

(3) Releases of existing loans, including prepayment penalties and recordation; escrow fee, tax statement, preparation of Deed, Note and Deed of Trust, expenses VA prohibits Buyer to pay (e.g., copies of restrictions, photos, excess cost of survey of Property), other expenses stipulated to be paid by Seller under other provisions of this contract.

C. Buyer's Expenses: Expenses incident to Loan (e.g., credit reports, recording fees, Mortgagee's Title Policy; Loan origination fee, that portion of survey cost Buyer can pay by VA regulation, Loan related inspection fees, premiums for 1 year's hazard insurance and any flood insurance, required reserve deposits for insurance premiums, ad valorem taxes and special assessments, interest from date of disbursement to 1 month prior to date of first monthly payment on the Note; premiums on nonrequired insurance, expenses stipulated to be paid by Buyer under other provisions of this contract.

D. If any sales expenses exceed the maximum amount herein stipulated to be paid by either party, either party may terminate this contract unless the other party agrees to pay such expenses. In no event shall Buyer pay charges and fees other than those expressly permitted by VA Regulations.

12. PRORATIONS: Insurance (at Buyer's option), taxes and any rents and maintenance fees shall be prorated to the Closing Date.

13. TITLE APPROVAL: If Abstract is furnished, Seller shall deliver same to Buyer within 20 days from the effective date hereof. Buyer shall have 20 days from date of receipt of Abstract to deliver a copy of the title opinion to Seller, stating any objections to title, and only objections so stated shall be considered. If Title Policy is furnished, the Title shall guarantee Buyer's title to be good and indefeasible subject only to (i) restrictive covenants affecting the Property, (ii) any discrepancies, conflicts or shortages in area or boundary lines or any encroachments, or any overlapping of improvements, (iii) all taxes for the current and subsequent years, (iv) any existing building and zoning ordinances, (v) rights of parties in possession, (vi) any liens created as security for the sale consideration, and (vii) any reservations or exceptions contained in the Deed. In either instance, if title objections are disclosed, Seller shall have 30 days to cure the same. Exceptions permitted in the Deed and zoning ordinances shall not be valid objections to title. Seller shall furnish at Seller's expense tax statements showing no delinquent taxes and a General Warranty Deed conveying title subject only to liens securing debt created as part of the consideration, taxes for the current year, usual restrictive covenants and utility easements common to the platted subdivision of which the Property is a part and any other reservations or exceptions acceptable to Buyer. The Note shall be secured by Vendor's and Deed of Trust liens. In case of dispute as to the form of Deed, such shall be upon a form prepared by the State Bar of _____ (State).

14. CASUALTY LOSS: If any part of Property is damaged or destroyed by fire or other casualty loss, Seller shall restore the same to its previous condition as soon as reasonably possible, but in any event by Closing Date, and if Seller is unable to do so without fault, this contract shall terminate and Earnest Money shall be refunded.

15. DEFAULT: If Buyer fails to comply herewith, Seller may either enforce specific performance or terminate this contract and receive the Earnest Money as liquidated damages.

If Seller is unable without fault to deliver Abstract or Title Policy or to make any noncasualty repairs required herein within the time herein specified, Buyer may either terminate this contract and receive the Earnest Money as the sole remedy, or extend the time up to 30 days. If Seller fails to comply herewith for any other reason, Buyer may (i) terminate this contract and receive the Earnest Money, thereby releasing Seller from this contract, (ii) enforce specific performance hereof, or (iii) seek such other relief as may be provided by law.

16. ATTORNEY'S FEES: Any signatory to this contract who is the prevailing party in any legal proceeding against any other signatory brought under or with relation to this contract or transaction shall be additionally entitled to recover court costs and reasonable attorney fees from the nonprevailing party.

17. ESCROW: Earnest Money is deposited with Escrow Agent with the understanding that Escrow Agent (i) does not have any liability for performance or nonperformance of any party, (ii) has the right to require the receipt, release and authorization in writing of all parties before paying the deposit to any party, and (iii) is not liable for interest or other charge on the funds held. If any party unreasonably fails to agree in writing to an appropriate release of Earnest Money, then such party shall be liable to the other parties to the extent provided in paragraph 16. At closing, Earnest Money shall be applied to any cash down payment required, next to Buyer's closing costs and any excess refunded to Buyer. Before Buyer shall be entitled to refund of Earnest Money, any actual and VA allowable expenses incurred or paid on Buyer's behalf shall be deducted therefrom and paid to the creditors entitled thereto.

18. REPRESENTATIONS: Seller represents that there will be no Title I liens, unrecorded liens or Uniform Commercial Code liens against any of the Property on Closing Date. If any representation above is untrue this contract may be terminated by Buyer and the Earnest Money shall be refunded without delay. Representations shall survive closing.

19. AGREEMENT OF PARTIES: This contract contains the entire agreement of the parties and cannot be changed except by their written consent.

20. CONSULT YOUR ATTORNEY: This is intended to be a legally binding contract. READ IT CAREFULLY. If you do not understand the effect of any part, consult your attorney BEFORE signing. Attorneys to represent parties may be designated below.

Seller's Atty: _____   Buyer's Atty: _____

EXECUTED in multiple originals effective the _____ day of _____ , 19_____ .

_____
Seller

_____
Seller

_____
Seller's Address

_____
Buyer

_____
Buyer

_____
Buyer's Address

ASSUMPTION OF LOAN—
RESIDENTIAL EARNEST-MONEY CONTRACT (RESALE)

1. PARTIES _____ (Seller) agrees to

   sell and convey to _____ (Buyer)

   and Buyer agrees to buy from Seller the following property situated in _____

   County, _____ (State), known as _____ (Address).

2. PROPERTY: Lot _____, Block _____, _____ Addition, City of

   _____, or as described on attached exhibit, together with the following

   fixtures, if any; curtain rods, drapery rods, venetian blinds, window shades, screens and shutters,

   awnings, wall-to-wall carpeting, mirrors fixed in place, attic fans, permanently installed heating and

   air-conditioning units and equipment, lighting and plumbing fixtures, TV antennas, mailboxes,

   water softener, shrubbery and all other property owned by Seller and attached to the above de-

   scribed real property. All property sold by this contract is called "Property."

3. CONTRACT SALES PRICE:

   A. _____ Exact _____ Approximate Cash down payment payable at closing ....

   ....$_____

   B. Buyer's assumption of the unpaid balance of a promissory note (the Note) payable in present

   monthly installments of $_____, including principal and interest and any reserve de-

   posits, with Buyer's first installment payable to _____

   _____ on _____, 19_____, in the assumed principal balance of

   which at closing (allowing for an agreed $250.00 variance) will be............$_____

   C. Any balance of Sales Price to be evidenced by a second lien note payable to [check (1) or (2)

   below]:

   _____ (1) Seller bearing interest at the rate of _____% per annum, in

   _____ lump sum on or before _____

   _____ principal and interest installments of $_____, or more per

   _____, with first installment payable on _____.

   _____ (2) Third Party in principal and interest installments not in excess of

   $_____ per month, and in the _____ Exact _____ Approximate

   (check "Approximate" only if A above and D below are "Exact") amount of ....

   ....$_____

   D. The _____ Exact _____ Approximate total Sales Price (Sum of A, B, and C above ....

   ....$_____

4. FINANCING CONDITIONS: If a Noteholder on assumption (i) requires Buyer to pay an assumption fee in excess of $_____ and Seller declines to pay such excess, (ii) raises the existing interest rate above _____%, or (iii) requires approval of Buyer or can accelerate the Note and Buyer does not receive from the Noteholder written approval and acceleration waiver prior to the Closing Date, Buyer may terminate this contract and the Earnest Money shall be refunded. Buyer shall apply for the approval and waiver under (iii) above within 7 days from the effective date hereof and shall make every reasonable effort to obtain the same.

5. EARNEST MONEY: $_____ is herewith tendered and is to be deposited as Earnest Money with _____ as Escrow Agent, upon execution of the contract by both parties. Additional Earnest Money, if any, shall be deposited with the Escrow Agent on or before _____, 19_____ in the amount of $_____.

6. TITLE: Seller at Seller's expense shall furnish either:

_____A. Owner's Policy of Title Insurance (the Title Policy) issued by _____ in the amount of the Sales Price and dated at or after closing:

OR

_____B. Complete Abstract of Title (the Abstract) certified by _____ to current date.

NOTICE TO BUYER AS REQUIRED BY LAW, YOU should have the Abstract covering the Property examined by an attorney of YOUR selection, or YOU should be furnished with or obtain a Title Policy.

7. PROPERTY CONDITION [Check "A" or "B"]:

_____A. Buyer accepts the Property in its present condition, subject only to _____

_____

_____B. Buyer requires inspections and repairs required by the Property Condition Addendum (the Addendum). Upon Seller's receipt of all loan approvals and inspection reports Seller shall commence and complete prior to closing all required repairs at Seller's expense.

All inspections, reports and repairs required of Seller by this contract and the Addendum shall not exceed $_____. If Seller fails to complete such requirements, Buyer may do so and Seller shall be liable up to the amount specified and the same paid from the proceeds of the sale. If such expenditures exceed the stated amount and Seller refuses to pay such excess, Buyer may pay the additional cost or accept the Property with limited repairs and this sale shall be closed as scheduled, or Buyer may terminate this contract and the Earnest Money shall be refunded.

8. CLOSING: The closing of the sale (the Closing Date) shall be on or before _____ 19_____, or within 7 days after objections to title have been cured, whichever date is later.

9. POSSESSION: The possession of the Property shall be delivered to Buyer on ——————— ————————————————— in its present or required improved condition, ordinary wear and tear excepted. Any possession by Buyer prior to or by Seller after Closing Date shall establish a landlord tenant at sufferance relationship between the parties.

10. SPECIAL PROVISIONS:

[Insert terms and conditions of a factual nature applicable to this sale, e.g., personal property included in sale (curtains, draperies, valances, etc.), prior purchase or sale of other property, lessee's surrender of possession, and the like.]

11. PRORATION: Taxes, insurance, rents, interest and maintenance fees, if any, ——————— SHALL ——————— SHALL NOT be prorated to the Closing Date. If these are not prorated, all funds held in reserve for payment of taxes, maintenance fees and insurance and the insurance policy shall be transferred to the Buyer by Seller without cost to Buyer.

12. SALES EXPENSES TO BE PAID IN CASH AT OR PRIOR TO CLOSING: Preparing Deed, preparing and recording Deed of Trust to Secure Assumption, all inspections, reports and repairs required of Seller herein and in the Addendum and ½ of escrow fee shall be Seller's expense. All other costs and expenses incurred in connection with this contract which are not recited herein to be the obligation of Seller, shall be the obligation of Buyer. Unless otherwise paid, before Buyer shall be entitled to refund of Earnest Money, any such costs and expenses shall be deducted therefrom and paid to the creditors entitled thereto. If any sales expenses exceed the maximum amount herein stipulated to be paid by either party, either party may terminate this contract unless the other party agrees to pay such excess.

13. TITLE APPROVAL: If Abstract is furnished, Seller shall deliver same to Buyer within 20 days from the effective date hereof. Buyer shall have 20 days from date of receipt of Abstract to deliver a copy of the title opinion to Seller, stating any objections to title, and only objections so stated shall be considered. If Title Policy is furnished, the Title shall guarantee Buyer's title to be good and indefeasible subject only to (i) restrictive covenants affecting the Property, (ii) any discrepancies, conflicts or shortages in area or boundary lines or any encroachments, or any overlapping of improvements, (iii) all taxes for the current and subsequent years, (iv) any existing building and zoning ordinances, (v) rights of parties in possession, (vi) any liens created as security for the sale consideration, and (vii) any reservations or exceptions contained in the Deed. In either instance, if title objections are disclosed, Seller shall have 30 days to cure the same. Exceptions permitted in the

Deed and zoning ordinances shall not be valid objections to title. Seller shall furnish at Seller's expense tax statements showing no delinquent taxes and a General Warranty Deed conveying title subject only to liens securing debt created as part of the consideration, taxes for the current year, usual restrictive covenants and utility easements common to the platted subdivision of which the Property is a part and any other reservations or exceptions acceptable to Buyer. Each note herein provided shall be secured by Vendor's and Deed of Trust liens. A Vendor's lien shall be retained and a Deed of Trust to Secure Assumption required, which shall be automatically released on execution and delivery of a release by Noteholder. In the case of dispute as to the form of Deed, Note(s) or Deed(s) of Trust, such shall be upon a form prepared by the State Bar of _____ (State).

14. CASUALTY LOSS: If any part of Property is damaged or destroyed by fire or other casualty loss, Seller shall restore the same to its previous condition as soon as reasonably possible, but in any event by Closing Date, and if Seller is unable to do so without fault, this contract shall terminate and Earnest Money shall be refunded.

15. DEFAULT: If Buyer fails to comply herewith, Seller may either enforce specific performance or terminate this contract and receive the Earnest Money as liquidated damages.

    If Seller is unable without fault to deliver Abstract or Title Policy or to make any noncasualty repairs required herein within the time herein specified, Buyer may either terminate this contract and receive the Earnest Money as the sole remedy, or extend the time up to 30 days. If Seller fails to comply herewith for any other reason, Buyer may (i) terminate this contract and receive the Earnest Money, thereby releasing Seller from this contract, (ii) enforce specific performance hereof, or (iii) seek such other relief as may be provided by law.

16. ATTORNEY'S FEES: Any signatory to this contract who is the prevailing party in any legal proceeding against any other signatory brought under or with relation to this contract or transaction shall be additionally entitled to recover court costs and reasonable attorney fees from the nonprevailing party.

17. ESCROW: Earnest Money is deposited with Escrow Agent with the understanding that Escrow Agent (i) does not have any liability for performance or nonperformance of any party, (ii) has the right to require the receipt, release and authorization in writing of all parties before paying the deposit to any party, and (iii) is not liable for interest or other charge on the funds held. If any party unreasonably fails to agree in writing to an appropriate release of Earnest Money, then such party shall be liable to the other parties to the extent provided in paragraph 16. At closing, Earnest Money shall be applied to any cash down payment required, next to Buyer's closing costs and any excess refunded to Buyer. Before Buyer shall be entitled to refund of Earnest Money, any actual expenses incurred or paid on Buyer's behalf shall be deducted therefrom and paid to the creditors entitled thereto.

18. REPRESENTATIONS: Seller represents that unless securing payment of the Note there will be no Title I liens, unrecorded liens or Uniform Commercial Code liens against any of the Property on Closing Date, that loan(s) will be without default, and reserve deposits will not be deficient. If any representation above is untrue this contract may be terminated by Buyer and the Earnest Money shall be refunded without delay. Representations shall survive closing.

19. THIRD PARTY FINANCING: If financing by Third Party under 3C(2) above is required herein, Buyer shall have 15 days from effective date hereof to obtain the same, and failure to secure the same after reasonable effort shall render this contract null and void, and the Earnest Money refunded without delay.

20. AGREEMENT OF PARTIES: This contract contains the entire agreement of the parties and cannot be changed except by their written consent.

21. CONSULT YOUR ATTORNEY: This is intended to be a legally binding contract. READ IT CARE-FULLY. If you do not understand the effect of any part, consult your attorney BEFORE signing. Attorneys to represent parties may be designated below.

_____
Seller's Atty:

_____
Seller

_____
Seller

_____
Seller's Address

_____
Buyer's Atty:

_____
Buyer

_____
Buyer

_____
Buyer's Address

CONTRACT FOR DEED
ALL CASH OR OWNER FINANCED—RESIDENTIAL EARNEST-MONEY CONTRACT
(RESALE)

1. PARTIES ——————————————————————————— (Seller) agrees to

   sell and convey to ————————————————————————— (Buyer)

   and Buyer agrees to buy from Seller the following property situated in ——————

   County, ———— (State), known as —————————————————

   ———————— (Address).

2. PROPERTY: Lot ——————, Block ——————, ——————— Addition, City

   of ——————————————, or as described on attached exhibit, together with the follow-

   ing fixtures, if any; curtain rods, drapery rods, venetian blinds, window shades, screens and shut-

   ters, awnings, wall-to-wall carpeting, mirrors fixed in place, attic fans, permanently installed heat-

   ing and air-conditioning units and equipment, lighting and plumbing fixtures, TV antennas,

   mailboxes, water softeners, shrubbery and all other property owned by Seller and attached to the

   above described real property. All property sold by this contract is called "Property."

3. CONTRACT SALES PRICE:

   A. Cash down payment payable at closing ....$————

   B. Note described in 4B below (the Note) ....$————

   C. Sales Price payable to Seller (Sum of A and B) ....$————

4. FINANCING CONDITIONS:

   ————A. This is an all cash sale; no financing is involved.

   ————B. The Note in the principal sum shown in 3B above, dated as of the Closing Date, to be

   executed and delivered by Buyer and payable to the order of Seller, bearing interest at

   the rate of ———— percent per annum from date thereof until maturity, matured un-

   paid principal and interest to bear interest at the rate of 10% per annum, principal and

   interest to be due and payable

   ————(1) In —————— installments of $—————— or more each, be-

   ginning on or before ————————— after date of the Note, and

   [Check "a" or "b"]

   ————a. continuing regularly and at the same intervals thereafter until

   fully paid.

   ————b. continuing regularly and at the same intervals thereafter until

   ———————— 19————, when the entire balance of princi-

   pal and accrued interest shall be due and payable.

_____(2) In a lump sum on or before _____ after date of the Note.

_____C. This contract is subject to Buyer furnishing Seller evidence that Buyer has a history of good credit.

5. EARNEST MONEY: $_____ is herewith tendered and is to be deposited as Earnest Money with _____ as Escrow Agent, upon execution of the contract by both parties. Additional Earnest Money, if any, shall be deposited with the Escrow Agent on or before _____, 19_____ in the amount of $_____.

6. TITLE: Seller at Seller's expense shall furnish either:

_____A. Owner's Policy of Title Insurance (the Title Policy) issued by _____ _____ in the amount of the Sales Price and dated at or after closing:

OR

_____B. Complete Abstract of Title (the Abstract) certified by _____ _____ to current date.

NOTICE TO BUYER AS REQUIRED BY LAW, YOU should have the Abstract covering the Property examined by an attorney of YOUR selection, or YOU should be furnished with or obtain a Title Policy.

7. PROPERTY CONDITION [Check "A" or "B"]:

_____A. Buyer accepts the Property in its present condition, subject only to _____ _____

_____B. Buyer requires inspections and repairs required by the Property Condition Addendum (the Addendum). Seller shall commence and complete prior to closing all required repairs at Seller's expense.

All inspections, reports and repairs required of Seller by this contract and the Addendum shall not exceed $_____. If Seller fails to complete such requirements, Buyer may do so and Seller shall be liable up to the amount specified and the same paid from the proceeds of the sale. If such expenditures exceed the stated amount and Seller refuses to pay such excess, Buyer may pay the additional cost or accept the Property with limited repairs and this sale shall be closed as scheduled, or Buyer may terminate this contract and the Earnest Money shall be refunded to Buyer.

8. CLOSING: The closing of the sale (the Closing Date) shall be on or before _____ 19_____, or within 7 days after objections to title have been cured, whichever date is later.

9. POSSESSION: The possession of the Property shall be delivered to Buyer on _____ _____ in its present or required improved condition, ordinary wear and tear excepted. Any possession by Buyer prior to or by Seller after Closing Date shall establish a landlord tenant at sufferance relationship between the parties.

10. SPECIAL PROVISIONS:

[Insert terms and conditions of a factual nature applicable to this sale, e.g., personal property included in sale (curtains, draperies, valances, etc.), prior purchase or sale of other property, lessee's surrender of possession and the like.]

11. SALES EXPENSES TO BE PAID IN CASH AT OR PRIOR TO CLOSING:

   A. Seller's Expenses:

   (1) Any inspections, reports and repairs required of Seller herein, and in the Addendum.

   (2) All cost of releasing existing loans and recording the releases; tax statements, ½ of any escrow fees, preparation of Deed, copies of restrictions and easements, other expenses to be paid by Seller under other provisions of this contract.

   B. Buyer's Expenses: All expenses incident to any loan (e.g., preparation of Note, Deed of Trust and other loan documents, recording fees, Mortgagee's Title Policy, credit reports, ½ of any escrow fee, one year premium for hazard insurance unless insurance is prorated, and expenses stipulated to be paid by Buyer under other provisions of this contract.

   C. If any sales expenses exceed the maximum amount herein stipulated to be paid by either party, either party may terminate this contract unless the other party agrees to pay such excess.

12. PRORATIONS: Insurance (at Buyer's option), taxes and any rents and maintenance fees shall be prorated to the Closing Date.

13. TITLE APPROVAL: If Abstract is furnished, Seller shall deliver same to Buyer within 20 days from the effective date hereof. Buyer shall have 20 days from date of receipt of Abstract to deliver a copy of the title opinion to Seller, stating any objections to title, and only objections so stated shall be considered. If Title Policy is furnished, the Title shall guarantee Buyer's title to be good and indefeasible subject only to (i) restrictive covenants affecting the Property, (ii) any discrepancies, conflicts or shortages in area or boundary lines or any encroachments, or any overlapping of improvements, (iii) all taxes for the current and subsequent years, (iv) any existing building and zoning ordinances, (v) rights of parties in possession, (vi) any liens created as security for the sale consid-

eration, and (vii) any reservations or exceptions contained in the Deed. In either instance, if title objections are disclosed, Seller shall have 30 days to cure the same. Exceptions permitted in the Deed and zoning ordinances shall not be valid objections to title. Seller shall furnish at Seller's expense tax statements showing no delinquent taxes and a General Warranty Deed conveying title subject only to liens securing debt created as part of the consideration, taxes for the current year, usual restrictive covenants and utility easements common to the platted subdivision of which the Property is a part and any other reservations or exceptions acceptable to Buyer. The Note shall be secured by Vendor's and Deed of Trust liens. In case of dispute as to the form of Deed, Deed of Trust or Note, such shall be upon a form prepared by the State Bar of ———————— (State).

14. CASUALTY LOSS: If any part of Property is damaged or destroyed by fire or other casualty loss, Seller shall restore the same to its previous condition as soon as reasonably possible, but in any event by Closing Date, and if Seller is unable to do so without fault, this contract shall terminate and Earnest Money shall be refunded.

15. DEFAULT: If Buyer fails to comply herewith, Seller may either enforce specific performance or terminate this contract and receive the Earnest Money as liquidated damages.

If Seller is unable without fault to deliver Abstract or Title Policy or to make any noncasualty repairs required herein within the time herein specified, Buyer may either terminate this contract and receive the Earnest Money as the sole remedy, or extend the time up to 30 days. If Seller fails to comply herewith for any other reason, Buyer may (i) terminate this contract and receive the Earnest Money, thereby releasing Seller from this contract, (ii) enforce specific performance hereof, or (iii) seek such other relief as may be provided by law.

16. ATTORNEY'S FEES: Any signatory to this contract who is the prevailing party in any legal proceeding against any other signatory brought under or with relation to this contract or transaction shall be additionally entitled to recover court costs and reasonable attorney fees from the nonprevailing party.

17. ESCROW: Earnest Money is deposited with Escrow Agent with the understanding that Escrow Agent (i) does not have any liability for performance or nonperformance of any party, (ii) has the right to require the receipt, release and authorization in writing of all parties before paying the deposit to any party, and (iii) is not liable for interest or other charge on the funds held. If any party unreasonably fails to agree in writing to an appropriate release of Earnest Money, then such party shall be liable to the other parties to the extent provided in paragraph 16. At closing, Earnest Money shall be applied to any cash down payment required, next to Buyer's closing costs and any excess refunded to Buyer. Before Buyer shall be entitled to refund of Earnest Money, any actual expenses incurred or paid on Buyer's behalf shall be deducted therefrom and paid to the creditors entitled thereto.

18. REPRESENTATIONS: Seller represents that there will be no Title I liens, unrecorded liens or Uniform Commercial Code liens against any of the Property on Closing Date. If any representation above is untrue this contract may be terminated by Buyer and the Earnest Money shall be refunded without delay. Representations shall survive closing.

19. AGREEMENT OF PARTIES: This contract contains the entire agreement of the parties and cannot be changed except by their written consent.

20. CONSULT YOUR ATTORNEY: This is intended to be a legally binding contract. READ IT CAREFULLY. If you do not understand the effect of any part, consult your attorney BEFORE signing. Attorneys to represent parties may be designated below.

Seller's Atty: _____   Buyer's Atty: _____

EXECUTED in multiple originals effective the _____ day of _____, 19_____.

_____   _____
Seller   Buyer

_____   _____
Seller   Buyer

_____   _____
Seller's Address   Buyer's Address

SECOND MORTGAGE IN CONTRACT—
RESIDENTIAL EARNEST-MONEY CONTRACT (RESALE)

1. PARTIES —————————————————————————— (Seller) agrees to

   sell and convey to ———————————————————————— (Buyer)

   and Buyer agrees to buy from Seller the following property situated in —————————

   County, ————— (State), known as ———————————————————————

   ———————————————————————————— (Address).

2. PROPERTY: Lot ——————— , Block ——————— , ——————— Addition, City of

   ——————————————————— , or as described on attached exhibit, together with the following

   fixtures, if any; curtain rods, drapery rods, venetian blinds, window shades, screens and shutters,

   awnings, wall-to-wall carpeting, mirrors fixed in place, attic fans, permanently installed heating and

   air-conditioning units and equipment, lighting and plumbing fixtures, TV antennas, mailboxes,

   water softener, shrubbery and all other property owned by Seller and attached to the above de-

   scribed real property. All property sold by this contract is called "Property."

3. CONTRACT SALES PRICE:

   A. ——— Exact ——— Approximate Cash down payment payable at closing ....

   ....$————

   B. Buyer's assumption of the unpaid balance of a promissory note (the Note) payable in present

   monthly installments of $——————— , including principal and interest and any reserve

   deposits, with Buyer's first installment payable to ———————————————————

   ——————————— on ——————— , 19——— , in the assumed principal balance

   of which at closing (allowing for an agreed $250 variance) will be ....$————

   C. Any balance of Sales Price to be evidenced by a second lien note payable to [check (1) or (2)

   below]:

   ———(1) Seller bearing interest at the rate of ———% per annum, in

   ———lump sum on or before ———————————————

   ———principal and interest installments of $——————— , or more per

   ———————————————————— , with first installment payable on

   ——————————————— .

   ———(2) Third Party in principal and interest installments not in excess of

   $——————— per month and in the ——— Exact ——— Approximate

   (check "Approximate" only if A above and D below are "Exact") amount of ....

   ....$————

   D. The ——— Exact ——— Approximate total Sales Price (Sum of A, B, and C above) ....

   ....$————

4. FINANCING CONDITIONS: If a Noteholder on assumption (i) requires Buyer to pay an assumption fee in excess of $_____ and Seller declines to pay such excess, (ii) raises the existing interest rate above _____%, or (iii) requires approval of Buyer or can accelerate the Note and Buyer does not receive from the Noteholder written approval and acceleration waiver prior to the Closing Date, Buyer may terminate this contract and the Earnest Money shall be refunded. Buyer shall apply for the approval and waiver under (iii) above within 7 days from the effective date hereof and shall make every reasonable effort to obtain the same.

5. EARNEST MONEY: $_____ is herewith tendered and is to be deposited as Earnest Money with _____ as Escrow Agent, upon execution of the contract by both parties. Additional Earnest Money, if any, shall be deposited with the Escrow Agent on or before _____ , 19_____ in the amount of $_____ .

6. TITLE: Seller at Seller's expense shall furnish either:

_____A. Owner's Policy of Title Insurance (the Title Policy) issued by _____

_____ in the amount of the Sales Price and dated at or after closing:

OR

_____B. Complete Abstract of Title (the Abstract) certified by _____

_____ to current date.

NOTICE TO BUYER AS REQUIRED BY LAW, YOU should have the Abstract covering the Property examined by an attorney of YOUR selection, or YOU should be furnished with or obtain a Title Policy.

7. PROPERTY CONDITION [Check "A" or "B"]:

_____A. Buyer accepts the Property in its present condition, subject only to _____

_____

_____B. Buyer requires inspections and repairs required by the Property Condition Addendum (the Addendum). Upon Seller's receipt of all loan approvals and inspection reports Seller shall commence and complete prior to closing all required repairs at Seller's expense.

All inspections, reports and repairs required of Seller by this contract and the Addendum shall not exceed $_____ . If Seller fails to complete such requirements, Buyer may do so and Seller shall be liable up to the amount specified and the same paid from the proceeds of the sale. If such expenditures exceed the stated amount and Seller refuses to pay such excess, Buyer may pay the additional cost or accept the Property with limited repairs and this sale shall be closed as scheduled, or Buyer may terminate this contract and the Earnest Money shall be refunded.

8. CLOSING: The closing of the sale (the Closing Date) shall be on or before _____ 19_____ , or within 7 days after objections to title have been cured, whichever date is later.

9. POSSESSION: The possession of the Property shall be delivered to Buyer on —————————————————————————— in its present or required improved condition, ordinary wear and tear excepted. Any possession by Buyer prior to or by Seller after Closing Date shall establish a landlord tenant at sufferance relationship between the parties.

10. SPECIAL PROVISIONS:

[Insert terms and conditions of a factual nature applicable to this sale, e.g., personal property included in sale (curtains, draperies, valances, etc.), prior purchase or sale of other property, lessee's surrender of possession, and the like.]

11. PRORATION: Taxes, insurance, rents, interest and maintenance fees, if any, ————SHALL ————SHALL NOT be prorated to the Closing Date. If these are not prorated, all funds held in reserve for payment of taxes, maintenance fees and insurance and the insurance policy shall be transferred to the Buyer by Seller without cost to Buyer.

12. SALES EXPENSES TO BE PAID IN CASH AT OR PRIOR TO CLOSING: Preparing Deed, preparing and recording Deed of Trust to Secure Assumption, all inspections, reports and repairs required of Seller herein and in the Addendum and ½ of escrow fee shall be Seller's expense. All other costs and expenses incurred in connection with this contract which are not recited herein to be the obligation of Seller, shall be the obligation of Buyer. Unless otherwise paid, before Buyer shall be entitled to refund of Earnest Money, any such costs and expenses shall be deducted therefrom and paid to the creditors entitled thereto. If any sales expenses exceed the maximum amount herein stipulated to be paid by either party, either party may terminate this contract unless the other party agrees to pay such excess.

13. TITLE APPROVAL: If Abstract is furnished, Seller shall deliver same to Buyer within 20 days from the effective date hereof. Buyer shall have 20 days from date of receipt of Abstract to deliver a copy of the title opinion to Seller, stating any objections to title, and only objections so stated shall be considered. If Title Policy is furnished, the Title shall guarantee Buyer's title to be good and indefeasible subject only to (i) restrictive covenants affecting the Property, (ii) any discrepancies, conflicts or shortages in area or boundary lines or any encroachments, or any overlapping of improve-

ments, (iii) all taxes for the current and subsequent years, (iv) any existing building and zoning ordinances, (v) rights of parties in possession, (vi) any liens created as security for the sale consideration, and (vii) any reservations or exceptions contained in the Deed. In either instance, if title objections are disclosed, Seller shall have 30 days to cure the same. Exceptions permitted in the Deed and zoning ordinances shall not be valid objections to title. Seller shall furnish at Seller's expense tax statements showing no delinquent taxes and a General Warranty Deed conveying title subject only to liens securing debt created as part of the consideration, taxes for the current year, usual restrictive covenants and utility easements common to the platted subdivision of which the Property is a part and any other reservations or exceptions acceptable to Buyer. Each note herein provided shall be secured by Vendor's and Deed of Trust liens. A Vendor's lien shall be retained and a Deed of Trust to Secure Assumption required, which shall be automatically released on execution and delivery of a release by Noteholder. In the case of dispute as to the form of Deed, Note(s) or Deed(s) of Trust, such shall be upon a form prepared by the State Bar of _____ (State).

14. CASUALTY LOSS: If any part of Property is damaged or destroyed by fire or other casualty loss, Seller shall restore the same to its previous condition as soon as reasonably possible, but in any event by Closing Date, and if Seller is unable to do so without fault, this contract shall terminate and Earnest Money shall be refunded.

15. DEFAULT: If Buyer fails to comply herewith, Seller may either enforce specific performance or terminate this contract and receive the Earnest Money as liquidated damages.

   If Seller is unable without fault to deliver Abstract or Title Policy or to make any noncasualty repairs required herein within the time herein specified, Buyer may either terminate this contract and receive the Earnest Money as the sole remedy, or extend the time up to 30 days. If Seller fails to comply herewith for any other reason, Buyer may (i) terminate this contract and receive the Earnest Money, thereby releasing Seller from this contract, (ii) enforce specific performance hereof, or (iii) seek such other relief as may be provided by law.

16. ATTORNEY'S FEES: Any signatory to this contract who is the prevailing party in any legal proceeding against any other signatory brought under or with relation to this contract or transaction shall be additionally entitled to recover court costs and reasonable attorney fees from the nonprevailing party.

17. ESCROW: Earnest Money is deposited with Escrow Agent with the understanding that Escrow Agent (i) does not have any liability for performance or nonperformance of any party, (ii) has the right to require the receipt, release and authorization in writing of all parties before paying the deposit to any party, and (iii) is not liable for interest or other charge on the funds held. If any party unreasonably fails to agree in writing to an appropriate release of Earnest Money, then such party shall be liable to the other parties to the extent provided in paragraph 16. At closing, Earnest Money shall

be applied to any cash down payment required, next to Buyer's closing costs and any excess refunded to Buyer. Before Buyer shall be entitled to refund of Earnest Money, any actual expenses incurred or paid on Buyer's behalf shall be deducted therefrom and paid to the creditors entitled thereto.

18. REPRESENTATIONS: Seller represents that unless securing payment of the Note there will be no Title I liens, unrecorded liens or Uniform Commercial Code liens against any of the Property on Closing Date, that loan(s) will be without default, and reserve deposits will not be deficient. If any representation above is untrue this contract may be terminated by Buyer and the Earnest Money shall be refunded without delay. Representations shall survive closing.

19. THIRD PARTY FINANCING: If financing by Third Party under 3C(2) above is required herein, Buyer shall have 15 days from effective date hereof to obtain the same, and failure to secure the same after reasonable effort shall render this contract null and void, and the Earnest Money refunded without delay.

20. AGREEMENT OF PARTIES: This contract contains the entire agreement of the parties and cannot be changed except by their written consent.

21. CONSULT YOUR ATTORNEY: This is intended to be a legally binding contract. READ IT CAREFULLY. If you do not understand the effect of any part, consult your attorney BEFORE signing.
    Attorneys to represent parties may be designated below.

Seller's Atty: _____   Buyer's Atty: _____

EXECUTED in multiple originals effective the _____ day of _____, 19_____.

Seller _____   Buyer _____

Seller _____   Buyer _____

Seller's Address   Buyer's Address

ALL CASH OR OWNER FINANCED—
RESIDENTIAL EARNEST-MONEY CONTRACT
(RESALE)

1. PARTIES _____ (Seller) agrees to

   sell and convey to _____ (Buyer)

   and Buyer agrees to buy from Seller the following property situated in _____

   County, _____ (State), known as _____

   _____ (Address).

2. PROPERTY: Lot _____ , Block _____ , _____ Addition, City of

   _____ , or as described on attached exhibit, together with the following

   fixtures, if any; curtain rods, drapery rods, venetian blinds, window shades, screens and shutters,

   awnings, wall-to-wall carpeting, mirrors fixed in place, attic fans, permanently installed heating and

   air-conditioning units and equipment, lighting and plumbing fixtures, TV antennas, mailboxes,

   water softeners, shrubbery and all other property owned by Seller and attached to the above de-

   scribed real property. All property sold by this contract is called "Property."

3. CONTRACT SALES PRICE:

   A. Cash down payment payable at closing ....$_____

   B. Note described in 4B below (the Note) ....$_____

   C. Sales Price payable to Seller (Sum of A and B) ....$_____

4. FINANCING CONDITIONS:

   _____A. This is an all cash sale; no financing is involved.

   _____B. The Note in the principal sum shown in 3B above, dated as of the Closing Date, to be

   executed and delivered by Buyer and payable to the order of Seller, bearing interest at

   the rate of _____ percent per annum from date thereof until maturity, matured un-

   paid principal and interest to bear interest at the rate of 10% per annum, principal and

   interest to be due and payable

   _____(1) In _____ installments of $_____ or more each, be-

   ginning on or before _____ after date of the Note, and

   [Check "a" or "b"]

   _____a. continuing regularly and at the same intervals thereafter until

   fully paid.

   _____b. continuing regularly and at the same intervals thereafter until

   _____ 19_____ , when the entire balance of princi-

   pal and accrued interest shall be due and payable.

_____(2) In a lump sum on or before _____ after date of the
Note.

_____C. This contract is subject to Buyer furnishing Seller evidence that Buyer has a history of
good credit.

5. EARNEST MONEY: $_____ is herewith tendered and is to be deposited as Earnest
Money with _____ as Escrow Agent, upon execution of the con-
tract by both parties. Additional Earnest Money, if any, shall be deposited with the Escrow Agent on
or before _____ , 19_____ in the amount of $_____ .

6. TITLE: Seller at Seller's expense shall furnish either:

_____A. Owner's Policy of Title Insurance (the Title Policy) issued by _____
_____ in the amount of the Sales Price and dated at or after closing:

OR

_____B. Complete Abstract of Title (the Abstract) certified by _____
_____ to current date.

NOTICE TO BUYER AS REQUIRED BY LAW, YOU should have the Abstract covering the Property
examined by an attorney of YOUR selection, or YOU should be furnished with or obtain a Title Policy.

7. PROPERTY CONDITION [Check ''A'' or ''B'']:

_____A. Buyer accepts the Property in its present condition, subject only to _____
_____

_____B. Buyer requires inspections and repairs required by the Property Condition Addendum
(the Addendum). Seller shall commence and complete prior to closing all required repairs at Seller's expense.

All inspections, reports and repairs required of Seller by this contract and the Addendum shall not
exceed $_____ . If Seller fails to complete such requirements, Buyer may do so and
Seller shall be liable up to the amount specified and the same paid from the proceeds of the sale. If
such expenditures exceed the stated amount and Seller refuses to pay such excess, Buyer may pay
the additional cost or accept the Property with limited repairs and this sale shall be closed as sched-
uled, or Buyer may terminate this contract and the Earnest Money shall be refunded to Buyer.

8. CLOSING: The closing of the sale (the Closing Date) shall be on or before _____
19_____ , or within 7 days after objections to title have been cured, whichever date is later.

9. POSSESSION: The possession of the Property shall be delivered to Buyer on
_____ in its present or required improved condition, ordinary wear and tear
excepted. Any possession by Buyer prior to or by Seller after Closing Date shall establish a landlord
tenant at sufferance relationship between the parties.

10. SPECIAL PROVISIONS:

[Insert terms and conditions of a factual nature applicable to this sale, e.g., personal property included in sale (curtains, draperies, valances, etc.), prior purchases or sale of other property, lessee's surrender of possession and the like.]

11. SALES EXPENSES TO BE PAID IN CASH AT OR PRIOR TO CLOSING:

A. Seller's Expenses:

(1) Any inspections, reports and repairs required of Seller herein, and in the Addendum.

(2) All cost of releasing existing loans and recording the releases; tax statements, ½ of any escrow fees, preparation of Deed, copies of restrictions and easements, other expenses to be paid by Seller under other provisions of this contract.

B. Buyer's Expenses: All expenses incident to any loan (e.g., preparation of Note, Deed of Trust and other loan documents, recording fees, Mortgagee's Title Policy, credit reports, ½ of any escrow fee, one year premium for hazard insurance unless insurance is prorated, and expenses stipulated to be paid by Buyer under other provisions of this contract.

C. If any sales expenses exceed the maximum amount herein stipulated to be paid by either party, either party may terminate this contract unless the other party agrees to pay such excess.

12. PRORATIONS: Insurance (at Buyer's option), taxes and any rents and maintenance fees shall be prorated to the Closing Date.

13. TITLE APPROVAL: If Abstract is furnished, Seller shall deliver same to Buyer within 20 days from the effective date hereof. Buyer shall have 20 days from date of receipt of Abstract to deliver a copy of the title opinion to Seller, stating any objections to title, and only objections so stated shall be considered. If Title Policy is furnished, the Title shall guarantee Buyer's title to be good and indefeasible subject only to (i) restrictive covenants affecting the Property, (ii) any discrepancies, conflicts or shortages in area or boundary lines or any encroachments, or any overlapping of improvements, (iii) all taxes for the current and subsequent years, (iv) any existing building and zoning

ordinances, (v) rights of parties in possession, (vi) any liens created as security for the sale consideration, and (vii) any reservations or exceptions contained in the Deed. In either instance, if title objections are disclosed, Seller shall have 30 days to cure the same. Exceptions permitted in the Deed and zoning ordinances shall not be valid objections to title. Seller shall furnish at Seller's expense tax statements showing no delinquent taxes and a General Warranty Deed conveying title subject only to liens securing debt created as part of the consideration, taxes for the current year, usual restrictive covenants and utility easements common to the platted subdivision of which the Property is a part and any other reservations or exceptions acceptable to Buyer. The Note shall be secured by Vendor's and Deed of Trust liens. In case of dispute as to the form of Deed, Deed of Trust or Note, such shall be upon a form prepared by the State Bar of ——————— (State).

14. CASUALTY LOSS: If any part of Property is damaged or destroyed by fire or other casualty loss, Seller shall restore the same to its previous condition as soon as reasonably possible, but in any event by Closing Date, and if Seller is unable to do so without fault, this contract shall terminate and Earnest Money shall be refunded.

15. DEFAULT: If Buyer fails to comply herewith, Seller may either enforce specific performance or terminate this contract and receive the Earnest Money as liquidated damages.

   If Seller is unable without fault to deliver Abstract or Title Policy or to make any noncasualty repairs required herein within the time herein specified, Buyer may either terminate this contract and receive the Earnest Money as the sole remedy, or extend the time up to 30 days. If Seller fails to comply herewith for any other reason, Buyer may (i) terminate this contract and receive the Earnest Money, thereby releasing Seller from this contract, (ii) enforce specific performance hereof, or (iii) seek such other relief as may be provided by law.

16. ATTORNEY'S FEES: Any signatory to this contract who is the prevailing party in any legal proceeding against any other signatory brought under or with relation to this contract or transaction shall be additionally entitled to recover court costs and reasonable attorney fees from the nonprevailing party.

17. ESCROW: Earnest Money is deposited with Escrow Agent with the understanding that Escrow Agent (i) does not have any liability for performance or nonperformance of any party, (ii) has the right to require the receipt, release and authorization in writing of all parties before paying the deposit to any party, and (iii) is not liable for interest or other charge on the funds held. If any party unreasonably fails to agree in writing to an appropriate release of Earnest Money, then such party shall be liable to the other parties to the extent provided in paragraph 16. At closing, Earnest Money shall be applied to any cash down payment required, next to Buyer's closing costs and any excess refunded to Buyer. Before Buyer shall be entitled to refund of Earnest Money, any actual expenses incurred or paid on Buyer's behalf shall be deducted therefrom and paid to the creditors entitled thereto.

18. REPRESENTATIONS: Seller represents that there will be no Title I liens, unrecorded liens or Uniform Commercial Code liens against any of the Property on Closing Date. If any representation above is untrue this contract may be terminated by Buyer and the Earnest Money shall be refunded without delay. Representations shall survive closing.

19. AGREEMENT OF PARTIES: This contract contains the entire agreement of the parties and cannot be changed except by their written consent.

20. CONSULT YOUR ATTORNEY: This is intended to be a legally binding contract. READ IT CARE-FULLY. If you do not understand the effect of any part, consult your attorney BEFORE signing. Attorneys to represent parties may be designated below.

Seller's Atty: _____   Buyer's Atty: _____

EXECUTED in multiple originals effective the _____ day of _____ , 19_____ .

_____   _____
Seller   Buyer

_____   _____
Seller   Buyer

_____   _____
Seller's Address   Buyer's Address

WRAPAROUND MORTGAGE
ALL CASH OR OWNER FINANCED—RESIDENTIAL EARNEST-MONEY CONTRACT
(RESALE)

1. PARTIES _____ (Seller) agrees to

sell and convey to _____ (Buyer)

and Buyer agrees to buy from Seller the following property situated in _____

County, _____ (State), known as _____

_____ (Address).

2. PROPERTY: Lot _____, Block _____, _____ Addition, City of

_____, or as described on attached exhibit, together with the following

fixtures, if any; curtain rods, drapery rods, venetian blinds, window shades, screens and shutters,

awnings, wall-to-wall carpeting, mirrors fixed in place, attic fans, permanently installed heating and

air-conditioning units and equipment, lighting and plumbing fixtures, TV antennas, mailboxes,

water softeners, shrubbery and all other property owned by Seller and attached to the above de-

scribed real property. All property sold by this contract is called "Property."

3. CONTRACT SALES PRICE:

   A. Cash down payment payable at closing .... $_____

   B. Note described in 4B below (the Note) .... $_____

   C. Sales Price payable to Seller (Sum of A and B) .... $_____

4. FINANCING CONDITIONS:

   _____A. This is an all cash sale; no financing is involved.

   _____B. The Note in the principal sum shown in 3B above, dated as of the Closing Date, to be

   executed and delivered by Buyer and payable to the order of Seller, bearing interest at

   the rate of _____ percent per annum from date thereof until maturity, matured un-

   paid principal and interest to bear interest at the rate of 10% per annum, principal and

   interest to be due and payable

   _____(1) In _____ installments of $_____ or more

   each, beginning on or before _____ after date of the

   Note, and [Check "a" or "b"]

   _____a. continuing regularly and at the same intervals thereafter until

   fully paid.

   _____b. continuing regularly and at the same intervals thereafter until

   _____ 19_____, when the entire balance of princi-

   pal and accrued interest shall be due and payable.

————(2) In a lump sum on or before ———————————— after date of the Note.

————C. This contract is subject to Buyer furnishing Seller evidence that Buyer has a history of good credit.

5. EARNEST MONEY: $———————— is herewith tendered and is to be deposited as Earnest Money with ———————————————————— as Escrow Agent, upon execution of the contract by both parties. Additional Earnest Money, if any, shall be deposited with the Escrow Agent on or before ———————— , 19———— in the amount of $———————— .

6. TITLE: Seller at Seller's expense shall furnish either:

————A. Owner's Policy of Title Insurance (the Title Policy) issued by ————————————— ————————————— in the amount of the Sales Price and dated at or after closing:

OR

————B. Complete Abstract of Title (the Abstract) certified by ————————————— ————————————— to current date.

NOTICE TO BUYER AS REQUIRED BY LAW, YOU should have the Abstract covering the Property examined by an attorney of YOUR selection, or YOU should be furnished with or obtain a Title Policy.

7. PROPERTY CONDITION [Check "A" or "B"]:

————A. Buyer accepts the Property in its present condition, subject only to ————————————— —————————————

————B. Buyer requires inspections and repairs required by the Property Condition Addendum (the Addendum). Seller shall commence and complete prior to closing all required repairs at Seller's expense.

All inspections, reports and repairs required of Seller by this contract and the Addendum shall not exceed $———————— . If Seller fails to complete such requirements, Buyer may do so and Seller shall be liable up to the amount specified and the same paid from the proceeds of the sale. If such expenditures exceed the stated amount and Seller refuses to pay such excess, Buyer may pay the additional cost or accept the Property with limited repairs and this sale shall be closed as scheduled, or Buyer may terminate this contract and the Earnest Money shall be refunded to Buyer.

8. CLOSING: The closing of the sale (the Closing Date) shall be on or before ———————— 19———— , or within 7 days after objections to title have been cured, whichever date is later.

9. POSSESSION: The possession of the Property shall be delivered to Buyer on ————————————— in its present or required improved condition, ordinary wear and tear excepted. Any possession by Buyer prior to or by Seller after Closing Date shall establish a landlord tenant at sufferance relationship between the parties.

10. SPECIAL PROVISIONS:

[Insert terms and conditions of a factual nature applicable to this sale, e.g., personal property included in sale (curtains, draperies, valances, etc.), prior purchase or sale of other property, lessee's surrender of possession and the like.]

11. SALES EXPENSES TO BE PAID IN CASH AT OR PRIOR TO CLOSING:

    A. Seller's Expenses:

       (1) Any inspections, reports and repairs required of Seller herein, and in the Addendum.

       (2) All cost of releasing existing loans and recording the releases; tax statements, ½ of any escrow fees, preparation of Deed, copies of restrictions and easements, other expenses to be paid by Seller under other provisions of this contract.

    B. Buyer's Expenses: All expenses incident to any loan (e.g., preparation of Note, Deed of Trust and other loan documents, recording fees, Mortgagee's Title Policy, credit reports, ½ of any escrow fee, one year premium for hazard insurance unless insurance is prorated, and expenses stipulated to be paid by Buyer under other provisions of this contract.

    C. If any sales expenses exceed the maximum amount herein stipulated to be paid by either party, either party may terminate this contract unless the other party agrees to pay such excess.

12. PRORATIONS: Insurance (at Buyer's option), taxes and any rents and maintenance fees shall be prorated to the Closing Date.

13. TITLE APPROVAL: If Abstract is furnished, Seller shall deliver same to Buyer within 20 days from the effective date hereof. Buyer shall have 20 days from date of receipt of Abstract to deliver a copy of the title opinion to Seller, stating any objections to title, and only objections so stated shall be considered. If Title Policy is furnished, the Title shall guarantee Buyer's title to be good and indefeasible subject only to (i) restrictive covenants affecting the Property, (ii) any discrepancies, conflicts or shortages in area or boundary lines or any encroachments, or any overlapping of improvements, (iii) all taxes for the current and subsequent years, (iv) any existing building and zoning

ordinances, (v) rights of parties in possession, (vi) any liens created as security for the sale consideration, and (vii) any reservations or exceptions contained in the Deed. In either instance, if title objections are disclosed, Seller shall have 30 days to cure the same. Exceptions permitted in the Deed and zoning ordinances shall not be valid objections to title. Seller shall furnish at Seller's expense tax statements showing no delinquent taxes and a General Warranty Deed conveying title subject only to liens securing debt created as part of the consideration, taxes for the current year, usual restrictive covenants and utility easements common to the platted subdivision of which the Property is a part and any other reservations or exceptions acceptable to Buyer. The Note shall be secured by Vendor's and Deed of Trust liens. In case of dispute as to the form of Deed, Deed of Trust or Note, such shall be upon a form prepared by the State Bar of —————— (State).

14. CASUALTY LOSS: If any part of Property is damaged or destroyed by fire or other casualty loss, Seller shall restore the same to its previous condition as soon as reasonably possible, but in any event by Closing Date, and if Seller is unable to do so without fault, this contract shall terminate and Earnest Money shall be refunded.

15. DEFAULT: If Buyer fails to comply herewith, Seller may either enforce specific performance or terminate this contract and receive the Earnest Money as liquidated damages.

    If Seller is unable without fault to deliver Abstract or Title Policy or to make any noncasualty repairs required herein within the time herein specified, Buyer may either terminate this contract and receive the Earnest Money as the sole remedy, or extend the time up to 30 days. If Seller fails to comply herewith for any other reason, Buyer may (i) terminate this contract and receive the Earnest Money, thereby releasing Seller from this contract, (ii) enforce specific performance hereof, or (iii) seek such other relief as may be provided by law.

16. ATTORNEY'S FEES: Any signatory to this contract who is the prevailing party in any legal proceeding against any other signatory brought under or with relation to this contract or transaction shall be additionally entitled to recover court costs and reasonable attorney fees from the nonprevailing party.

17. ESCROW: Earnest Money is deposited with Escrow Agent with the understanding that Escrow Agent (i) does not have any liability for performance or nonperformance of any party, (ii) has the right to require the receipt, release and authorization in writing of all parties before paying the deposit to any party, and (iii) is not liable for interest or other charge on the funds held. If any party unreasonably fails to agree in writing to an appropriate release of Earnest Money, then such party shall be liable to the other parties to the extent provided in paragraph 16. At closing, Earnest Money shall be applied to any cash down payment required, next to Buyer's closing costs and any excess refunded to Buyer. Before Buyer shall be entitled to refund of Earnest Money, any actual expenses incurred or paid on Buyer's behalf shall be deducted therefrom and paid to the creditors entitled thereto.

18. REPRESENTATIONS: Seller represents that there will be no Title I liens, unrecorded liens or Uniform Commercial Code liens against any of the Property on Closing Date. If any representation above is untrue this contract may be terminated by Buyer and the Earnest Money shall be refunded without delay. Representations shall survive closing.

19. AGREEMENT OF PARTIES: This contract contains the entire agreement of the parties and cannot be changed except by their written consent.

20. CONSULT YOUR ATTORNEY: This is intended to be a legally binding contract. READ IT CAREFULLY. If you do not understand the effect of any part, consult your attorney BEFORE signing. Attorneys to represent parties may be designated below.

Seller's Atty: _____   Buyer's Atty: _____

EXECUTED in multiple originals effective the _____ day of _____ , 19_____ .

_____
Seller

_____
Seller

_____
Seller's Address

_____
Buyer

_____
Buyer

_____
Buyer's Address

VA GUARANTEED LOAN WITH SECOND MORTGAGE—RESIDENTIAL EARNEST-MONEY CONTRACT (RESALE)

1. PARTIES _____ (Seller) agrees to sell and convey to _____ (Buyer) and Buyer agrees to buy from Seller the following property situated in _____ County, _____ (State), known as _____ (Address).

2. PROPERTY: Lot _____ Block _____, _____ Addition, City of _____ , or as described on attached exhibit, together with the following fixtures, if any: curtain rods, drapery rods, venetian blinds, window shades, screens and shutters, awnings, wall-to-wall carpeting, mirrors fixed in place, attic fans, permanently installed heating and air-conditioning units and equipment, lighting and plumbing fixtures, TV antennas, mailboxes, water softeners, shrubbery and all other property owned by Seller and attached to the above described real property. All property sold by this contract is called "Property."

3. CONTRACT SALES PRICE:

   A. Cash down payment payable at closing ....$_____

   B. Note described in 4 below (the Note) in the amount of ....$_____

   C. Sales price payable to Seller on Loan funding after closing (Sum of A and B)........................

   ....$_____

4. FINANCING CONDITIONS: This contract is subject to approval for Buyer of a VA loan (the Loan) of not less than the amount of the Note, amortizable monthly for not less than _____ years, with interest at maximum rate allowable at time of Loan funding. Buyer shall apply for the Loan within _____ days from the effective date of this contract and shall make every reasonable effort to obtain approval. If the Loan has not been approved by the Closing Date, this contract shall terminate and the Earnest Money shall be refunded to Buyer without delay. VA NOTICE TO BUYER: "It is expressly agreed that, notwithstanding any other provisions of this contract, the Buyer shall not incur any penalty by forfeiture of earnest money or otherwise or be obligated to complete the purchase of the Property described herein, if the contract purchase price or cost exceeds the reasonable value of the Property established by the Veterans Administration. The Buyer shall, however, have the privilege and option of proceeding with the consummation of this contract without regard to the amount of the reasonable value established by the Veterans Administration." Buyer agrees that should Buyer elect to complete the purchase at an amount in excess of the reasonable value established by VA, Buyer shall pay such excess amount in cash from a source which Buyer agrees to disclose to the VA and which Buyer represents will not be from borrowed funds except as approved by VA. If VA reasonable value of the Property is less than the Sales Price (3C above), Seller

may reduce the Sales Price to an amount equal to the VA reasonable value and both parties agree to close the sale at such lower Sales Price with appropriate adjustments to 3A and 3B above.

5. EARNEST MONEY: $_____ is herewith tendered and is to be deposited as Earnest Money with _____, as Escrow Agent, upon execution of the contract by both parties. Additional Earnest Money, if any, shall be deposited with the Escrow Agent on or before _____, 19_____, in the amount of $_____ .

6. TITLE: Seller at Seller's expense shall furnish either:

_____A. Owner's Policy of Title Insurance (the Title Policy) issued by _____ _____ in the amount of the Sales Price and dated at or after closing:

OR

_____B. Complete Abstract of Title (the Abstract) certified by _____ _____ to current date.

NOTICE TO BUYER AS REQUIRED BY LAW, YOU should have the Abstract covering the Property examined by an attorney of YOUR selection, or YOU should be furnished with or obtain a Title Policy.

7. PROPERTY CONDITION [Check "A" OR "B"]:

_____A. Buyer accepts the Property in its present condition, subject only to VA required repairs and _____ _____

_____B. Buyer requires inspections and repairs required by the Property Condition Addendum (the Addendum) and those required by VA. Upon Seller's receipt of the Loan approval and inspection reports Seller shall commence and complete prior to closing all required repairs at Seller's expense.

All inspections, reports and repairs required of Seller by this contract and the Addendum shall not exceed $_____ . If Seller fails to complete such requirements, Buyer may do so and Seller shall be liable up to the amount specified and the same paid from the proceeds of the sale. If such expenditures exceed the stated amount and Seller refuses to pay such excess, Buyer may pay the additional cost or accept the Property with the limited repairs and this sale shall be closed as scheduled, or Buyer may terminate this contract and the Earnest Money shall be refunded to Buyer.

8. CLOSING: The closing of the sale (the Closing Date) shall be on or before _____ 19_____ , or within 7 days after objections to title have been cured, whichever date is later; however, if necessary to complete Loan requirements, the Closing Date shall be extended daily up to 15 days.

9. POSSESSION: The possession of the Property shall be delivered to Buyer on _____ in

its present or required improved condition, ordinary wear and tear excepted. Any possession by Buyer prior to or by Seller after Closing Date shall establish a landlord tenant at sufferance relationship between the parties.

10. SPECIAL PROVISIONS:

[Insert terms and conditions of a factual nature applicable to this sale, e.g., prior purchase or sale of other property, lessee surrender of possession and the like.]

11. SALES EXPENSES TO BE PAID IN CASH AT OR PRIOR TO CLOSING:

    A. Loan appraisal fees shall be paid by _____ .

    B. Seller's Expenses:

        (1) Seller's Loan discount points not exceeding _____ .

        (2) VA required repairs and any other inspections, reports and repairs required of Seller herein, and in the Addendum.

        (3) Releases of existing loans, including prepayment penalties and recordation: escrow fee, tax statement, preparation of Deed, Note and Deed of Trust, expenses VA prohibits Buyer to pay (e.g., copies of restrictions, photos, excess cost of survey of Property), other expenses stipulated to be paid by Seller under other provisions of this contract.

    C. Buyer's Expenses: Expenses incident to Loan (e.g., credit reports, recording fees, Mortgagee's Title Policy; Loan origination fee, that portion of survey cost Buyer can pay by VA regulation, Loan related inspection fees, premiums for 1 year's hazard insurance and any flood insurance, required reserve deposits for insurance premiums, ad valorem taxes and special assessments, interest from date of disbursement to 1 month prior to date of first monthly payment on the Note; premiums on non-required insurance, expenses stipulated to be paid by Buyer under other provisions of this contract.

    D. If any sales expenses exceed the maximum amount herein stipulated to be paid by either party, either party may terminate this contract unless the other party agrees to pay such excess. In no event shall Buyer pay charges and fees other than those expressly permitted by VA Regulations.

12. PRORATIONS: Insurance (at Buyer's option), taxes and any rents and maintenance fees shall be prorated to the Closing Date.

13. TITLE APPROVAL: If Abstract is furnished, Seller shall deliver same to Buyer within 20 days from the effective date hereof. Buyer shall have 20 days from date of receipt of Abstract to deliver a copy of the title opinion to Seller, stating any objections to title, and only objections so stated shall be considered. If Title Policy is furnished, the Title shall guarantee Buyer's title to be good and indefeasible subject only to (i) restrictive covenants affecting the Property, (ii) any discrepancies, conflicts or shortages in area or boundary lines or any encroachments, or any overlapping of improvements, (iii) all taxes for the current and subsequent years, (iv) any existing building and zoning ordinances, (v) rights of parties in possession, (vi) any liens created as security for the sale consideration, and (vii) any reservations or exceptions contained in the Deed. In either instance, if title objections are disclosed, Seller shall have 30 days to cure the same. Exceptions permitted in the Deed and zoning ordinances shall not be valid objections to title. Seller shall furnish at Seller's expense tax statements showing no delinquent taxes and a General Warranty Deed conveying title subject only to liens securing debt created as part of the consideration, taxes for the current year, usual restrictive covenants and utility easements common to the platted subdivision of which the Property is a part and any other reservations or exceptions acceptable to Buyer. The Note shall be secured by Vendor's and Deed of Trust liens. In case of dispute as to the form of Deed, such shall be upon a form prepared by the State Bar of _____ (State).

14. CASUALTY LOSS: If any part of Property is damaged or destroyed by fire or other casualty loss, Seller shall restore the same to its previous condition as soon as reasonably possible, but in any event by Closing Date, and if Seller is unable to do so without fault, this contract shall terminate and Earnest Money shall be refunded.

15. DEFAULT: If Buyer fails to comply herewith, Seller may either enforce specific performance or terminate this contract and receive the Earnest Money as liquidated damages.

    If Seller is unable without fault to deliver Abstract or Title Policy or to make any noncasualty repairs required herein within the time herein specified, Buyer may either terminate this contract and receive the Earnest Money as the sole remedy, or extend the time up to 30 days. If Seller fails to comply herewith for any other reason, Buyer may (i) terminate this contract and receive the Earnest Money, thereby releasing Seller from this contract, (ii) enforce specific performance hereof, or (iii) seek such other relief as may be provided by law.

16. ATTORNEY'S FEES: Any signatory to this contract who is the prevailing party in any legal proceeding against any other signatory brought under or with relation to this contract or transaction shall be additionally entitled to recover court costs and reasonable attorney fees from the nonprevailing party.

17. ESCROW: Earnest Money is deposited with Escrow Agent with the understanding that Escrow Agent (i) does not have any liability for performance or nonperformance of any party, (ii) has the right to

require the receipt, release and authorization in writing of all parties before paying the deposit to any party, and (iii) is not liable for interest or other charge on the funds held. If any party unreasonably fails to agree in writing to an appropriate release of Earnest Money, then such party shall be liable to the other parties to the extent provided in paragraph 16. At closing, Earnest Money shall be applied to any cash down payment required, next to Buyer's closing costs and any excess refunded to Buyer. Before Buyer shall be entitled to refund of Earnest Money, any actual and VA allowable expenses incurred or paid on Buyer's behalf shall be deducted therefrom and paid to the creditors entitled thereto.

18. REPRESENTATIONS: Seller represents that there will be no Title I liens, unrecorded liens or Uniform Commercial Code liens against any of the Property on Closing Date. If any representation above is untrue this contract may be terminated by Buyer and the Earnest Money shall be refunded without delay. Representations shall survive closing.

19. AGREEMENT OF PARTIES: This contract contains the entire agreement of the parties and cannot be changed except by their written consent.

20. CONSULT YOUR ATTORNEY: This is intended to be a legally binding contract. READ IT CAREFULLY. If you do not understand the effect of any part, consult your attorney BEFORE signing. Attorneys to represent parties may be designated below.

Seller's Atty: _____   Buyer's Atty: _____

EXECUTED in multiple originals effective the _____ day of _____, 19____.

_____   _____
Seller   Buyer

_____   _____
Seller   Buyer

_____   _____
Seller's Address   Buyer's Address

PROPERTY CONDITION ADDENDUM
ADDENDUM TO EARNEST-MONEY CONTRACT BETWEEN THE UNDERSIGNED PARTIES CONCERNING THE PROPERTY AT

_____

_____

(Street Address and City)

CHECK APPLICABLE BOXES:

———— A.   TERMITES: Seller, at Seller's expense, shall furnish to Buyer at or prior to closing a written report by a Structural Pest Control Business Licensee, dated within 30 days before Closing Date and stating that there is no visible evidence of active termites or visible damage to the improvements from the same in need of repair. Such report shall not cover fences, trees, and shrubs.

———— B.   CONDITION OF PROPERTY:

Buyer shall have the right at Buyer's expense (i) within ———— days from the effective date of this contract to have any of the STRUCTURAL items indicated below, and (ii) within ———— days from the effective date of this contract to have any of the EQUIPMENT AND SYSTEMS items indicated below, inspected by inspectors of Buyer's choice and to give Seller within such time periods a written report of required repairs to any of the items checked below which are not performing the function for which intended or which are in need of immediate repair. Failure to do so shall be deemed a waiver of Buyer's inspection and repair rights and Buyer agrees to accept Property in its present condition.

ITEMS THAT BUYER MAY REQUIRE TO BE INSPECTED (check applicable boxes):

STRUCTURAL:

———— foundation ———— roof ———— load bearing walls ———— floors ———— ceilings ———— basement ———— water penetration ———— and _____

_____

_____

EQUIPMENT AND SYSTEMS:

———— plumbing system (including any water heaters, wells and septic system), ———— central heating and air conditioning, ———— electrical system, ———— heating and cooling units in the walls, floor, ceilings, roof or windows, ———— any built-in range, oven, dishwasher, disposer, kitchen exhaust fan, trash compactor, ———— swimming pool and related mechanical equipment, ———— sprinkler systems ———— and _____

_____

_____

Repairs required by inspections and reports shall be at Seller's expense.

_____C. Seller shall make the following repairs in addition to those required above: _____

_____

_____

_____

All inspections shall be made by trained and qualified persons who regularly provide such service and all repairs shall be by trained and qualified persons who are, whenever possible, manufacturer-approved service persons or are licensed or bonded whenever such license or bond is required by law. For these purposes and for reinspections after repairs have been completed, Seller shall permit access to the Property at any reasonable time.

_____D. Where gas supplier, regulations or ordinances require inspection on transfer of gas service, Seller consents to transfer gas service to Buyer's name within 7 days prior to closing. Seller shall arrange and pay at closing for any repairs necessary if gas leak is discovered. Buyer's failure to request such transfer in time to complete the inspection prior to closing shall release the Seller of liability for repair of gas leaks.

_____   _____
Seller   Buyer

_____   _____
Seller   Buyer

CONTINGENCY CLAUSE ADDENDUM—SALE OF BUYER'S HOME

ADDENDUM TO EARNEST-MONEY CONTRACT BETWEEN THE UNDERSIGNED PARTIES DATED _____ AND CONCERNING THE PROPERTY LOCATED AT

_____.

1. This Contract is contingent upon the closing and funding of Buyer's home located at

   _____ , _____

   (State), on or before 6:00 p.m. on the _____ day of _____ , 19_____. If such sale and funding does not occur within such time period this Contract shall be null and void and the Earnest Money returned to Buyer.

2. It is further agreed Seller's home will continue to be shown and offered for sale and should Seller receive a written offer to purchase such home from a third party purchaser which is acceptable to Seller, Seller or his agent will notify Buyer in writing by certified mail, telegram, or personal delivery, that Seller requires removal of said contingency. Buyer will have _____ hours following receipt of such notice to deliver in writing, by personal delivery or telegram, to Seller's agent (designated below) notice of Buyer's election to (i) waive this contingency, immediately deposit with Escrow Agent $_____ as additional Earnest Money and close the sale under the terms of this Contract, or (ii) declare this contract null and void and receive a refund of the Earnest Money.

3. If Buyer fails to elect and notify Seller's agent within such time period, Seller shall receive the Earnest Money and this contract shall be null and void.

4. If Buyer waives this contingency and is then unable to secure funding of a new loan or assumption approval of an existing loan, as the case may be, for this purchase because of ownership of the above referred to home, Seller shall receive the entire amount of the Earnest Money as increased.

_____   _____
SELLER   BUYER

_____   _____
SELLER   BUYER

                                           _____
                                           BUYER'S ADDRESS & TELEPHONE #

abstract of title—A summary of the public records relating to the title to a particular piece of land. An attorney or title insurance company reviews an abstract of title to determine whether there are any title defects which must be cleared before a buyer can purchase clear, marketable, and insurable title.

acceleration clause—A condition in a mortgage that may require the balance of the loan to become due immediately if regular mortgage payments are not made or for breach of other conditions of the mortgage

agreement of sale—Known by various names, such as earnest-money contract, contract of purchase, contract of sale, purchase agreement, or sales agreement, according to location or jurisdiction. A contract in which a seller agrees to sell and a buyer agrees to buy, under certain specific terms and conditions spelled out in writing and signed by both parties.

AIREA (American Institute of Real Estate Appraisers)—A national accreditation organization for real-estate appraisers affiliated with the National Association of Realtors

amortize—To pay a loan with interest in equal installments, usually monthly

appraisal—An expert judgment or estimate, in writing, of the quality or value of real estate as of a given date

appraiser—An expert who estimates the quality or value of real estate for a fee. FHA and VA mortgages often use FHA and VA appraisers.

appreciation—Increase in value of a house due to improvements in the neighborhood or any other reason

assessed value—The value of real estate as determined by the tax assessor for the purpose of taxation

assessment—A tax imposed by the government for a specific purpose such as municipal improvements

assumption of mortgage—An obligation undertaken by the purchaser of property to be personally liable for payment of an existing mortgage. In an assumption, the purchaser is substituted for the original mortgagor in the mortgage instrument, and the original mortgagor is released from further liability in the assumption. Since the mortgagor is to be released from further liability in the assumption, the mortgagee's (bank's) consent is usually required. The original mortgagor should always obtain a written release from further liability if he desires to be fully released under the assumption. Failure to obtain such a release

renders the original mortgagor liable if the person assuming the mortgage fails to make the monthly payments. An "assumption of mortgage" is often confused with "purchasing subject to a mortgage." When one purchases subject to a mortgage, the purchaser agrees to make the monthly mortgage payments on an existing mortgage, but the original mortgagor (borrower) remains personally liable if the purchaser fails to make the monthly payments. Since the original mortgagor remains liable in the event of default, the mortgagee's (bank's) consent is not required for a sale subject to a mortgage.

balloon payment—A payment under a loan agreement that is larger in amount than the other installments and which becomes due at a date agreed upon by the buyer and seller. Balloon payments enable a buyer to purchase a home at a lower down payment and lower monthly payments than would otherwise be possible.

binder—A simplistic written form acknowledged in some states in which the buyer and seller tentatively agree on the conditions and terms of a real-estate contract

building codes—Local regulations governing the construction of buildings. Such regulations apply to size, location, and use of buildings and other such matters under public jurisdiction.

building line—Distances from the ends and/or sides of the lot beyond which construction may not extend. The building line may be established by a filed plat of the subdivision, by restrictive covenants in deeds or leases, by building codes, or by zoning ordinances.

carrying charges—Mortgages, insurance, taxes, and other expenditures involved in the ownership of property

certificate of title—A certificate issued by a title company or a written opinion rendered by an attorney establishing that the seller has good marketable and insurable title to the property which he is offering for sale. A certificate of title offers no protection against any hidden defects in the title which an examination of the records could not reveal. The issuer of a certificate of title is liable only for damages due to negligence. The protection offered a homeowner under a certificate of title is not as great as that offered in a title insurance policy.

closing—The transaction at which the seller of a property transfers the deed to the property to the buyer. A closing is usually held in the office of either the buyer's or the seller's attorney or at the bank that is financing the loan.

closing costs—The expenses incurred apart from the cost of the property at the closing. Closing costs include title insurance, points, survey charges, attorney's fees, escrow fees, and others. Certain costs may be the responsibility of either the buyer or the seller. Such costs are paid only once, on the closing day, and may be negotiated between buyer and seller in the agreement of sale.

closing date—The actual day of the closing, as specified in the agreement of sale

cloud on title—An outstanding claim or encumbrance which adversely affects the marketability of title

commission—Money paid to a real-estate agent or broker by the seller as compensation for finding a buyer and completing the sale. Usually it is a percentage of the sale price—6% to 7% on houses, 10% on land.

conventional mortgage—A mortgage loan not insured by HUD or guaranteed by the Veterans Administration. It is subject to conditions established by the lending institution and state statutes. The mortgage rates may vary with different institutions and between states. States have various interest limits.

conveyance—An instrument (deed) by which title to property is conveyed from one party to another

covenant—A written agreement or promise between two parties usually relating to the deed

creative financing—Refers to financing plans that offer increased options to buyers, including lower interest rates, lower monthly payments for the first few years of a loan, longer loan terms, and sometimes lower down-payment requirements.

deed—A formal written instrument by which title to real property is transferred from one owner to another. The deed should contain an accurate description of the property being conveyed, be signed and witnessed according to the laws of the state where the property is located, and be delivered to the purchaser at closing day. There are two parties to a deed: the grantor and the grantee.

deed of trust—Like a mortgage, a security instrument whereby real property is given as security for a debt. In a deed of trust there are three parties to the instrument: the borrower, the trustee, and the lender (or beneficiary). In such a transaction, the borrower transfers the legal title for the property to the trustee, who holds the property in trust as security for the payment of the debt to the lender or beneficiary. If the borrower pays the debt as agreed, the deed of trust becomes void. If, however, he defaults in the payment of the debt, the trustee may sell the property at a public sale, under the terms of the deed of trust. In most jurisdictions where the deed of trust is in force, the borrower is subject to having his property sold without benefit of legal proceedings. A few states have begun in recent years to treat the deed of trust like a mortgage.

default—Failure to make mortgage payments as agreed to in a commitment based on the terms and at the designated time set forth in the mortgage or the deed of trust. It is the mortgagor's responsibility to remember the due date and send the payment prior to the due date, not after. If payment is not received 30 days after the due date, the mortgage is in default. In the event of default, the mortgage may give the lender the right to accelerate payments, take posession and receive rents, and start foreclosure. Defaults may also come about by the failure to observe all conditions in the deed of trust.

deposit—The amount of money the buyer gives the seller as evidence of the buyer's serious intent to purchase the seller's property. See earnest money.

depreciation—Decline in value of a house due to wear and tear, adverse changes in the neighborhood, or any other reason

documentary stamps—A state tax, in the form of stamps, required on deeds and mortgages when real-estate title passes from one owner to another. The number of stamps required varies with each state.

down payment—The amount of money to be paid by the purchaser to the seller upon the signing of the agreement of sale (earnest-money contract). The agreement of sale will refer to the down payment amount and will acknowledge receipt of the down payment. The down payment is usually a percentage of the total purchase price and varies according to the market conditions, availability and type of financing, and the confidence the purchaser and the seller have in each other's intent to close the sale. The down payment may not be refundable if the purchaser fails to buy the property without good cause. If the purchaser wants the down payment to be refundable, he should insert a clause in the agreement of sale specifying the conditions under which the deposit will be refunded, if the agreement does not already contain such clause. If the seller cannot deliver good title, the agreement of sale usually requires the seller to return the down payment and to pay interest and expenses incurred by the purchaser.

earnest money—The deposit money given to the seller or his agent by the potential buyer to show that he is serious about buying the house. If the sale goes through, the earnest money is applied toward the down payment. If the sale does not go through, the earnest money will be forfeited or lost unless the agreement of sale (earnest-money contract) expressly provides that it is refundable.

earnest-money contract—A written agreement in which a seller agrees to sell property and a buyer agrees to buy property according to specified terms and conditions signed by both parties. See agreement of sale.

easement rights—A right-of-way granted to a person or company authorizing access to or over the owner's land, such as an electric company obtaining a right-of-way across private property

encroachment—An obstruction, building, or part of a building that intrudes beyond a legal boundary onto neighboring private or public land, or a building extending beyond the building line

encumbrance—A legal right or interest in land that affects a good or clear title, and diminishes the land's value. It can take numerous forms, such as zoning ordinances, easement rights, claims, mortgages, liens, charges, a pending legal action, unpaid taxes, or restrictive covenants. An encumbrance does not legally prevent transfer of the property to another. A title seach is all that is usually done to reveal the existence of such encumbrances, and it is up to the buyer to determine whether he wants to purchase with the encumbrance, or what can be done to remove it. It is strongly recommended that the buyer secure title insurance.

equity—The value of a homeowner's unencumbered interest in real estate. Equity is computed by subtracting from the property's fair market value the total of the unpaid mortgage balance and any outstanding liens or other debts against the property. A homeowner's equity increases as he pays off his mortgage or as the property appreciates in value. When the mortgage and all other debts against the property are paid in full the homeowner has 100% equity in his property.

escalation clause—A clause in a mortgage which permits the mortgagee to raise or lower the interest rate of the mortgage according to the prevailing money market without the borrower's consent

escrow—Funds paid by one party to another (the escrow agent) to hold until the occurrence of a specified event, after which the funds are released to a designated individual. In FHA mortgage transactions an escrow account usually refers to the funds a mortgagor pays the lender at the time of the periodic mortgage payments. The money is held in a trust fund, provided by the lender for the buyer. Such funds shold be adequate to cover yearly anticipated expenditures for mortgage insurance premiums, taxes, insurance premiums, and special assessments.

fair market value—The value of property on the open market

FHA mortgage—A mortgage insured by the Federal Housing Administration in which the loan is given by a commercial lender. The FHA establishes the interest rates and down payments and may offer lower down-payment requirements to qualified lower-income buyers.

first mortgage—The principal mortgage of a property. A first mortgage is a first lien on the property and has first claim on monies resulting from a foreclosure.

FNMA (Federal National Mortgage Association)—A privately owned, for-profit corporation established in 1938 which acts as a mortgage bank. Popularly known as Fannie Mae, FNMA is the largest purchaser of home loans in the United States.

foreclosure—A legal term applied to any of the various methods of enforcing payment of the debt secured by a mortgage or deed of trust, by taking and selling the mortgaged property, and depriving the mortgagor of possession

general warranty deed—A deed which conveys not only all the grantor's interests in and title to the property to the grantee, but also warrants that if the title is defective or has a "cloud" on it (such as mortgage claims, tax liens, title claims, judgments, or mechanic's liens against it), the grantee may hold the grantor liable

grantee—The party in the deed who is buyer or recipient

grantor—That party in the deed who is the seller or giver

guaranty—A pledge or promise to answer for the payment of a debt or the performance of an obligation

hazard insurance—Protects against damages caused to property by fire, windstorms, and other common hazards

HUD—U.S. Department of Housing and Urban Development. The Housing Production and Mortgage Credit/Federal Housing Administration within HUD insures home mortgage loans made by lenders and sets minimum standards for such homes.

improvement—An outlay that extends the useful life of the property, such as the installation of a new heating system. An improvement can be depreciated over its useful life.

interest—A charge paid for borrowing money

joint tenancy—The term decribing property owned jointly by two or more persons, usually a husband and wife. A joint tenancy property can be sold only with the approval of both joint tenants. Either joint tenant can assume full title to the property if the other dies.

lien—A claim by one person on the property of another as security for money owed. Such claims may include obligations not met or satisfied, judgments, or unpaid taxes, materials, or labor.

MAI (Member of the Appraisal Institute)—A designation of the AIREA. An appraiser who holds the MAI designation is certified to appraise all types of property.

marketable title—A title that is free and clear of objectionable liens, clouds, or other title defects

mortgage—A lien or claim against real property given by the buyer to the lender as security for money borrowed. Under government-insured or loan guaranty provisions, the payments may include escrow amounts covering taxes, hazard insurance, water charges, and special assessments. Mortgages generally run from 10 to 30 years, during which the loan is to be paid off.

mortgage commitment—A written notice from the bank or other lending institution saying it will advance mortgage funds in a specified amount to enable a buyer to purchase a house

mortgage insurance premium—The payment made by a borrower to the lender for transmittal to HUD to help defray the cost of the FHA mortgage insurance program and to provide a reserve fund to protect lenders against loss in insured mortgage transactions. In FHA-insured mortgages this represents an annual rate of 0.5% paid by the mortgagor on a monthly basis.

mortgage note—A written agreement to repay a loan. The agreement is secured by a mortgage, serves as proof of an indebtedness, and states the manner in which it shall be paid. The note states the actual amount of the debt that the mortgage secures and renders the mortgagor personally responsible for repayment.

mortgagee—The lender in a mortgage agreement

mortgagor—The borrower in a mortgage agreement

note—Also called a promissory note. A written document in which a borrower promises to repay an acknowledged debt within a stated period of time. A note may be secured by a mortgage and is usually signed by the buyer at the closing.

open-end mortgage—A mortgage with a provision that permits borrowing additional money in the future without refinancing the loan or paying additional financing charges. Open-end provisions often limit such borrowing to no more than would raise the balance to the original loan figure.

option—The right to buy a designated property at a specific price within a specified time

plat—A map or chart of a lot, subdivision, or community drawn by a surveyor showing boundary lines, buildings, improvements on the land, and easements

points—Sometimes called "discount points," "loan fees," or "origination fees." A point is one percent of the amount of the mortgage loan. Points are charged by a lender to raise the yield on his loan at a time when money is tight, interest rates are high, and there is a legal limit to the interest rate that can be charged on a mortgage. Buyers are prohibited from paying points on HUD or VA guaranteed loans (sellers can pay, however). On a conventional mortgage, points may be paid by either buyer or seller or split between them.

prepayment—Payment of mortgage loan, or part of it, before due date. Mortgage agreements often restrict the right of prepayment either by limiting the amount that can be prepaid in any one year or by charging a penalty for prepayment. The FHA and VA do not permit such restrictions in their insured mortgages.

prepayment penalty—The amount of the penalty a lender charges when a borrower repays a mortgage loan before its due date

principal—The basic element of the loan as distinguished from interest and mortgage insurance premium. Principal is the amount upon which interest is paid.

quitclaim deed—A deed which transfers whatever interest the maker of the deed may have in the particular parcel of land. A quitclaim deed is often given to clear the title when the grantor's interest in a property is questionable. By accepting such a deed the buyer assumes all the risks. Such a deed makes no warranties as to the title, but simply transfers to the buyer whatever interest the grantor has.

real-estate broker—A middleman or agent licensed by the state who buys and sells real estate for a company, firm, or individual on a commission basis. The broker does not have title to the property, but generally represents the owner.

real property—Real estate; the land and everything on it or attached to it, including houses, trees, etc.

realtor—A member of the National Association of Realtors who is licensed by the state to sell real estate

refinancing—The process of paying off one loan with the proceeds from another loan

repair—An expense that keeps property in efficient operating condition, such as fixing a leak in the faucet. Repairs are fully tax deductible from the profit on the sale of a home.

restrictive covenants—Private restrictions limiting the use of real property. Restrictive covenants are created by deed and may run with the land, binding all subsequent purchasers of the land, or may be personal and binding only between the original buyer and seller. The determination whether a covenant runs with the land or is personal is governed by the language of the covenant, the intent of the parties, and the law in the state where the land is situated. Restrictive covenants that run with the land are encumbrances and may affect the value and marketability of title. Restrictive covenants may limit the density of buildings per acre, regulate the size, style, or price range of buildings to be erected, or prevent particular businesses from operating or minority groups from owning or occupying homes in a given area. This latter discriminatory covenant is unconstitutional and has been declared unenforceable by the U.S. Supreme Court.

RM (Residential Member)—A designation of the

AIREA. An appraiser who holds the RM designation is certified to appraise single-family residences.

second mortgage—A mortgage given over and above the first mortgage the buyer obtains. Second mortgages have second claim on monies realized in the event of a foreclosure.

special assessments—A special tax imposed on property, individual lots or all property in the immediate area, for road construction, sidewalks, sewers, street lights, etc.

special lien—A lien that binds a specified piece of property, unlike a general lien, which is levied against all one's assets. It creates a right to retain something of value belonging to another person as compensation for labor, material, or money expended in that person's behalf. In some localities, it is called particular lien or specific lien.

special warranty deed—A deed in which the grantor conveys title to the grantee and agrees to protect the grantee against title defects of claims asserted by the grantor and those persons whose right to assert a claim against the title arose during the period the grantor held title to the property. In a special warranty deed the grantor guarantees to the grantee that he has done nothing during the time he held title to the property which has impaired, or which might in the future impair, the grantee's title.

survey—A map or plat made by a licensed surveyor showing the results of measuring the land with its elevations, improvements, boundaries, and its relationship to the surrounding tracts of land. A survey is often required by the lender to assure him that a building is actually sited on the land according to its legal description.

tax—As applied to real estate, an enforced charge imposed on persons, property, or income, to be used to support the state. The governing body in turn utilizes the funds in the best interest of the general public.

title—As generally used, the rights of ownership and possession of particular property. In real-estate usage, title may refer to the instruments or documents by which a right of ownership is established (title documents), or it may refer to the ownership interest one has in real estate.

title insurance—Protects lenders and homeowners against loss of their interest in property due to legal defects in title. Title insurance may be issued to either the mortgagor, as an "owner's title policy," or to the mortgagee (lender), as a "mortgagee's title policy." Insurance benefits will be paid only to the "named insured" in the title policy, so it is important that an owner purchase an "owner's title policy" if he desires the protection of title insurance.

title search—A check of the title records, generally at the local courthouse, to make sure the buyer is purchasing a house from the legal owner and there are no liens, overdue special assessments, or other claims or outstanding restrictive covenants filed in the record, which would adversely affect the marketability or value of title

trustee—A party who is given legal responsibility to hold property in the best interest of or "for the benefit of" another. The trustee is one placed in a position of responsibility for another, a responsibility enforceable in a court of law.

usury—The practice of charging interest rates in excess of those permitted by law

VA mortgage—A mortgage given by a commercial lender under rules and regulations established by the Veterans Administration. The VA regulates the interest rate and guarantees the loan up to a maximum of $110,000 in case of default. VA mortgages are characterized by no down payments or low down payments.

valuation—An estimate of the value of a property

vendee—The buyer in a real-estate transaction

vendor—The seller in a real-estate transaction

waiver—The voluntary relinquishing of a claim, right, or privilege

warranty—A guarantee by the seller that the title to the property is as represented in the deed

zoning ordinances—The acts of an authorized local government establishing building codes and setting forth regulations for property land usage